Getting Started in
Technical
Analysis

The Getting Started in Series

Getting Started in
Technical Analysis

Jack D. Schwager

John Wiley & Sons, Inc.

New York • Chichester • Weinheim • Brisbane • Singapore • Toronto

This book is printed on acid-free paper. ♾

Copyright © 1999 by Jack D. Schwager. All rights reserved.

Published by John Wiley & Sons, Inc.

Published simultaneously in Canada.

TradeStation® is a registered trademark of Omega Research, Inc.

This publication is designed to provide accurate and authoritative information in regard to the subject matter covered. It is sold with the understanding that the publisher is not engaged in rendering professional services. If professional advice or other expert assistance is required, the services of a competent professional person should be sought.

Library of Congress Cataloging-in-Publication Data:
Schwager, Jack D., 1948–
    Getting started in technical analysis / Jack D. Schwager
      p. cm.—(Getting started in)
    Includes index.
    ISBN 0-471-29542-6 (pbk. : alk. paper)
    1. Stock price forecasting.   2. Investment analysis.   3. Stocks—
Charts, diagrams, etc. I. Title. II. Series.
HG4637.S37   1998
332.63'222—dc21   98-23565

Printed in the United States of America.

10 9 8 7 6 5 4

Contents

Preface

Trading success cannot be capsulized in a simple indicator, formula, or system—the pronouncements of countless books, advertisements, and brochures notwithstanding. This book is written by a trader, from a trader's perspective, rather than being yet another compendium of analytical techniques, indicators, or systems, using idealized illustrations.

In explaining various analytical techniques and methods, I have tried to keep in the forefront key questions that are often ignored by writers of books on technical analysis: How can the methods described be applied in actual trading? What works and doesn't work in the real world? What are the implications of a method's failure? How can trading systems be designed and tested to maximize their *future* performance rather than their *past* performance?

This is a practical book. I have used many of the methods described in this volume to construct a very profitable trading approach—yes, with real money. Why then am I willing to share this information? Because, to use a building metaphor, I am supplying the tools, but not the architectural design—that is left to the individual reader. I believe that readers who are serious about using technical analysis to become more successful traders and who understand that this goal requires individual work will find much here that is useful.

JACK D. SCHWAGER

Unless otherwise indicated, the charts in this book are reproduced courtesy of Prudential Securities, Inc.

Getting Started in
Technical Analysis

The Great Fundamental versus Technical Analysis Debate

Curiously, however, the broken technician is never apologetic about his method. If anything, he is more enthusiastic than ever. If you commit the social error of asking him why he is broke, he will tell you quite ingeniously that he made the all-too-human error of not believing his own charts. To my great embarrassment, I once choked conspicuously at the dinner table of a chartist friend of mine when he made such a comment. I have since made it a rule never to eat with a chartist. It's bad for digestion.

       —Burton G. Malkiel, *A Random Walk Down Wall Street*

One evening, while having dinner with a fundamentalist, I accidentally knocked a sharp knife off the edge of the table. He watched the knife twirl through the air, as it came to rest with the pointed end sticking into his shoe. "Why didn't you move your foot?" I exclaimed. "I was waiting for it to come back up," he replied.

       —Ed Seykota (an avowed technician)

Most speculators, especially those active primarily in stocks, are accustomed to trading from a fundamental perspective. Fundamental analysis involves the use of economic data—for example, P/E ratios or book values in the case of stocks, or crop reports or import/export figures in the case of commodity futures—to forecast prices, or equivalently, to gauge whether a market is overvalued or undervalued.

Technical analysis, by comparison, is the study of price activity—more specifically, price patterns—to identify favorable trade opportunities. The logical basis for this approach has two major elements. First, that the price of a particular stock, commodity, or financial future reflects all the knowable information about that asset at any given time and the opinions of all market participants regarding that information. Second, that the fundamental information and market opinions reflected by price will result in recurring price patterns that provide clues to potential *future* price movement. Hence, by analyzing historical price patterns, the technical analyst looks for price behavior that suggests the possible initiation, conclusion, or continuation of a trend.

Which method—fundamental analysis or technical analysis—is better? This question is the subject of great debate. Interestingly, the experts are no less divided on this issue than the novices are. In a pair of books in which I interviewed some of the world's best traders (*Market Wizards*, New York Institute of Finance, 1988, and *The New Market Wizards*, HarperBusiness, 1992), I was struck by the sharply divergent views on this issue.

Jim Rogers was characteristic of one extreme of the spectrum. During the 1970s, Jim Rogers and George Soros were the two principals of the Quantum Fund, perhaps the most successful Wall Street fund of its day. In 1980, Rogers left the fund to escape managerial responsibilities and to devote himself full-time to managing his own investments—an endeavor at which he again proved spectacularly successful. (The Quantum Fund continued to maintain its excellent performance under George Soros's directorship.) Over the years, Rogers has been on record with a high percentage of accurate market forecasts. As but one example, in my 1988 interview with him, Rogers correctly predicted both the massive collapse in the Japanese stock market and the continued multiyear downtrend in gold prices. Clearly, Jim Rogers is a man whose opinion merits serious attention.

When I queried Rogers about his opinion on chart reading (the classical method of technical analysis), he replied: "I haven't met a rich technician. Excluding, of course, technicians who sell their services and make a lot of money." That cynical response succinctly summarized Rogers's view about technical analysis.

Marty Schwartz is a trader whose opinion lies at the other extreme. At the time of our interview, Schwartz, an independent stock index futures trader, was considering managing outside money. In conjunction with this undertaking, he had just had his personal track record audited, and he allowed me to view the results. During the prior 10-year period, he had achieved an average return of 25%—monthly! Equally impressive, during this 120-month period, he witnessed only two losing months—minuscule declines of 2% and 3%. Again, here was an individual whose opinion on the market demanded serious respect.

Although I did not mention Rogers's comments to Schwartz, when I asked Schwartz whether he had made a complete transition from fundamental to technical analysis (Schwartz had started his financial career as a stock analyst), his response almost sounded like a direct rebuttal to Jim Rogers. "Absolutely. I always laugh at people who say, 'I've never met a rich technician.' I love that! It is such an arrogant, nonsensical response. I used fundamentals for nine years and got rich as a technician."

There you have it. Two extraordinarily successful market participants holding polar-opposite views regarding the efficacy of fundamental versus technical analysis. Whom do you believe?

In my own assessment, both Rogers's and Schwartz's viewpoints contain elements of truth. It is possible to succeed as a trader by being a pure fundamentalist, a pure technician, or a hybrid of the two. The two methods are certainly not mutually exclusive. In fact, many of the world's most successful traders use fundamental analysis to *determine the market direction* in which to trade and technical analysis to *time the entry and exit* of such trades.

One virtually universal trait I found among successful traders was that they had gravitated to an approach that best fit their personality. Some traders prefer very long-term approaches, while others are inclined toward day trading; some traders only feel comfortable following signals generated by an automated computer program, while others find such a mechanical method to be anathema; some traders thrive in the near-bedlam atmosphere of an exchange trading floor, while others succeed only if their decisions are made in the calm of a quiet office; and some traders find fundamental analysis a natural approach, while others instinctively lean to technical methods, and still others a blend of the two.

The truth is that while technical analysis and fundamental analysis are traditionally treated as polar opposites, they are in principle more closely related than the most vociferous proponents in either camp would lead you to believe. Technicians, for the most part, do not dismiss the relevance of fundamental factors; they simply believe that price data incorporates and reflects these factors, and that the best way to understand their impact on market behavior is to analyze price. The primary difference between the two approaches is that fundamental analysis is concerned with the *why* of market behavior, while technical analysis is more concerned with the *when*.

Essentially, then, there is no universal answer to the question: Which is better, fundamental analysis or technical analysis? Quite simply, it depends on the individual. For some, fundamental analysis provides the most comfortable and effective approach; for others, technical analysis is the preferred method; and for still others, the optimal procedure is a combination of the two. In fact, combining fundamental analysis with technical analysis can provide a particularly effective approach and is indeed descriptive of the general methodology used by some of the world's most successful traders. Each individual must determine his or her natural approach.

PART ONE

BASIC ANALYSIS TOOLS

Chapter 1

Charts: Forecasting Tool or Folklore?

Common sense is not so common.

—Voltaire

There is a story about a speculator whose desire to be a winner was intensified by each successive failure. He tried fundamental analysis, chart analysis, computerized trading systems, and even a number of esoteric techniques ranging from wave counting to astrology. Although each of these approaches seemed to work well on paper, once he started to place actual trades based on these methods an odd thing happened: His short positions inevitably seemed to be followed by towering bull markets, and steady uptrends had an uncanny tendency to reverse course after he went long. After years of frustration, he finally gave up in exasperation.

It was at this point that he heard of a famous guru who lived on a remote mountain in the Himalayas and who answered the questions of all pilgrims who sought him out. The trader boarded a plane to Nepal, hired guides, and set out on a two-month trek. Finally, completely exhausted, he reached the famous guru.

"Oh Wise One," he said, "I am a frustrated man. For many years I have sought the key to successful trading, but everything I have tried has failed. What is the secret?"

The guru paused for only a moment, and, staring at his visitor intently, answered, "BLASH." He said no more.

"Blash?" The trader returned home. He did not understand the answer. It filled his mind every waking moment, but he could not fathom its meaning. He repeated the story to many, until finally one listener interpreted the guru's response.

"It's quite simple," he said. "Buy low and sell high."

The guru's message is apt to disappoint readers seeking the key to trading wisdom. BLASH does not satisfy our concept of an insight, because it appears to be a matter of common sense. However, if, as Voltaire suggested, "Common sense is not so common," neither is it obvious. For example, consider the following question: What are the trading implications of a market reaching new highs? The "commonsense" BLASH theory would unambiguously indicate that subsequent trading activity should be confined to the short side.

Very likely, a large percentage of speculators would be comfortable with this interpretation. Perhaps the appeal of the BLASH approach is tied to the desire of most traders to demonstrate their brilliance. After all, any fool can buy the market after a long uptrend, but it takes genius to fade the trend and pick a top. In any case, few trading responses are as instinctive as the bias toward buying when prices are low and selling when prices are high.

As a result, many speculators have a strong predilection toward favoring the short side when a market trades at new high levels. There is only one thing wrong with this approach: it doesn't work. Why? Because a market's ability to reach and sustain new highs is usually evidence of powerful underlying forces that often push prices much higher. Common sense? Certainly. But note that the trading implications are exactly opposite to those of the "commonsense" BLASH approach.

The point of all of this is that many of our commonsense instincts about market behavior are wrong. Chart analysis provides a means of acquiring common sense in trading—a goal far more elusive than it sounds. For example, if prior to beginning trading an individual exhaustively researched historical price charts to determine the consequences of a market reaching new highs, he or she would have a strong advantage in avoiding one of the common pitfalls that await the novice trader. Similarly, other market truths can be gleaned through a careful study of historical price patterns.

It must be acknowledged, however, that the usefulness of charts as an indicator of *future* price direction is a fiercely contested subject. Rather than list the pros and cons of this argument, we note that a recent episode of a popular TV series on the financial markets succinctly highlighted some of the key issues in this debate.

MODERATOR: Hello, I'm Louis Puneyser of *Wallet Street Week*. Tonight we will depart from our normal interview format to provide a forum for a debate on the usefulness of commodity price charts. Can all those wiggly lines and patterns really predict the future? Or is Shakespeare's description of life also appropriate to chart analysis: "a tale told by an idiot, full of sound and fury, signifying nothing"? Our guests tonight are Faith N. Trend, a renowned technical analyst with the Wall Street firm of Churnum & Burnum, and Phillip A. Coin, a professor at Ivory Tower University and the author of *The Only Way to Beat the Market—Become a Broker*. Professor Coin, you belong to a group called the Random Walkers. Is that some sort of hiking club that decides its destinations by throwing darts at a trail map? (*He smiles smugly into the camera.*)

PROFESSOR COIN: Well no, Mr. Puneyser. The Random Walkers are a group of economists who believe that market price movements are random. That is, one can no more devise a system to predict market prices than one can devise a system to predict the sequence of colors that will turn up on a roulette wheel. Both events are strictly a matter of chance. Prices have no memory, and what happened yesterday has nothing to do with what will happen tomorrow. In other words, charts can only tell you what has happened in the past; they are useless in predicting the future.

MS. TREND: Professor, you overlook a very important fact: Daily prices are not drawn out of a bowl, but rather are the consequence of the collective activity of all market participants. Human behavior may not be as predictable as the motion of planets as governed by the laws of physics, but neither is it totally random. If this is not the case, your profession—economics—is doomed to the same fate as alchemy. (*Professor Coin squirms uncomfortably in his seat at this reference.*) Charts reveal basic behavioral patterns. Insofar as similar interactions between buyers and sellers will result in similar price patterns, the past can indeed be used as a guideline for the future.

PROFESSOR COIN: If past prices can be used to predict future prices, why have a myriad of academic studies concluded that tested technical rules failed to outperform a simple buy-and-hold policy once commissions were taken into account?

MS. TREND: The rules used in those studies are generally oversimplified. The studies demonstrate that those particular rules don't work. They don't prove that a richer synthesis of price information, such as chart analysis, or a more complex technical system, cannot be successfully exploited for making trading decisions.

PROFESSOR COIN: Why then are there no studies that conclusively demonstrate the viability of chart analysis as a forecasting tool?

MS. TREND: Your argument merely reflects the difficulties of quantifying chart theories rather than the deficiencies of the chartist approach. One man's top formation is another man's congestion area. An attempt to define anything but the simplest chart pattern mathematically will be unavoidably arbitrary. The problems become even more tangled when one realizes that at any given time, the chart picture may exhibit conflicting patterns. Thus, in a sense, it is not really possible to test many chart theories objectively.

PROFESSOR COIN: That's rather convenient for you, isn't it? If these theories can't be rigorously tested, of what use are they? How do you know that trading on charts will lead to better than a 50–50 success rate—that is, before commissions?

MS. TREND: If you mean that blindly following every chart signal will merely make your broker rich, I don't disagree. However, my point is that chart analysis is an art, not a science. A familiarity with basic chart theories is only the starting point. The true usefulness of charts depends on the individual trader's ability to synthesize successfully his or her own experience with standard concepts. In the right hands, charts can be extremely valuable in anticipating major market trends. There are many successful traders who base their decisions primarily on charts. What would you attribute their success to—a lucky streak?

PROFESSOR COIN: Yes. Exactly that, a lucky streak. If there are enough traders, some of them will be winners, whether they reach their decisions by reading charts or throwing darts at the commodity price page. It's not the method, just the laws of probability. Even in a casino, some percentage of the people are winners. You wouldn't say that their success is due to any insights or system.

MS. TREND: All that proves is that superior performance by some chartists *could* be due to chance. It doesn't disprove the contention that the skillful chartist is onto something that gives him or her an edge.

MODERATOR: I sense a lot of resistance here, and I think we could use some more support. Have either of you brought any evidence along that would tend to substantiate your positions?

PROFESSOR COIN: Yes! (*At this point, Professor Coin pulls a thick manuscript from his briefcase and thrusts it into Mr. Puneyser's hands. The moderator flips through the pages and shakes his head as he notices a profusion of funny little Greek letters.)*

MODERATOR: I had something a little less mathematical in mind. Even educational TV is not ready for this.

PROFESSOR COIN: Well, I also have this. (*He pulls out a sheet of paper and hands it to Ms. Trend.*) How would you interpret this chart, Ms. Trend? (*He unsuccessfully attempts to suppress a smirk.*)

MS. TREND: I'd say this looks like a chart based on a series of coin tosses. You know—heads, one box up, tails one box down.

PROFESSOR COIN: (*Whose smirk has turned into a very visible frown.*) How did you know that?

MS. TREND: Lucky guess.

PROFESSOR COIN: Well, anyway, that doesn't affect my argument. Look at this chart. Here's a trend. And this here—isn't that what you people call a head and shoulders formation?

MODERATOR: Speaking of head and shoulders, do either of you have an opinion on Procter & Gamble?

PROFESSOR COIN: (*Continuing.*) The same chart patterns you are so quick to point to on your price charts also show up in obviously random series.

MS. TREND: Yes, but that line of reasoning can lead to some odd conclusions. For instance, would you agree that the fact that working economists tend to have advanced degrees is not a chance occurrence?

PROFESSOR COIN: Of course.

MS. TREND: Well then, a random sample of the population is also likely to turn up some people with advanced degrees. Do you then conclude that the fact that an economist has an advanced degree is a coincidence?

PROFESSOR COIN: I still don't see any difference between price charts and my randomly generated chart.

MS. TREND: You don't? Does this look like a randomly generated chart? (*Ms. Trend holds up a July 1980 silver chart—see Figure 1.1.*)

PROFESSOR COIN: Well, not exactly, but . . .

MODERATOR: You might say that not every silver chart has a cloudy trend line.

MS. TREND: (*On the attack.*) Or this. (*She holds up the December 1994 coffee chart—see Figure 1.2.*) I could go on.

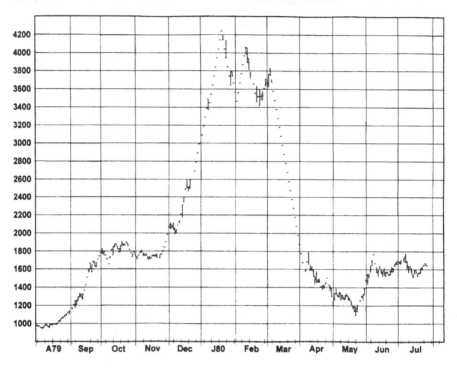

FIGURE 1.1 July 1980 silver.

MODERATOR: (*To Professor Coin.*) Ms. Trend really seems to be percolating. Are there any grounds for dismissing her examples?

PROFESSOR COIN: Well, I admit those examples are pretty extreme, but they still don't prove that past prices can predict future prices.

MODERATOR: Before our time reaches limit-up, so to speak, I would like to rechart our course. I wonder what your opinions are about fundamental analysts?

PROFESSOR COIN: Well, they're better than chartists since they can at least *explain* price moves. But I'm afraid their attempts to *forecast* prices are equally futile. You see, at any given moment, the market discounts all known information, so there is no way they can project prices unless they can anticipate unforeseen future developments such as droughts or export embargoes.

MS. TREND: Well, first I would like to address the implication that chart analysts ignore fundamentals. Actually, we believe that the price chart provides an unambiguous and immediate summary of the net impact of all fundamental and psychological factors. In contrast, accurate fundamental models, if they could be con-

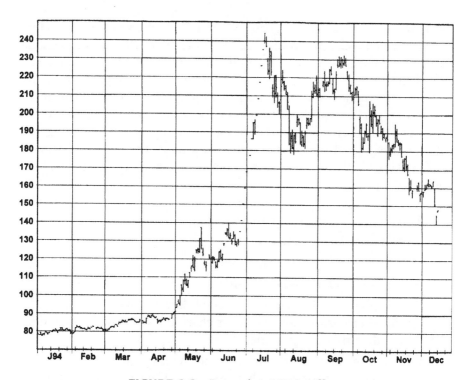

FIGURE 1.2 December 1994 coffee.

structed at all, would be extremely complex. Furthermore, the fundamental data for the forecast period would have to be estimated, thereby making the price projections extremely vulnerable to error.

MODERATOR: Then you might say you both agree with the statement that fundamentalists end up with holes in their shoes.

MS. TREND: Yes.

PROFESSOR COIN: Yes.

MODERATOR: Well, on that upbeat note of agreement, we end tonight's program.

In a sense, the argument between the "random walkers" and the chartists can never be clearly resolved. It must be understood that it is impossible to prove randomness; all that one can prove is that a given pattern does not exist. Because there is no consensus as to the precise mathematical definition of many chart patterns, the viability of these patterns as price indicators can neither be proven nor disproven.

For example, if one wanted to determine if *breakouts* from *trading ranges* represent valid trade signals, the first requirement would be to formulate a concise definition of a trading range and a breakout. Assume that the following definitions are adopted: (1) that the trading range is a price band that completely encloses all daily price changes during the past six-week period and that is no wider than 5% of the median price during that period; and (2) that a breakout is a closing price above the six-week trading range. Although the validity of breakouts as trading signals could be tested for these specific definitions, the definitions themselves will be challenged by many. Some of the objections might include the following:

1. The price band is too narrow.
2. The price band is too wide.
3. The six-week period is too long.
4. The six-week period is too short.
5. No allowance is made for isolated days beyond the confines of the range—an event that most chart analysts would agree does not disturb the basic pattern.
6. The direction of the trend prior to the trading range is not considered—a factor many chartists would view as a critical input in interpreting the reliability of a breakout.
7. The breakout should be required to exceed the boundary of the trading range by a minimum amount (e.g., 1% of the price level) in order to be viewed as valid.
8. Several closes above the trading range should be required to indicate a breakout.
9. A time lag should be used to test the validity of the breakout; for example, are prices still beyond the trading range one week after the initial penetration of the range?

The preceding list represents only a sample of the possible objections to our hypothetical definitions of a trading range and a breakout—and all of this for one of the most basic chart patterns. Imagine the ambiguities and complications in specifically defining a pattern such as a confirmed head and shoulders.

For their part, the chartists cannot win the argument, either. Although chart analysis is based on general principles, its application depends on individual interpretation. The successful chart-oriented trader might not have any doubts about the viability of chart analysis, but the random walk theoreticians would dismiss the chartist's success as a consequence of the laws of probability, since even a totally random trade selection process would yield a percentage of winners.

In short, the debate is not about to be concluded.

It is also important to realize that even if conclusive tests were possible, the conflicting claims of the random walkers and the chartists need not necessarily be contradictory. One way of viewing the situation is that markets may witness extended periods of random fluctuation, interspersed with shorter periods of nonrandom behavior. Thus, even if the price series as a whole appears random, it is entirely possible that there are periods within the data that exhibit definite patterns. The goal of the chart analyst is to identify those periods (i.e., major trends).

The time has come to admit my own biases. Personal experience has convinced me that charts are a valuable, if not essential, trading tool. However, such perceptions do not prove anything. The random walkers would argue that my conclusions could be based on selective memory—that is, a tendency to remember the successes of chart analysis and forget the failures—or just pure luck. And they are right. Such explanations could indeed be correct.

Each trader must evaluate chart analysis independently and draw his or her own conclusions. However, it should be strongly emphasized that charts are considered to be an extremely valuable trading tool by many successful traders, and therefore, the new trader should be wary of rejecting this approach simply on the basis of intuitive skepticism. Some of the principal potential benefits of using charts are listed below. (Note that a number of these uses remain valid even if one totally rejects the possibility that charts can be used to forecast prices.)

1. Charts provide a concise price history—an essential item of information for any trader.

2. Charts can provide the trader with a good sense of the market's *volatility*—an important consideration in assessing risk.

3. Charts are a very useful tool to the fundamental analyst. Long-term price charts enable the fundamentalist to isolate quickly the periods of major price moves. By determining the fundamental conditions or events that were peculiar to those periods, the fundamentalist can identify the key price-influencing factors. This information can then be used to construct a price behavior model.

4. Charts can be used as a timing tool, even by traders who formulate their trading decisions on the basis of other information (e.g., fundamentals).

5. Charts can be used as a money management tool by helping to define meaningful and realistic stop points.

6. Charts reflect market behavior that is subject to certain repetitive patterns. Given sufficient experience, some traders will uncover an innate ability to use charts successfully as a method of anticipating price moves.

7. An understanding of chart concepts is probably an essential prerequisite for developing profitable technical trading systems.

8. Cynics take notice: Under specific circumstances, a contrarian approach to classical chart signals can lead to very profitable trading opportunities. The specifics of this approach are detailed in Chapter 11.

In short, charts have something to offer everyone, from cynics to believers. The chapters of this section review and evaluate the key concepts of classical chart theory, as well as address the all-important question of how charts can be used as an effective trading tool.

Chapter

Types of Charts

You don't need a weatherman to know which way the wind blows.

—Bob Dylan

The price chart, of course, is the primary tool of the technical analyst. Although there are a variety of formats, most charts use a grid system in which the x-axis measures time while the y-axis measures price level. The time increment of the x-axis can vary according to the longer- or shorter-term perspective of the analyst. Charts can be constructed using price data for any interval: yearly, monthly, weekly, daily (the most common), and intraday (e.g., 60 minutes, 30 minutes, etc.).

BAR CHARTS

Bar charts are by far the most common type of price chart. In a bar chart, each day is represented by a vertical line that ranges from the daily low to the daily high. The day's closing value is indicated by a horizontal protrusion to the right of the bar. Additionally, the day's opening value is often (but not always) indicated by a horizontal protrusion to the left of the bar. Figure 2.1 is a daily bar chart of an individual stock.

In futures markets, the opening and closing prices shown on a bar chart are representative values (usually determined by exchange-authorized professional traders in a particular contract) that approximate the average price during the first and last minutes of the trading day, respectively. In the case of stocks, the opening and closing prices represent the actual first and last sales of the day as recorded by the specialist in a particular equity.

The daily bar chart is most useful for trading purposes, but bar

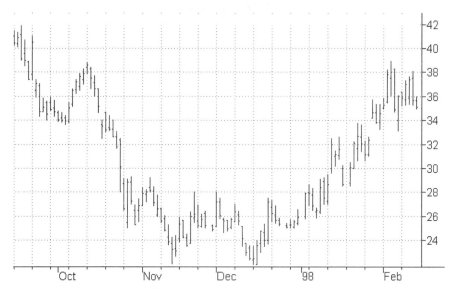

FIGURE 2.1 Daily bar chart: Micron Technology.
Chart created with TradeStation® by Omega Research, Inc.

charts for longer data periods provide an extremely important perspective. These longer-period bar charts (e.g., weekly, monthly) are entirely analogous to the daily bar chart, with each vertical line representing the price range and final price level for the period. (On weekly or monthly charts, the opening and closing prices are simply the opening price from the first trading period included in the bar and the closing price of the last trading period included in the bar. For example, each bar on a weekly chart would use Monday's opening price and Friday's closing price.) Figure 2.2 is a weekly bar chart of the stock pictured in Figure 2.1. The segment within the rectangle corresponds to the period captured in Figure 2.1. Figure 2.3 is a monthly bar chart for the same stock. The large and small rectangles enclose the periods depicted by Figure 2.2 and Figure 2.1, respectively.

Used in combination, the monthly, weekly, and daily bar charts provide a telephoto-type effect. The monthly and weekly charts would be used to provide a broad market perspective and to formulate a technical opinion regarding the potential long-term trend. The daily chart would then be employed to determine the timing of trades. If the long-term technical picture is sufficiently decisive, the trader may already have a strong market bias by the time he or she gets to the daily charts. For example, if the monthly and weekly charts suggest the market has witnessed a major long-term top, the trader will only monitor the daily charts for sell signals.

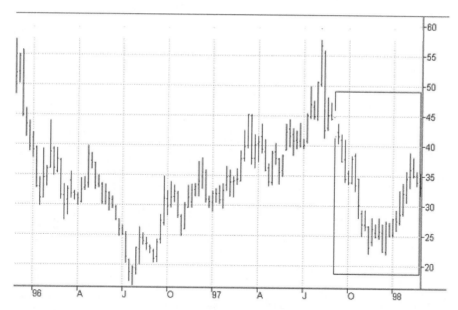

FIGURE 2.2 Weekly bar chart: Micron Technology.
Chart created with TradeStation® by Omega Research, Inc.

The difference in perspective between daily and weekly charts can be striking; hence, both types of charts should be examined. For example, the daily bar chart for the March 1995 silver contract (Figure 2.4) is dominated by a very bearish, massive *top pattern*. The weekly silver chart (Figure 2.5), however, provides a very different picture. Although in this chart the late 1993–1994 price pattern still looks toppy, the chart also reveals that prices are near the low end of a broad historical price range and that a major price base was apparently formed during the 1991 to early 1993 period. Thus, while both charts seem to imply a near-term bearish bias, the weekly chart provides strong reasons for viewing another price downswing as a potential major buying opportunity, whereas there is not even a hint of such a conclusion in the daily chart.

CLOSE-ONLY CHARTS

As the name implies, *close-only charts* are based on closing values and ignore high and low price information. Some price series can be depicted in only close-only chart formats because intraday data are not readily available. Two examples are (1) cash price series (Figure 2.6) and (2)

FIGURE 2.3 Monthly bar chart: Micron Technology.
Chart created with TradeStation® by Omega Research, Inc.

spreads (Figure 2.7). (A spread chart depicts the price difference between two instruments.)

Some chart traders may prefer close-only charts even when high/low/close data are available because they feel a clearer price picture can be obtained by using only the close. In their view, the inclusion of high/low data only serves to obfuscate the price chart. There is much to be said for the emphasis on the closing value as the embodiment of the day's essential price information. Nevertheless, many important chart patterns depend on the availability of high/low data and one should think twice before ignoring this information. Furthermore, as a practical matter, bar charts are far more readily available than close-only charts.

POINT-AND-FIGURE CHARTS

The essential characteristic of the *point-and-figure chart* is that it views all trading as a single continuous stream and hence ignores time. A point-and-figure chart (see Figure 2.8) consists of a series of columns of X's and O's. (Some types of charting software use rectangles or other symbols instead of O's.) Each X represents a price move of a given magnitude called the *box size*. As long as prices continue to rise, X's are added to a column for each increment equal to the box size. However, if prices decline by an

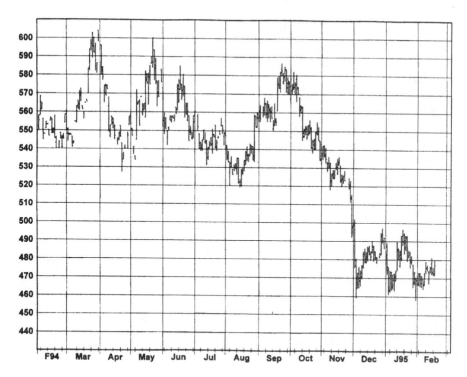

FIGURE 2.4 Daily bar chart perspective: March 1995 silver.

amount equal to or greater than the *reversal size* (usually quoted as a multiple of the box size), a new column of *O*'s is initiated and plotted in descending fashion. The number of *O*'s will depend on the magnitude of the reversal, but by definition must at least equal the reversal size. By convention, the first *O* in a column is always plotted one box below the last *X* in the preceding column. An analogous description would apply to price declines and upside reversals. The choice of box and reversal size is arbitrary. The larger the box size, the more short-term "noise" is filtered out of the point-and-figure chart.

Figure 2.8 uses a box size of .5 point and a reversal size of three boxes, or 1.5 points. In other words, as long as a price decline of 1.5 or more points does not occur, *X*'s continue to be added in a single column for every .5 point price rise that occurs. When a price decline of 1.5 or more points occurs, a new column of *O*'s is begun, with the first *O* placed one box below the last *X*.

As stated previously, the point-and-figure chart does not reflect time. One column may represent one day or two months. For example, Figure 2.9 is a bar chart corresponding to the point-and-figure chart in Figure

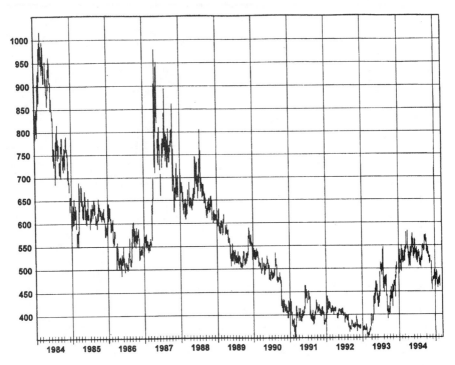

FIGURE 2.5 Weekly bar chart perspective: silver nearest futures.

2.8. Both the single day on the bar chart (denoted by the symbol "1") and the immediately subsequent five-day period on the bar chart (bracketed by arrows and labeled with the "2" symbol), correspond to single columns (similarly marked) on the point-and-figure chart.

CANDLESTICK CHARTS

Candlestick charts add dimension and color to the simple bar chart. The segment of the bar that represents the range between the open and close is represented by a two-dimensional *real body*, while the extensions beyond this range to the high and low are shown as lines (called *shadows*). A day on which the open and close are near opposite extremes of the daily range will have a large real body, whereas a day on which there is little net change between the open and close will have a small real body. The color of the real body indicates whether the close was higher than the open (white—Figure 2.10) or lower than the open (black—Figure 2.11). Figure 2.12 is a candlestick chart of the middle portion (late-May through early-September 1996) of Figure 2.9.

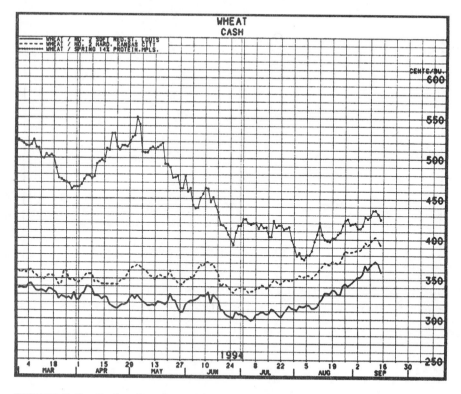

FIGURE 2.6 Cash price chart: wheat.
Source: Reprinted with permission, © 1995 BRIDGE/CRB, 30 South Wacker Drive, Suite 1810, Chicago, IL 60606.

While candlestick charts use the same price data as bar charts, their unique display of this data highlights distinct reversal and continuation patterns that candlestick analysts rely on to gauge market behavior. A detailed description of the myriad candlestick patterns and their respective interpretations is beyond the scope of this discussion. As one illustration, a candlestick that has the same opening and closing price is called a doji. An example is provided by the dramatic, wide-ranging day in Figure 2.12. Dojis are traditionally interpreted as manifestations of uneasiness or indecision in a market, and in a trending market may warn of an impending trend change. The doji is, by the way, the only candlestick that appears identical to its bar chart counterpart. (Compare Figure 2.12 to Figure 2.9.) Insofar as candlestick charts show more information than bar charts and offer an alternative visual depiction of price data, some traders may find these charts more natural or useful than conventional bar charts.

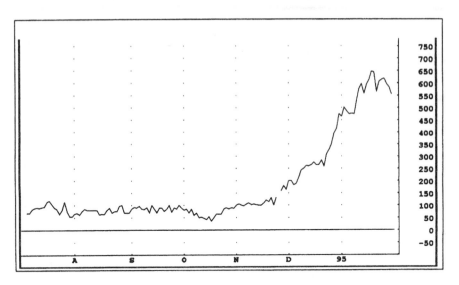

FIGURE 2.7 Spread chart: October/December cotton.
Source: FutureSource; copyright © 1986–1994; all rights reserved.

DATA

When analyzing any type of chart, it's important to understand the nature of the price data you're studying. The following sections address some of the often overlooked data issues for stock and futures traders, respectively.

FOR STOCK TRADERS ONLY:
STOCK SPLITS AND PRICE DATA

When the price of a stock splits, all past prices are adjusted proportionately so that the split itself does not cause any price change. For example, if a stock trading at $50 witnesses a 2:1 split, the current price becomes $25. If no adjustment were made, the chart would reflect a price move from $50 to $25. To avoid this absurdity and distortion, all past prices would be divided by 2 (the split ratio). Thus, while past prices prior to stock splits would not reflect the actual stock prices at the time, the series would be affected by only true price moves, as opposed to moves due to stock splits.

Although the method of adjusting stock price series for stock splits is sensible, it is important to realize that past price changes implied by a stock price series may dramatically understate the actual changes that oc-

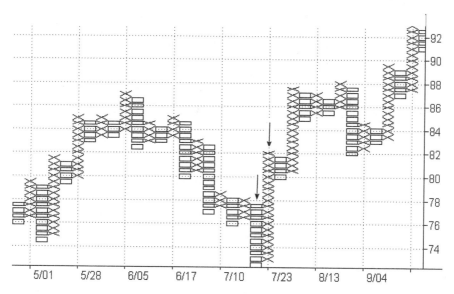

FIGURE 2.8 Point-and-figure chart: Citicorp.
Chart created with TradeStation® by Omega Research, Inc.

curred. For example, assume a stock witnessed three 2:1 splits. To adjust for these splits, prices between the second and third splits would be divided by 2; prices between the first and second splits would be divided by 4; and prices prior to all three splits would be divided by 8. Thus a price rise from $5 to $8 that occurred prior to all three splits would actually have represented a $24 per share gain, not a $3 per share gain. While this consideration may not alter price patterns, it can significantly distort trading system results based on computer tests applied to the entire price series. Although an explanation is beyond the scope of this book, in using standard split-adjusted price data in testing trading systems, distortions will be greatly mitigated by assuming a fixed-dollar position of shares in each trade (e.g., $1,000) as opposed to a fixed number of shares. For example, if the split-adjusted price is $5, the trade size would be 200 shares, while if the price is $50 the trade size would be 20 shares.

FOR FUTURES TRADERS ONLY: LINKED CONTRACT SERIES

Stock charts represent constant and unbroken data series. This is not the case with futures contracts. Commodity and financial futures are traded on a recurring cycle of contract months, each with finite life spans and distinct (but usually related) prices. For example, T-bond futures use

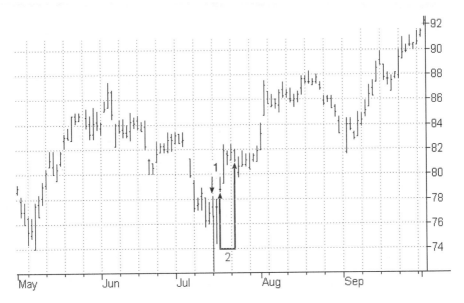

FIGURE 2.9 Bar chart corresponding to point-and-figure chart in Figure 2.8: Citicorp.
Chart created with TradeStation® by Omega Research, Inc.

what is commonly called the quarterly cycle, with contract months of March, June, September, and December. Crude oil, by comparison, has a contract for every month of the calendar year. A futures trader who holds a long-term position must "roll over" the trade—that is, liquidate the position in the expiring contract month and reestablish it in the next contract month. Thus, the time period covered by the typical weekly or monthly bar chart requires the use of a series of contracts. This is particularly important for the identification of longer-term top and bottom formations, as well as the determination of *support* and *resistance* levels.

A major problem facing the chart analyst in the futures markets is the relatively limited life spans of most futures contracts, and the even shorter periods in which these contracts have significant trading activity. For many futures contracts (e.g., currencies, stock indexes) trading activity is almost totally concentrated in the nearest one or two contract months. In fact, in some markets almost all trading is concentrated in the nearest position (e.g., most foreign bond futures), with the result that meaningful price data exist for only one to three months.

Such circumstances make it virtually impossible to apply most chart analysis techniques to individual contract charts. Even in those markets in which the individual contracts have a year or more of liquid data, part

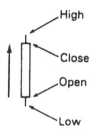

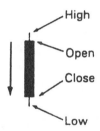

FIGURE 2.10 Candlestick chart: white real body (up day).

FIGURE 2.11 Candlestick chart: black real body (down day).

of a thorough chart study would still encompass analyzing multiyear weekly and monthly charts. Thus, the application of chart analysis unavoidably requires linking successive futures contracts into a single chart. In markets with very limited individual contract data, such linked charts will be a necessity in order to perform any meaningful chart analysis. In other markets, linked charts will still be required for analyzing multiyear chart patterns.

Nearest Futures

Normally, futures contracts are combined using the *nearest futures* approach: A contract is plotted until its expiration and then the subsequent contract is plotted until its expiration, and so on. However, a nearest futures chart may reflect significant distortions due to the price gaps between the expiring month and the subsequent contract.

Figure 2.13 provides a dramatic example of this type of distortion. Note the pattern of consolidations interspersed by single-week, sharp rallies that materialized every three months like clockwork. Was the Euromark during this period subject to some bullish event that occurred every three months? No. These regularly spaced, single-week "rallies" were not true price advances at all, but rather an illusory consequence of the transition from the nearest futures contract to the next contract, which during the period depicted consistently traded at a wide premium to the nearby month.

In fact, throughout almost the entire period shown in Figure 2.13, prices actually declined, in the sense that a continuously held long position that was rolled over to the next contract as each expiration approached would have lost money! This point is illustrated by Figure 2.14, which depicts the *continuous futures* chart for the same market during the same time period. (Price swings in a continuous futures chart, which is

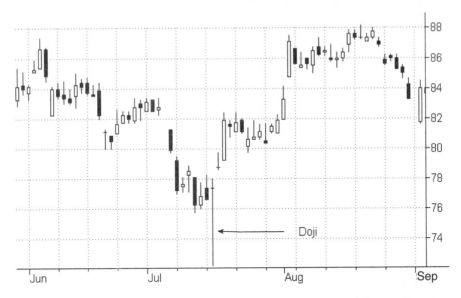

FIGURE 2.12 Candlestick chart corresponding to point-and-figure chart in Figure 2.8 and bar chart in Figure 2.9: Citicorp.
Chart created with TradeStation® by Omega Research, Inc.

defined later in this section, will exactly parallel the equity fluctuations in a continuously held long position.) The gains implied by the fixed-interval, sharp upswings in Figure 2.13 could not have been realized by a trader, because he would have liquidated a position in one contract month and replaced that position in another contract month that was much higher priced. In fact, it is this price difference between months that is responsible for the phantom price moves evident in the nearest futures chart at three-month intervals.

The fact that a nearest futures chart is vulnerable to great distortion, in the sense that price moves depicted in the chart may contrast dramatically with the results realized by an actual trader (as was the case in the Euromark illustration just provided), makes it necessary to consider an alternative linked-contract representation that does not share this defect. The continuous futures chart provides such an alternative approach.

Continuous Futures

Continuous futures is a series that links together successive contracts in such a way that the price gaps discussed earlier are eliminated. This is accomplished by adding the cumulative difference between the old and new contracts at rollover points to the new contract series. An example should

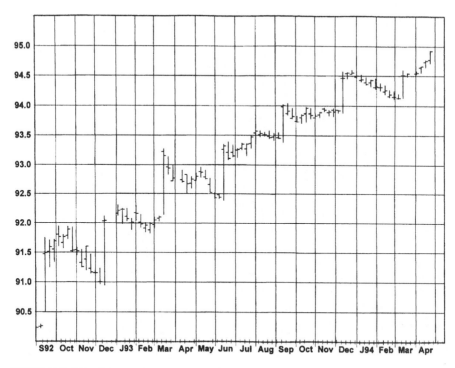

FIGURE 2.13 Distortion in nearest futures chart: Euromark weekly nearest futures.

help clarify this method. Assume we are constructing a continuous price series for COMEX gold using the June and December contracts.* If the price series begins at the start of the calendar year, initially the values in the series will be identical to the prices of the June contract expiring in that year. Assume that on the rollover date (which need not necessarily be the last trading day) June gold closes at $400 and December gold closes at $412. In this case, all subsequent prices based on the December contract would be adjusted downward by $12—the difference between the December and June contracts on the rollover date.

Assume that at the next rollover date December gold is trading at $450 and the subsequent June contract is trading at $464. The December contract price of $450 implies that the spread-adjusted continuous price

*The choice of a combination of contracts is arbitrary. One can use any combination of actively traded months in the given market. For example, in the case of COMEX gold, choices range from constructing a series based on all six actively traded contracts—February, April, June, August, October, and December—to a series based on only a single contract, such as December.

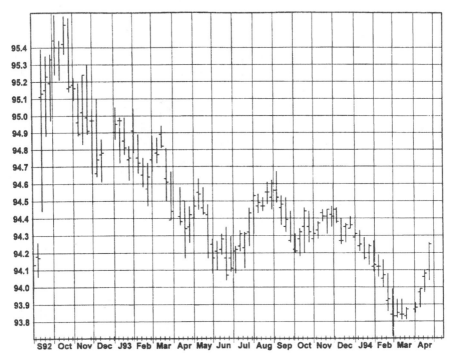

FIGURE 2.14 Continuous futures chart as accurate reflection of equity fluctuations: Euromark weekly nearest futures.

is $438. Thus, on this second rollover date, the June contract is trading $26 above the adjusted series. Consequently, all subsequent prices based on the second June contract would be adjusted downward by $26. This procedure would continue, with the adjustment for each contract dependent on the cumulative total of the present and prior transition point price differences. Typically, as a last step, it is convenient to shift the scale of the entire series by the cumulative adjustment factor, a step that will set the current price of the series equal to the price of the current contract without changing the shape of the series. The resulting price series would be free of the distortions due to spread differences that exist at the rollover points between contracts.

It should be noted that in markets in which there is a strong tendency for nearby contracts to trade at significant premiums at rollover points, it is entirely possible for a continuous futures series to eventually include negative prices for some past periods as cumulative adjustments mount. Although this might sound disconcerting, it does not present any problems for system testing. As for chart analysis, the trader would, of course, ignore any support points located at negative or unrealistically low price levels.

Constant Forward ("Perpetual") Series

A third type of linked future series that the reader may encounter is the *constant forward* (also known as "perpetual") series, which consists of quotes for prices a constant amount of time forward. A constant forward series can be constructed from futures price data through interpolation. For example, if we were calculating a 90-day constant forward series, and the 90-day forward date fell exactly one-third of the way between the expirations of the nearest two contracts, the constant forward price would be calculated as the sum of two-thirds of the nearest contract price and one-third of the subsequent contract price. As we moved forward in time, the nearest contract would be weighted less, but the weighting of the subsequent contract would increase proportionally. Eventually, the nearest contract would expire and drop out of the calculation, and the constant forward series would be based on an interpolation between the subsequent two contracts.

The constant forward series eliminates the problem of huge price gaps at rollovers and is certainly a significant improvement over a nearest futures price series. However, this type of series has two major drawbacks. First, since the series does not correspond to any real contract, one cannot actually trade a constant forward series. Second, and even more serious, the constant forward series does not reflect the impact of time evaporation on actual futures contracts. This deficiency can easily result in the price pattern of a constant forward futures series deviating significantly from the patterns exhibited by actual traded contracts—a highly undesirable feature.

Comparing the Series

It is important to understand that a linked futures price series can accurately reflect either price levels or price changes, but not both—much as a coin can land on either heads or tails, but not both. Nearest futures will accurately reflect actual historical levels, but not price swings. Continuous futures will precisely reflect price swings, but past continuous levels will not match actual historical levels. Constant forward futures are neither fish nor fowl—that is, they do not accurately reflect either price levels or price swings.

Since a continuous futures series is the only linked series that precisely reflects price swings and hence equity fluctuations in an actual trading account, it is the only linked series that can be used to generate accurate simulations in computer testing of trading systems. (Because of the aforementioned limited life span of individual contracts, these contracts cannot be used for testing any system that requires looking back at more than about six months of data as a whole spectrum of longer-term approaches do. Even when theoretically possible—for example, testing a short-term trading approach—using actual contract data requires using a large number of individual series, which is far more cumbersome than using a single linked series.)

Given the significant differences between nearest and continuous futures price series, the obvious question in the reader's mind is probably: Which series—nearest futures or continuous futures—would be most appropriate for chart analysis? To some extent, this is like asking, Which factor should a consumer consider before purchasing a new car: price or quality? The obvious answer is both; each factor provides important information about a characteristic that is not measured by the other. The fact that each type of price chart—nearest and continuous—has certain significant intrinsic weaknesses argues for combining both types of charts in a more complete analysis. Often these two types of charts will provide entirely different price pictures.

Nearest futures is the most common linked series provided by data vendors. Many vendors also provide an additional linked series—either continuous futures or constant forward futures. Given the very substantial differences between these series, always make sure you know which kind of linked data you are buying and using.

Chapter

Trends

The trend is your friend except at the end when it bends.

—Ed Seykota

DEFINING TRENDS BY HIGHS AND LOWS

Because market trends offer the best profit opportunities, the most basic goal of chart analysis is to define and identify price *trends*. One standard definition of an uptrend is a succession of higher highs and higher lows. For example, in Figure 3.1, during the March–September period, each *relative high* (RH) is higher than the preceding high and each *relative low* (RL) is higher than the preceding low. In essence, an uptrend can be considered intact until a previous relative low point (a "reaction" low) is broken. A violation of this condition serves as a warning that the trend may be over. For example, in Figure 3.1, the October penetration of the September relative low proves to be a harbinger of an ensuing decline. It should be emphasized, however, that the disruption of the pattern of higher highs and higher lows (or lower highs and lower lows) should be viewed as a clue, not absolute proof, of a possible long-term trend reversal. Figure 3.2 provides another example of an uptrend defined by successively higher highs and higher lows.

In similar fashion, a downtrend can be defined as a succession of lower lows and lower highs (see Figure 3.3). A downtrend can be considered intact until a previous relative high is exceeded.

Uptrends and downtrends are also often defined in terms of *trend lines*. An uptrend line connects a series of higher lows (see Figures 3.4 and 3.5); a downtrend line connects a series of lower highs (see Figure 3.6). Trend lines can sometimes extend for many years. For example, the trend line in Figure 3.7 highlights a seven-year uptrend.

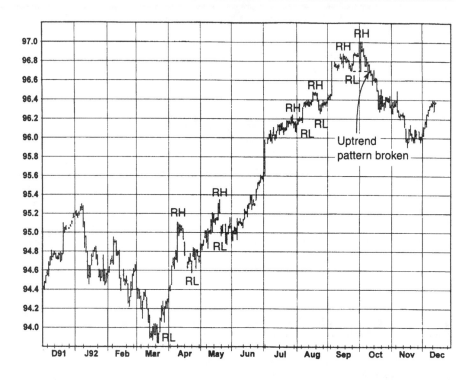

Note: RH = relative high; RL = relative low.

FIGURE 3.1 Uptrend as succession of higher highs and higher lows: December 1992 Eurodollar.

It is not uncommon for reactions against a major trend to begin near a line parallel to the trend line. Sets of parallel lines that enclose a trend are called *trend channels*. Figures 3.8 and 3.9 illustrate extended uptrend and downtrend channels.

TREND LINE RULES

The following rules are usually applied to trend lines and channels:

1. Declines approaching an uptrend line and rallies approaching a downtrend line are often good opportunities to initiate positions in the direction of the major trend.

2. The penetration of an uptrend line (particularly on a closing basis) is a sell signal; the penetration of a downtrend line is a buy signal. Normally, a minimum percentage price move or a mini-

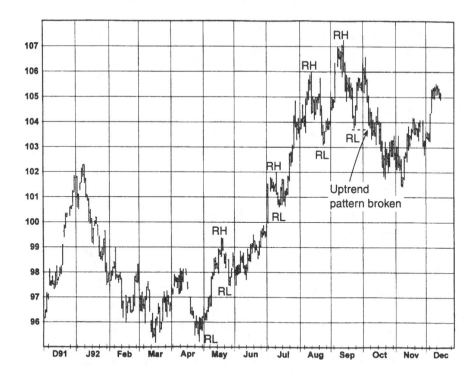

Note: RH = relative high; RL = relative low.

FIGURE 3.2 Uptrend as succession of higher highs and higher lows: December 1992 T-bond.

mum number of closes beyond the trend line is required to confirm a penetration.

3. The lower end of a downtrend channel and the upper end of an uptrend channel represent potential profit-taking zones for short-term traders.

Trend lines and channels are useful, but their importance is often overstated. It is easy to overestimate the reliability of trend lines when they are drawn with the benefit of hindsight. A consideration that is frequently overlooked is that trend lines often need to be redrawn as a bull or bear market is extended. Thus, although the penetration of a trend line will sometimes offer an early warning signal of a trend reversal, it is also common that such a development will merely require a redrawing of the trend line. For example, Figure 3.10 shows three trend lines, the first of which ("1") defines the steep uptrend in the April–June period. However, the mid-June penetration of this trend line did not result in a reversal, but merely necessitated a redrawing of the trend line ("2"). Similarly, the

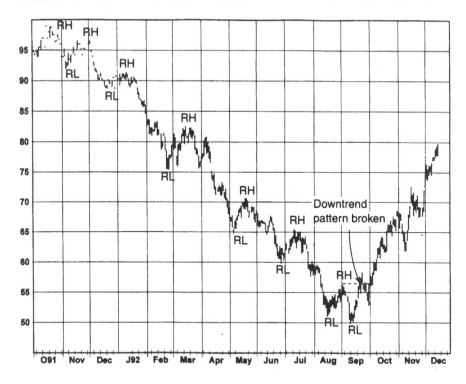

Note: RH = relative high; RL = relative low.

FIGURE 3.3 Downtrend as succession of lower highs and lower lows: December 1992 coffee.

dashed line ("3") represents an alternate trend line that could have been added to capture the July and August lows.

Figure 3.11 provides an example for a downtrend. The higher line in Figure 3.11 represents the downtrend line that would have been drawn with the benefit of hindsight. The lower line represents the downtrend line that was indicated until May (cover the portion of the chart from May onward to see the practicality of the original trend line). The May penetration of the trend line did not result in a trend reversal, but merely necessitated a redrawing of the trend line. In similar fashion, Figure 3.12 is identical to Figure 3.11, except the period depicted is extended by four months. The lower lines are reproduced from Figure 3.11 and represent the downtrend lines that were indicated until May and July, respectively. Again, the penetration of these trend lines did not result in trend reversals, but merely necessitated the redrawing of the trend line. These examples illustrate that trend lines may sometimes have to be redrawn several times.

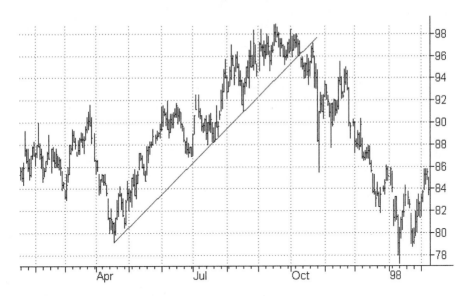

FIGURE 3.4 Uptrend line: Amoco.
Chart created with TradeStation® by Omega Research, Inc.

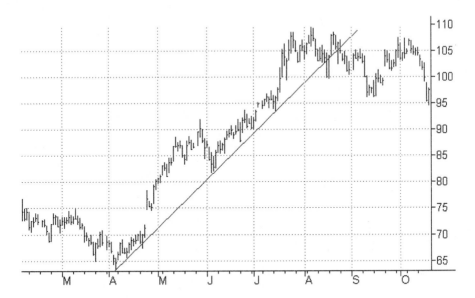

FIGURE 3.5 Uptrend line: IBM.
Chart created with TradeStation® by Omega Research, Inc.

FIGURE 3.6　Downtrend line: Motorola.
Chart created with TradeStation® by Omega Research, Inc.

FIGURE 3.7　Uptrend line: Xerox.
Chart created with TradeStation® by Omega Research, Inc.

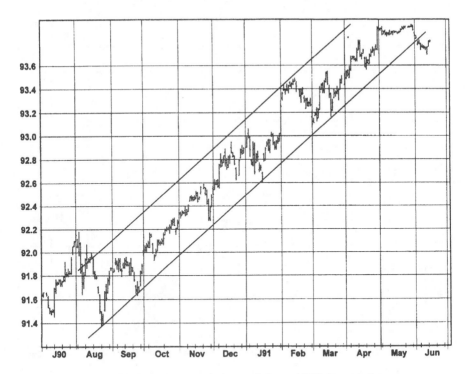

FIGURE 3.8 Uptrend channel: June 1991 Eurodollar.

The preceding examples are meant to drive home the point that the penetration of trend lines is more the rule than the exception. The simple fact is that trend lines tend to be penetrated, sometimes repeatedly, during their evolution, which is equivalent to saying that trend lines are frequently redefined as they extend. The important implications of this observation are that trend lines work much better in hindsight than in real time and that trend line penetrations often prove to be false signals. This latter consideration will be revisited in Chapter 11.

DRAWING TREND LINES

Trend lines are most commonly drawn by connecting significant lows (for uptrend lines) or highs (for downtrend lines). There is some debate regarding the number of highs or lows that must be joined to create a valid trend line. Two, of course, is the minimum, with the significance of the trend line rising proportionally to the number of highs or lows it connects. Ultimately, the process is unavoidably subjective. For example, a

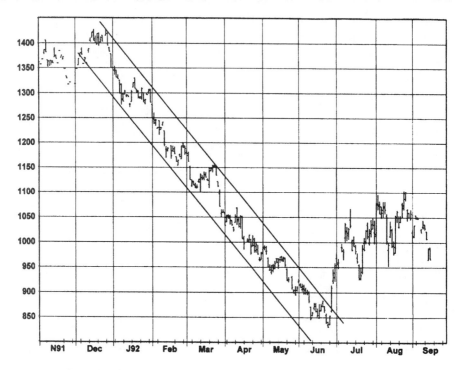

FIGURE 3.9 Downtrend channel: September 1992 cocoa.

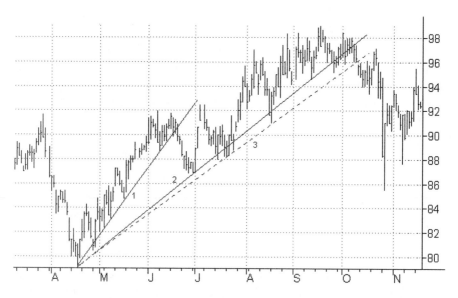

FIGURE 3.10 Uptrend line redefined: Amoco.
Chart created with TradeStation® by Omega Research, Inc.

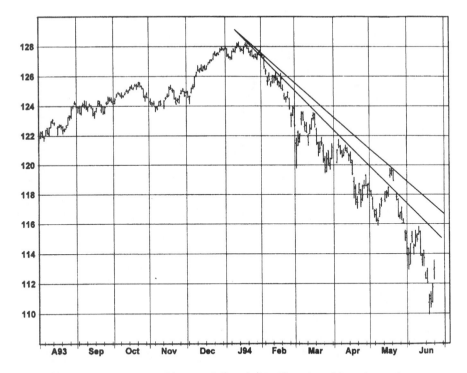

FIGURE 3.11   Downtrend line redefined: Matif notional bond continuous futures.

trend line connecting the approximate lows of six price bars (i.e., with some or all of the lows slightly penetrating the trend line) in an uptrend may more accurately define the trend than a line connecting the precise lows of two price bars. (For further discussion on this topic, see the next section, "Internal Trend Lines.")

It is, however, possible to define trend lines objectively. In his book, *The New Science of Technical Analysis* (John Wiley & Sons, New York, 1994), Thomas DeMark outlines such a method. The process of constructing his "TD lines" consists of connecting exactly two points: for uptrend lines, the most recent relative low and the most recent preceding lower relative low; for downtrend lines, the most recent relative high and the most recent preceding higher relative high. By basing trend line definitions on the most recent relative highs and lows, trend lines will be continually redefined as new relative highs and lows occur. This approach results in emphasizing the importance of recent prices over historical prices.

TD lines are highly dependent on the value of N used to define relative

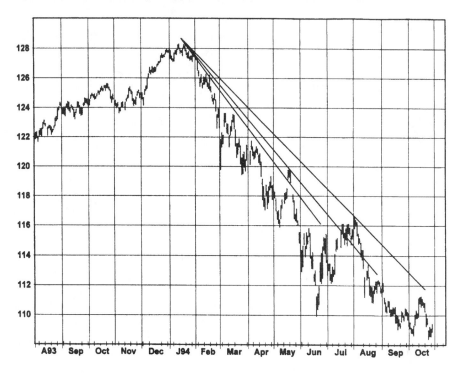

FIGURE 3.12 Downtrend line redefined twice: Matif notional bond continuous futures.

lows and highs. Figures 3.13 and 3.14 compare the TD lines generated by two different values of N (8 and 4) for the same market. In Figure 3.13 the TD line connects the most recent lows that are lower than the lows of the preceding and succeeding eight days; in Figure 3.14 the TD line connects the most recent lows that are lower than the lows of the preceding and succeeding four days. The higher the value of N selected, the fewer trend lines that will be generated and the more significant these trend lines will be. The trade-off is that the higher the value N, the slower the resulting trend line will be in yielding trading signals.

INTERNAL TREND LINES

Conventional trend lines are typically drawn to encompass extreme highs and lows. An argument can be made, however, that extreme highs and lows represent emotional excesses in the market, and as such may not represent the dominant trend in the market. An *internal trend line* does

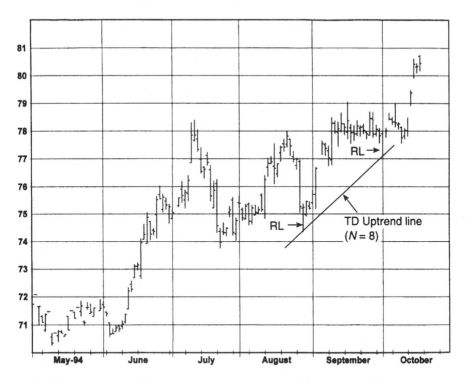

FIGURE 3.13   TD uptrend line ($N = 8$): December 1994 Swiss franc futures.

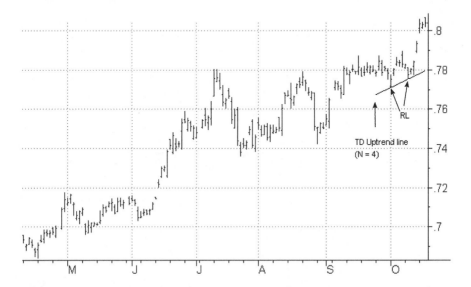

FIGURE 3.14   TD uptrend line ($N = 4$): Swiss franc futures.
Chart created with TradeStation® by Omega Research, Inc.

away with the implicit requirement of having to draw trend lines based on extreme price excursions. An internal trend line is a trend line drawn to best approximate the majority of relative highs or relative lows without any special consideration being given to extreme points. Figures 3.15–3.17 provide examples of both conventional and internal trend lines. (To avoid cluttering the charts, in most cases, only one or two of the conventional trend lines that would have been implied in the course of the price move are shown.)

One shortcoming of internal trend lines is that they are unavoidably arbitrary, perhaps even more so than conventional trend lines, which at least are anchored by the extreme high or low. Nevertheless, in my experience, internal trend lines are far more useful than conventional trend lines in defining potential support and resistance areas. An examination of Figures 3.15–3.17 will reveal that the internal trend lines depicted in these charts generally provided a better indication of where the market would hold in declines and stall in advances than did the conventional trend lines.

FIGURE 3.15 Internal trend line versus conventional trend line: March 1991 cotton.

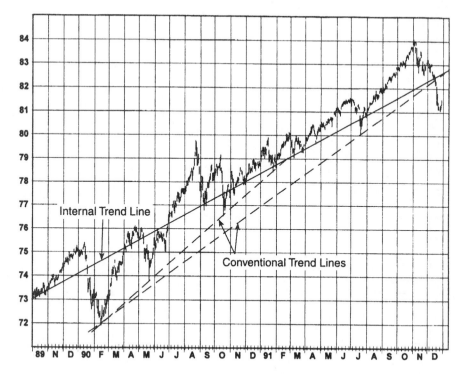

FIGURE 3.16 Internal trend line versus conventional trend lines: Canadian dollar continuous futures.

However, the anecdotal observation of a single individual hardly represents scientific proof. In fact, given the subjective nature of internal trend lines, a scientific test of their validity would be very difficult to construct. My point, however, is that internal trend lines are a concept that should certainly be explored by the serious chart analyst. By doing so, I am sure many readers will also find internal trend lines at least a worthwhile addition to their chart analysis tool kits.

MOVING AVERAGES

Moving averages provide a very simple means of smoothing a price series and making any trends more discernible. A simple moving average is defined as the average close of the past N days, ending in the current day. For example, a 40-day moving average would be equal to the average of the past 40 closes (including the current day). Typically, moving averages are calculated using daily closes. However, moving averages could also be

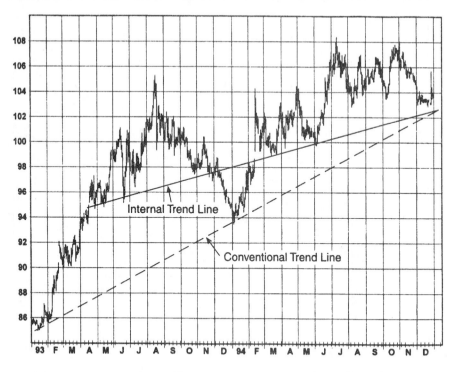

FIGURE 3.17 Internal trend line versus conventional trend line: Japanese yen continuous futures.

based on opens, highs, lows, or an average of the daily open, high, low, and close. Also, moving averages can be calculated for time intervals of data other than daily, in which case the "close" would refer to the final price quote in the given time interval.

The term *moving average* refers to the fact that the set of numbers being averaged is continuously moving through time. Figure 3.18 illustrates a 40-day moving average superimposed on a price series. Note that the moving average clearly reflects the trend in the price series and smooths out the meaningless fluctuations in the data. In choppy markets moving averages will tend to oscillate in a general sideways pattern (see, for example, the October 1993 to May 1994 period in Figure 3.19). The degree to which a moving average smooths a price series is commensurate to its length: A 40-day moving average will remove much more short-term "noise" than a 5-day moving average.

One very simple method of using moving averages to define trends is based on the direction of change in a moving average's value relative to the previous day. For example, a moving average (and by implication the

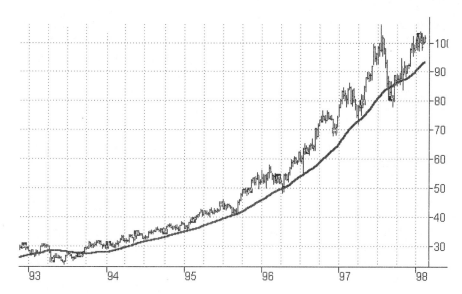

FIGURE 3.18 Moving average (40-day) in trending market: Gillette. Chart created with TradeStation® by Omega Research, Inc.

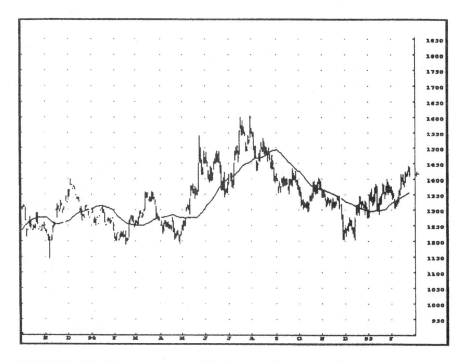

FIGURE 3.19 Moving average (40-day) in sideways market: March 1995 cocoa.
Source: FutureSource; copyright © 1986–1994; all rights reserved.

trend) would be considered to be *rising* if today's value was higher than yesterday's value and *declining* if today's value was lower.

Note that the basic definition of a rising moving average is equivalent to the simple condition that today's close is higher than the close N days ago. Why? Because yesterday's moving average is identical to today's moving average with the exception that it includes the close N days ago and does not include today's close. Therefore, if today's close is higher than the close of N days ago, then today's moving average will be higher than yesterday's moving average. Similarly, a declining moving average is equivalent to the condition that today's close is lower than the close N days ago.

The smoothing properties of moving averages are achieved at the expense of introducing lags in the data. By definition, since moving averages are based on an average of past prices, turning points in moving averages

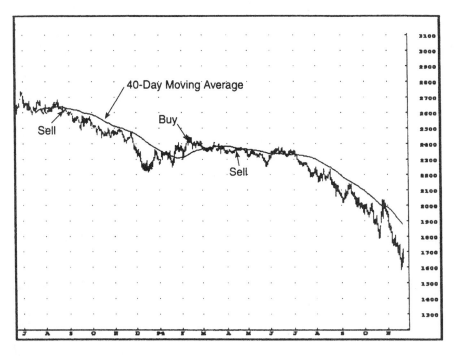

Notes: Buy = 10-tick rise in moving average off its low. Sell = 10-tick decline in moving average off its high.

FIGURE 3.20 Moving-average-based signals in trending market: December 1994 natural gas.

Source: FutureSource; copyright © 1986–1994; all rights reserved.

will always lag the corresponding transitions in the price series. This characteristic is readily evident in both Figures 3.18 and 3.19.

In trending markets, moving averages can provide a very simple and effective method of identifying trends. Figure 3.20 denotes buy signals at points at which the moving average reversed to the upside by at least 10 ticks and sell signals at points at which the moving average turned down by the same minimum amount. (The reason for using a minimum threshold reversal to define turns in the moving average is to keep trend signals from flipping back and forth, or *whipsawing*, repeatedly at times when the moving average is near zero.) As can be seen in Figure 3.20, this extremely simple technique generated superb trading signals. During the 17-month period shown, this method generated only three signals: The first signal captured a major portion of the August–December decline; the second resulted in only a slight loss; and the third caught virtually the entire massive 1994 price slide. You can't ask for much more than that.

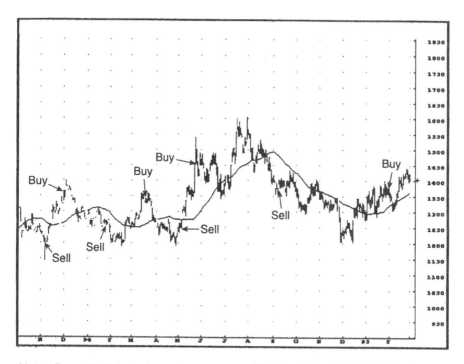

Notes: Buy = 10-tick rise in moving average off its low. Sell = 10-tick decline in moving average off its high.

FIGURE 3.21 Moving-average-based signals in sideways market: March 1995 cocoa.
Source: FutureSource; copyright © 1986–1994; all rights reserved.

The problem is that while moving averages do well in trending markets, they are apt to generate many false signals in choppy, sideways markets. For example, Figure 3.21 duplicates Figure 3.19, indicating buy signals and sell signals at points where the moving average turned up or down by at least 10 ticks. The same method that worked so well in Figure 3.20—buying on upturns in the moving average and selling on downturns in the moving average—proves to be a disastrous strategy in this market, yielding six consecutive losses and one break-even trade.

There are many other ways of calculating a moving average besides the simple moving average described in this section. Some of these other methods, as well as the application of moving averages in trading systems, are discussed in Chapter 14 and the Appendix.

Trading Ranges and Support and Resistance

There is the plain fool, who does the wrong thing at all times everywhere, but there is the Wall Street fool, who thinks he must trade all the time.

In a narrow market, when prices are not getting anywhere to speak of but move in a narrow range, there is no sense in trying to anticipate what the next big movement is going to be—up or down.

—Edwin Lefèvre

TRADING RANGES: TRADING CONSIDERATIONS

A *trading range* is a horizontal corridor that contains price fluctuations for an extended period. Generally speaking, markets tend to spend most of their time in trading ranges. Unfortunately, trading ranges are very difficult to trade profitably. In fact, most technical traders will probably find that the best strategy they can employ for trading ranges is to minimize their participation in such markets—a procedure that is easier said than done.

Although there are methodologies that can be profitable in trading ranges—oscillators, for example (see Chapter 6)—the problem is that these same approaches are disastrous for trending markets, and while trading ranges are easily identifiable for the past, they are nearly impossible to predict. Also, it should be noted that most chart patterns (e.g., gaps, flags, etc.) are relatively meaningless if they occur within a trading range. (Chart patterns are discussed in Chapter 5.) Furthermore, it should be emphasized that fading minor trends within a trading range can lead to disaster unless losses are limited (e.g., liquidation of position if prices penetrate range boundary by a specified minimum amount, or the market trades beyond the range for a minimum number of days, or both).

Trading ranges can often last for years. Figure 4.1 shows a four-year trading range in an individual stock, while Figure 4.2 depicts part of a multiyear trading range in the Dow Jones Industrial Average that preceded the bull market of the 1980s and 1990s. (The shorter set of lines in Figure 4.2 highlight an even tighter trading range that followed the 1974 stock market low.) Figures 4.3 and 4.4 show multiyear trading ranges in the lumber market. Note in these latter two illustrations that trading range periods will differ in nearest and continuous futures charts, although there will typically be some significant overlap.

Once a trading range is established, the upper and lower boundaries tend to define *support* and *resistance* areas. This topic is discussed in greater detail later in the chapter. Breakouts from trading ranges can provide important trading signals—an observation that is the subject of the next section.

TRADING RANGE BREAKOUTS

A *breakout* from a trading range (see, for example, Figures 4.5 and 4.6) suggests an impending price move in the direction of the breakout. The significance and reliability of a breakout are often enhanced by the following factors:

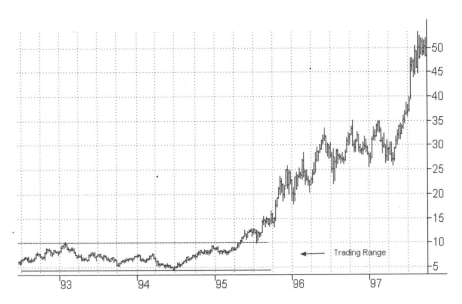

FIGURE 4.1 Multiyear trading range: Sun Microsystems.
Chart created with TradeStation® by Omega Research, Inc.

FIGURE 4.2 Multiyear trading range: Dow Industrials.
Chart created with TradeStation® by Omega Research, Inc.

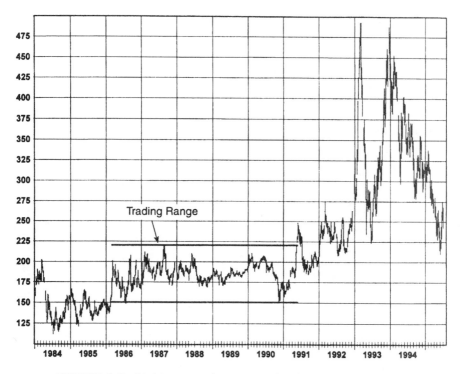

FIGURE 4.3 Multiyear trading range: lumber nearest futures.

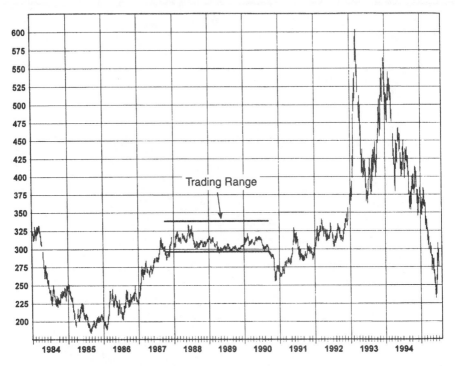

FIGURE 4.4 Multiyear trading range: lumber continuous futures.

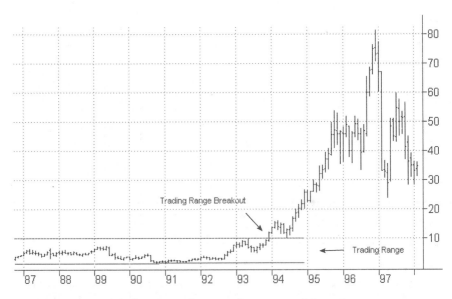

FIGURE 4.5 Upside breakout from trading range: 3Com Corp.
Chart created with TradeStation® by Omega Research, Inc.

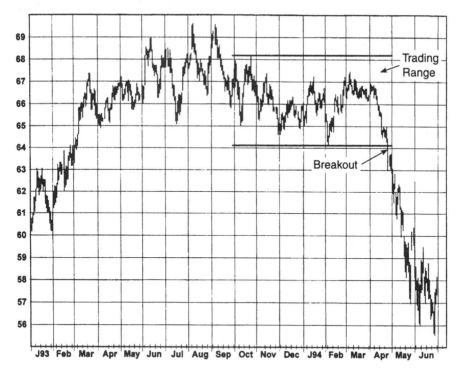

FIGURE 4.6 Downside breakout from trading range: cattle continuous futures.

1. *Duration of the Trading Range.* The longer the duration of a trading range, the more potentially significant the eventual breakout. This point is illustrated using a weekly chart example in Figure 4.7 and a daily chart example in Figure 4.8.

2. *Narrowness of Range.* Breakouts from narrow ranges tend to provide particularly reliable trade signals (see Figures 4.9 and 4.10). Furthermore, such trades can be especially attractive because the meaningful stop point implies a relatively low dollar risk.

3. *Confirmation of Breakout.* It is rather common for prices to break out from a trading range by only a small amount, or for only a few days, and then fall back into the range. One reason for this is that stop orders are frequently clustered in the region beyond a trading range. Consequently, a move slightly beyond the range can sometimes trigger a string of stops. Once this initial flurry of orders is filled, the breakout will fail unless there are solid fundamental reasons and underlying buying (or

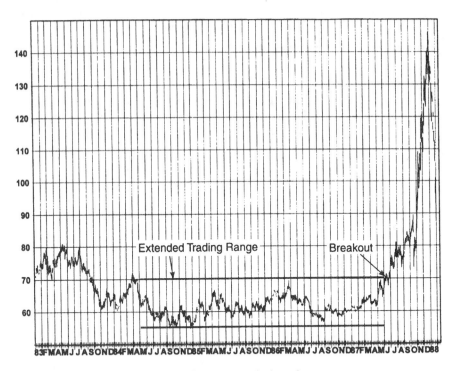

FIGURE 4.7 Upside breakout from extended trading range: copper nearest futures.

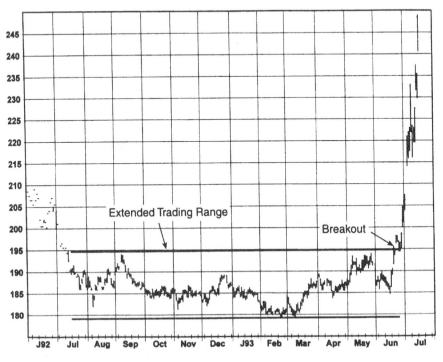

FIGURE 4.8 Upside breakout from extended trading range: July 1993 meal.

56

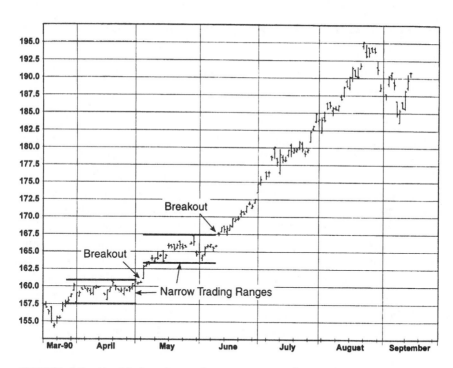

FIGURE 4.9 Upside breakouts from narrow trading ranges: September 1990 British pound.

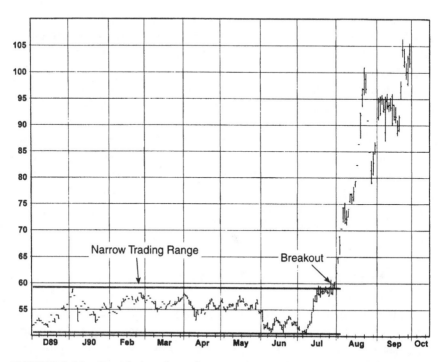

FIGURE 4.10 Upside breakout from narrow trading range: October 1990 unleaded gas.

overhead selling in the case of a downside breakout) to sustain the trend.

In view of these behavioral considerations, the reliability of a breakout from a trading range as a signal for an impending trend is significantly improved if prices are still beyond the range after a number of days (e.g., five). Other types of confirmation can also be used—minimum percent penetration, given number of *thrust days* (discussed in Chapter 5), and so on. Although waiting for a confirmation following breakouts will lead to worse fills on some valid signals, it will help avoid many false signals. The net balance of this trade-off will depend on the confirmation condition used and must be evaluated by the individual trader. The key point, however, is that the trader should experiment with different confirmation conditions, rather than blindly follow all breakouts. This advice is perhaps even more valid now (1998) than a decade ago, as the increased use of technical analysis seems to have resulted in an increased frequency of false breakouts.

SUPPORT AND RESISTANCE

Once a trading range is established (at least one to two months of sideways price movement), prices will tend to meet resistance at the upper end of the range and support at the lower end of the range. After prices break out from a trading range, the interpretation of support and resistance is turned on its head. Specifically, once prices witness a sustained breakout above a trading range, the upper boundary of that range becomes a zone of price support. The extended lines in Figures 4.11 and 4.12 indicate the support levels implied by the upper boundaries of the prior trading ranges. In the case of a sustained breakout below a trading range, the lower boundary of that range becomes a zone of price resistance. The extended lines in Figures 4.13 and 4.14 indicate the resistance levels implied by the lower boundaries of preceding trading ranges.

PRIOR MAJOR HIGHS AND LOWS

Normally, resistance will be encountered in the vicinity of previous major highs and support in the vicinity of major lows. Figures 4.15, 4.16, and 4.17 each illustrate both behavioral patterns. For example, in Figure 4.15 note that the major 1988 peak formed just below the 1985 high, while the 1989 low provided a support level that held both the 1991 and 1992 lows.

FIGURE 4.11 Support near top of prior trading range: Hitachi. Chart created with TradeStation® by Omega Research, Inc.

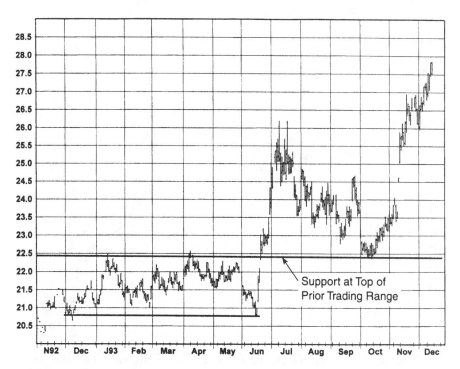

FIGURE 4.12 Support near top of prior trading range: December 1993 soybean oil.

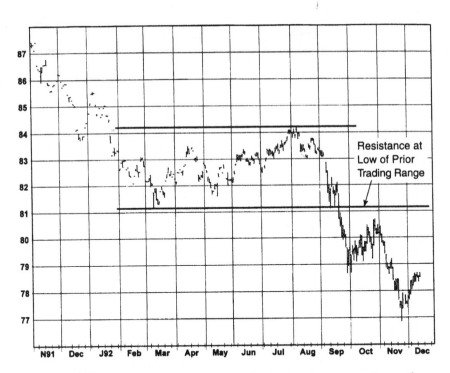

FIGURE 4.13 Resistance near bottom of prior trading range: December 1992 Canadian dollar.

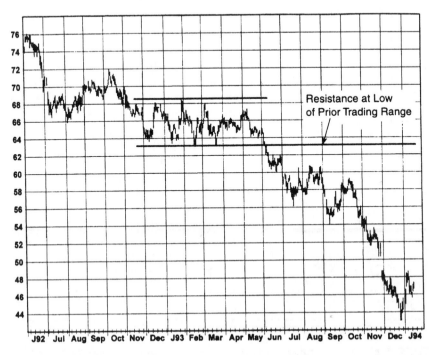

FIGURE 4.14 Resistance near bottom of prior trading range: unleaded gas continuous futures.

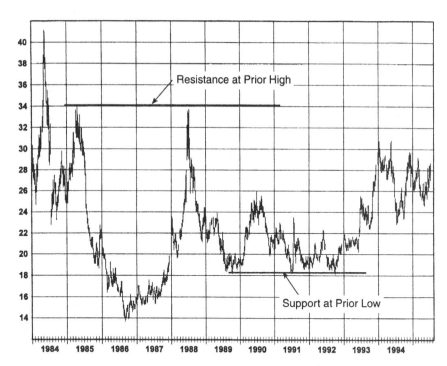

FIGURE 4.15 Resistance at prior high and support at prior low: soybean oil nearest futures.

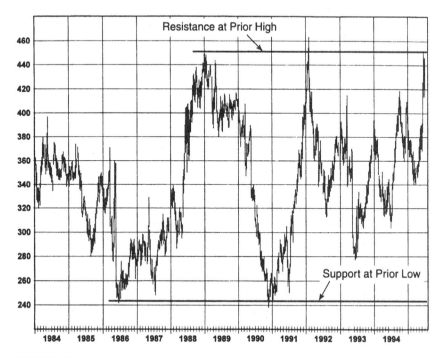

FIGURE 4.16 Resistance at prior high and support at prior low: wheat nearest futures.

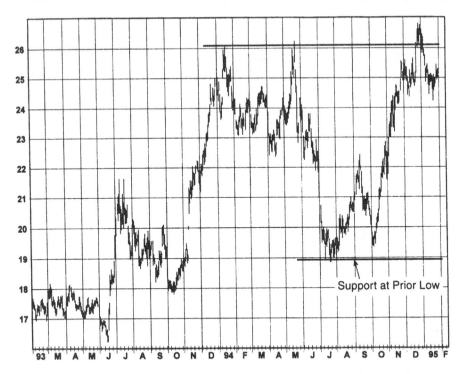

FIGURE 4.17 Resistance at prior high and support at prior low: soybean oil continuous futures.

In Figure 4.16 the late 1990 low held just below the 1986 bottom, while the 1992 reversal formed just above the early 1989 peak. Although the concept of resistance near prior peaks and support near prior lows is perhaps most important for weekly charts, such as Figures 4.15 and 4.16, the principle also applies to daily charts, such as Figure 4.17. In this latter chart, note that the May 1994 and December 1994 price reversals occurred just above the January 1994 peak, while the October 1994 low formed just slightly above the July 1994 low.

It should be emphasized that a prior high does not imply that subsequent rallies will fail at or below that point, but rather that resistance can be anticipated in the general vicinity of that point. Similarly, a prior low does not imply that subsequent declines will hold at or above that point, but rather that support can be anticipated in the general vicinity of that point. Some technical analysts treat prior highs and lows as points endowed with sacrosanct significance. If a prior high for a stock was 65, then they consider 65 to be major resistance, and if, for example, the market rallies to 66, they consider resistance to be broken. This is nonsense. Support and resistance should be considered approximate areas, not precise points. Note that although prior major highs and lows proved highly significant as resistance and support in all three charts—Figures 4.15, 4.16, and 4.17—only in Figure 4.15 did subsequent price rallies and breaks actually reverse at or before reaching these points. The type of price action represented by these charts is fairly typical.

The penetration of a previous high can be viewed as a buy signal, and the penetration of a prior low can be viewed as a sell signal. Similar to the case of breakouts from trading ranges, however, penetrations of highs and lows should be significant in terms of price magnitude, time duration, or both, to be viewed as trading signals. For example, as should be clear following the preceding discussion regarding Figures 4.16 and 4.17, a one-period (one-day for daily chart, one-week for weekly chart) modest penetration of a prior high or low would not prove anything. A stronger confirmation than a mere penetration of a prior high or low should be required before assuming such an event represents a buy or sell signal. Some examples of possible confirmation conditions include a minimum number of closes beyond the prior high or low, a minimum percent price penetration, or both requirements.

Figures 4.18 and 4.19 illustrate penetrations of previous highs as

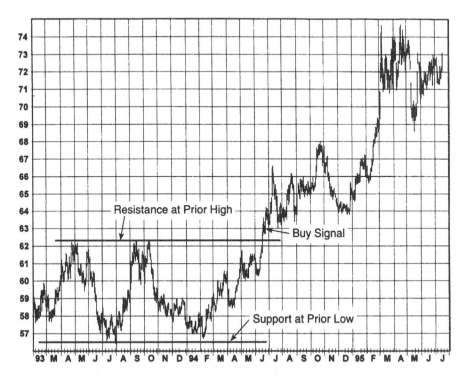

FIGURE 4.18 Penetration of previous high as buy signal: deutsche mark continuous futures.

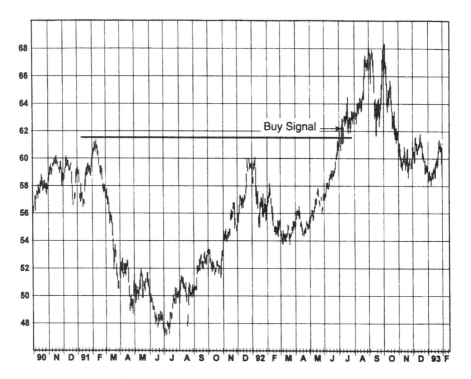

FIGURE 4.19 Penetration of previous high as buy signal: deutsche mark continuous futures.

buy signals, assuming a confirmation condition of three closes above the high. Similarly, Figures 4.20 and 4.21 provide examples of penetrations of previous lows as sell signals, using an analogous confirmation condition. Incidentally, note that Figure 4.18 also provides a good example of a prior high acting as resistance (before it is actually penetrated) and a previous low holding as support, while Figure 4.21 offers a classic example of a previous high representing major resistance.

Following a sustained penetration of a prior high or low, the area of a prior high becomes support and the area of a previous low becomes resistance. For example, in Figure 4.22, which reproduces Figure 4.19, the February 1991 high, which is penetrated in July 1992, successfully holds as a support area at the September 1992 low. The September low, which is subsequently penetrated in October, then proves to be a resistance area that stops the late November–early December rebound. In Figure 4.23, which reproduces Figure 4.20, the 1987 low, which is penetrated in 1989, proves to be a potent resistance area that stems repeated rally attempts in 1990 and 1991. (Incidentally, note that this chart also provides an excellent example of resistance at a prior high, with the major 1994 rally

FIGURE 4.20 Penetration of previous low as sell signal: coffee nearest futures.

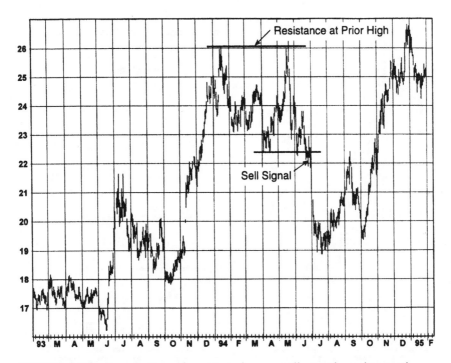

FIGURE 4.21 Penetration of previous low as sell signal: soybean oil continuous futures.

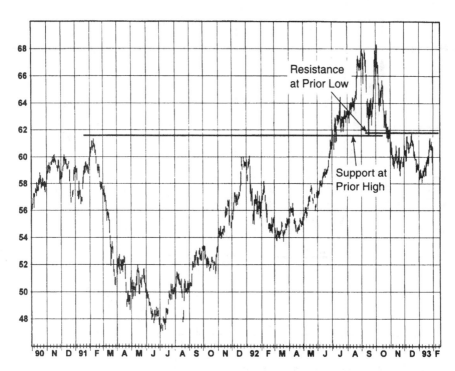

FIGURE 4.22 Support at prior relative high and resistance at prior relative low: deutsche mark continuous futures.

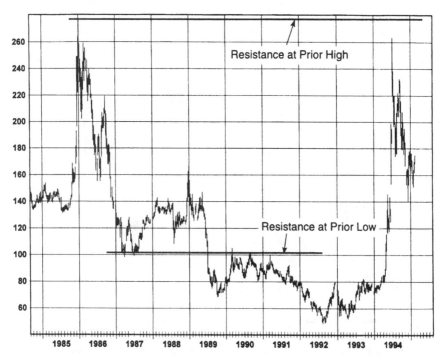

FIGURE 4.23 Resistance at prior relative low: coffee nearest futures.

stalling only moderately below the early 1986 peak.) Finally, in Figure 4.24, which reproduces Figure 4.21, the April 1994 low, which is penetrated in June, proves to be a major resistance area that leads to a price reversal in September.

CONCENTRATIONS OF RELATIVE HIGHS AND RELATIVE LOWS

The previous section dealt with support and resistance at prior major highs and lows—single peaks and nadirs. In this section we are concerned with support and resistance in price zones with concentrations of relative highs and relative lows rather than absolute tops and bottoms. Specifically, there is often a tendency for relative highs and relative lows to be concentrated in relatively narrow zones. These zones imply support regions if current prices are higher and resistance areas if

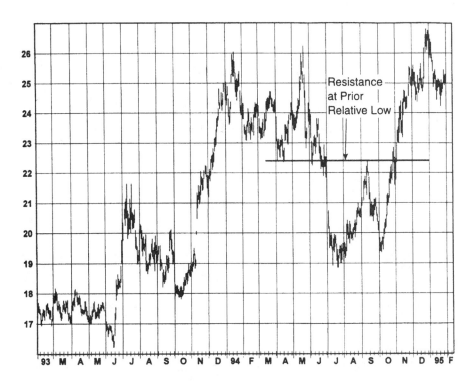

FIGURE 4.24 Resistance at prior relative low: soybean oil continuous futures.

current prices are lower. This approach is particularly useful for anticipating support and resistance areas in long-term charts. Figure 4.25 provides a weekly chart example of support being encountered at a prior concentration of relative lows and relative highs. Figure 4.26 provides a weekly chart example of resistance being encountered at a prior concentration of relative highs and relative lows.

The approach of using concentrations of prior relative highs and lows to define support and resistance can also be applied to daily charts of sufficient duration (e.g., two years). For example, Figures 4.27 and 4.28 show a daily continuous futures chart (most individual contract charts are too short for this method to be effectively applied) and a daily stock chart with resistance zones defined by prior relative highs and lows.

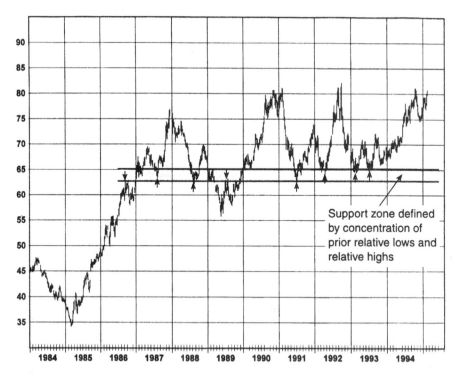

Note: ↑ = relative low; ↓ = relative high.

FIGURE 4.25 Support zone defined by concentration of prior relative lows and highs: Swiss franc nearest futures.

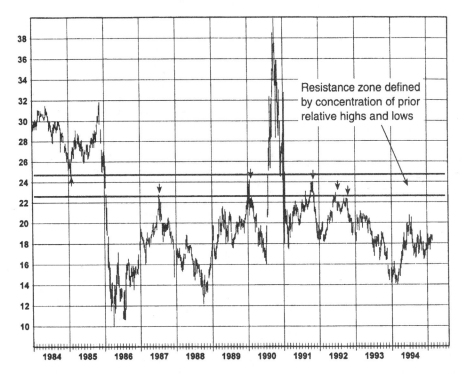

Note: ↑ = relative low; ↓ = relative high.

FIGURE 4.26 Resistance zone defined by concentration of prior relative highs and lows: crude oil nearest futures.

PRICE ENVELOPE BANDS

Another method of identifying support and resistance levels is the *price envelope band*, which is derived from a moving average. The upper boundary of the price envelope band is defined as the moving average plus a given percent of the moving average. Similarly, the lower boundary of the price envelope band is defined as the moving average minus a given percent of the moving average. For example, if the current moving average value on a stock chart is 100 and the percent value is defined as 3%, the upper band value would be 103 and the lower band value would be 97. By selecting an appropriate percent boundary for a given moving average, an envelope band can be defined so that it encompasses most of the price activity, with the upper boundary approximately coinciding

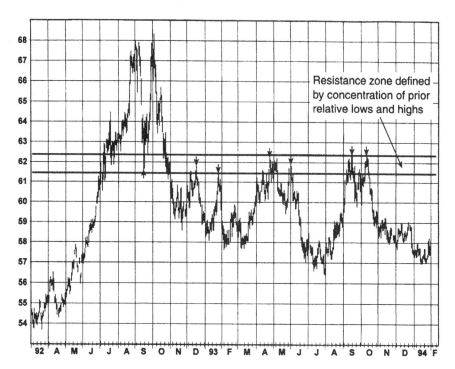

Note: ↑ = relative low; ↓ = relative high.

FIGURE 4.27 Resistance zone defined by concentration of prior relative highs and lows: deutsche mark continuous futures.

FIGURE 4.28 Resistance zone defined by concentration of prior relative highs and lows: Aetna Life.
Chart created with TradeStation® by Omega Research, Inc.

with relative highs and the lower boundary approximately coinciding with relative lows.

Figure 4.29 illustrates a price envelope band for the March 1994 T-bond contract using a 20-day moving average and a 2.5% value. As can be seen, the price envelope provides a good indication of support and resistance levels. An alternative way of expressing the same concept is that the price envelope indicates *overbought* and *oversold* levels (see Chapter 6). Price envelope bands can also be applied to data for other than daily time intervals. For example, Figure 4.30 illustrates a 1.2% price envelope band applied to 90-minute bars for the same market shown in Figure 4.29 (but of course for a shorter time period). Bollinger Bands are a well-known version of price envelope bands; they simply add and subtract a standard deviation calculation instead of a percentage calculation from a moving average.

It should be noted, however, that the price envelope is not as effective a tool as it might appear to be. Although it provides a reasonably good indication of when the market may be nearing a turning point, during ex-

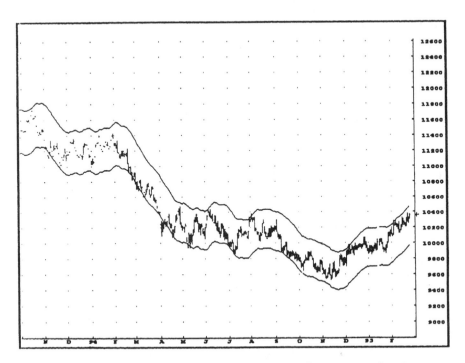

FIGURE 4.29 Price envelope band as indication of support and resistance in daily bar chart: March 1995 T-bond.
Source: FutureSource; copyright © 1986–1994; all rights reserved.

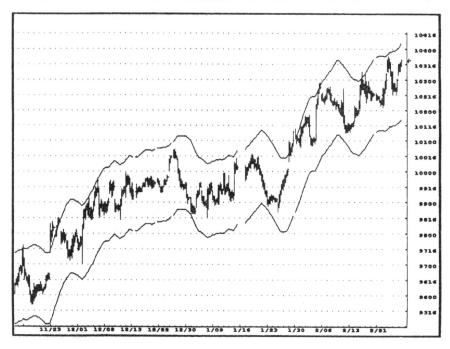

FIGURE 4.30 Price envelope band as indication of support and resistance in 90-minute bar chart: March 1995 T-bond.
Source: FutureSource; copyright © 1986–1994; all rights reserved.

tended trends prices can continue to hug one end of the price envelope. This pattern, for example, is evident in Figure 4.29 during the late February–April 1994 period. During this time, the price envelope repeatedly suggested that prices were oversold, while prices continued to slide steadily lower. Thus while it is true that price excursions beyond the price envelope band tend to be limited and temporary, the fact that prices are near one of the boundaries of the envelope does not necessarily mean that a price turning point is imminent. On balance, the price envelope provides one method of gauging potential areas of support and resistance, but it is by no means infallible.

Chapter

Chart Patterns

Never confuse brilliance with a bull market.

—Paul Rubin

When people think of technical analysis, they often first think of well-known visual chart patterns like head and shoulders, triangles, pennants, gaps, and so on. Such patterns—whether they consist of one bar or several dozen—suggest different kinds of price behavior depending on their specific market context. This chapter will discuss not only the structure of chart patterns, but also the factors that impact their interpretation and application.

ONE-DAY PATTERNS

Gaps

A *gap* day is one in which the low is above the previous day's high or the high is below the previous day's low. There are four basic types of gaps:

1. *Common Gap.* This type of gap occurs within a trading range and is not particularly significant. Figures 5.1, 5.2, and 5.3 show a few of the common gaps occurring in these charts.
2. *Breakaway Gap.* This type of gap occurs when prices surge beyond the extreme of a trading range, leaving an area in which no trading activity has occurred (see Figures 5.1 and 5.2). A breakaway gap that is not filled within a few days is one of the most significant and reliable chart signals.
3. *Runaway Gap.* This type of gap occurs when a trend accelerates and is a characteristic of strong bull and bear markets. In

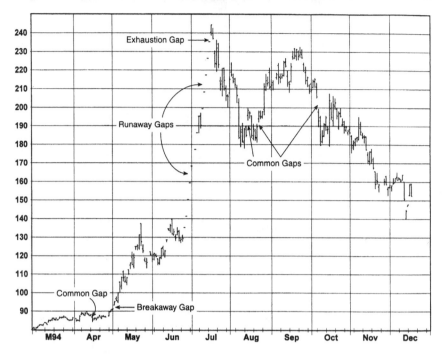

FIGURE 5.1   Price gaps: December 1994 coffee.

FIGURE 5.2   Price gaps: February 1995 hogs.

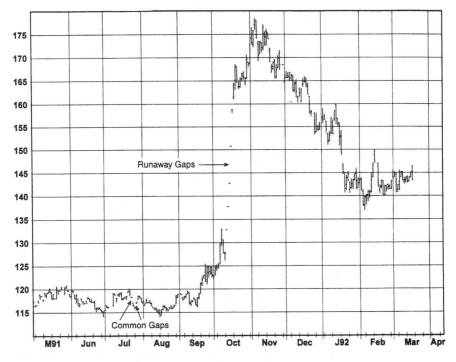

FIGURE 5.3 Price gaps: March 1992 FCOJ.

particularly powerful bull and bear markets a series of runaway gaps can occur on consecutive days (see Figures 5.1, 5.2, and 5.3).

4. *Exhaustion Gap.* This type of gap occurs after an extended price move and is soon followed by a trend reversal (see Figures 5.1 and 5.2). The exhaustion gap may sound like a particularly useful technical signal until one realizes that the difference between an exhaustion gap and a runaway gap is hindsight. However, in some instances, an exhaustion gap can be recognized at a very early point in the trend reversal—see discussion of *island reversals* in the section entitled "Top and Bottom Formations" later in this chapter.

Spikes

A *spike high* is a day whose high is sharply above the high of the preceding and succeeding days. Frequently, the closing price on a spike high day will be near the lower end of the day's trading range. A spike high is meaningful only if it occurs after a price advance, in which case it can often signify at least a temporary climax in buying pressure, and hence can be viewed as a potential relative high. Sometimes spike highs will prove to be major tops.

Generally speaking, the significance of a spike high will be enhanced by the following factors:

1. A wide difference between the spike high and the highs of the preceding and succeeding days.

2. A close near the low of the day's range.

3. A substantive price advance preceding the spike's formation.

The more extreme each of these conditions, the greater the likelihood that a spike high will prove to be an important relative high or even major top.

Similarly, a *spike low* is a day whose low is sharply below the low of the preceding and succeeding days. Frequently, the closing price on a spike low day will be near the upper end of the day's trading range. A spike low is meaningful only if it occurs after a price decline, in which case it can often signify at least a temporary climax in selling pressure, and hence can be viewed as a potential relative low. Sometimes spike lows will prove to be major bottoms.

Generally speaking, the significance of a spike low will be enhanced by the following factors:

1. A wide difference between the lows of the preceding and succeeding days and the spike low.

2. A close near the high of the day's range.

3. A substantive price decline preceding the spike's formation.

The more extreme each of these conditions, the greater the likelihood that a spike low will prove to be an important relative low or even major bottom.

Figures 5.4–5.6 contain several illustrations of spike highs and spike lows. Figure 5.4 shows an example of three spike highs occurring within an approximate two-month time span, the first defining a relative high and the latter two occurring in close proximity with near-equal highs and combining to form a major top. Figures 5.5 and 5.6 each contain examples of both a relative high and a relative low formed by spikes.

The preceding descriptions of spike highs and lows listed three essential characteristics that typify such days. However, the definition of these conditions was somewhat imprecise. Specifically, how great must

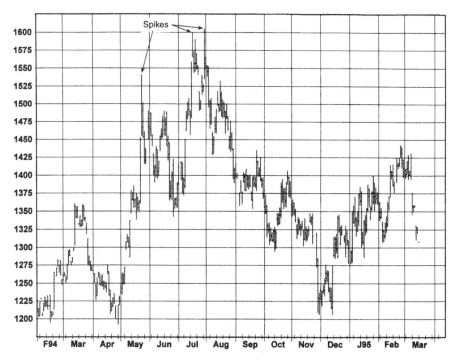

FIGURE 5.4 Spike highs: March 1995 cocoa.

the difference be between a day's high (or low) and the highs (or lows) of the preceding and succeeding days in order for it to qualify as a spike high (or low)? How near must the close be to the low (or high) for a day to be considered a spike high (or low)? How large must a preceding advance (or decline) be for a day to be viewed as a possible spike high (or low)? The answer to these questions is that there are no precise specifications; in each case, the choice of a qualifying condition is a subjective one. However, Figures 5.4–5.6 should provide an intuitive sense of the types of days that qualify as spikes. The Appendix, however, illustrates one method for constructing a mathematically precise definition for spike days.

Reversal Days

The standard definition of a *reversal high day* is a day that witnesses a new high in an upmove and then reverses to close below the preceding day's close. Analogously, a *reversal low day* is a day that witnesses a new low in a decline and then reverses to close above the preceding day's close. The

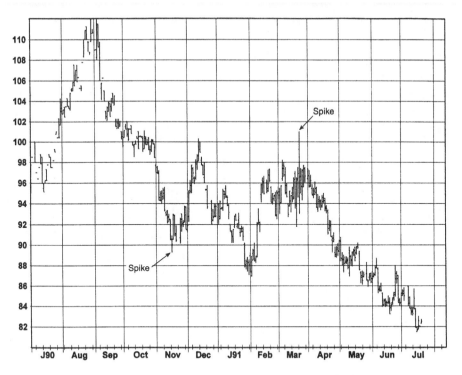

FIGURE 5.5 Spike low and spike high: July 1991 coffee.

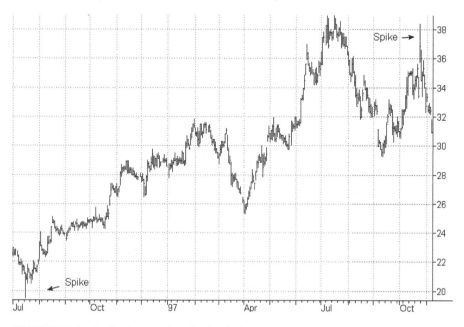

FIGURE 5.6 Spike low and spike high: Avon.
Chart created with TradeStation® by Omega Research, Inc.

following discussion focuses on reversal high days, but mirror-image comments would apply to reversal low days.

Similar to spike highs, a reversal high day is generally interpreted as suggesting a buying climax and hence a relative high. However, the condition required for a reversal high day by the standard definition is a relatively weak one, meaning that reversal high days are fairly common. Hence, while many market highs are reversal days, the problem is that the majority of reversal high days are not highs. Figure 5.7, which illustrates this point, is fairly typical. Note that two consecutive reversal high days occurred in October 1997 at the peak of the March–October advance and would have provided an excellent sell signal. Note also, however, that these reversal days were preceded by seven other reversal days that would have provided sell signals of varying degrees of prematurity (to avoid counting reversal high days during downswings, only those that occurred after the market had surpassed the previous reversal high day are marked). Figure 5.8 provides another example of how commonplace premature reversal day signals can be. In this case, a reversal day actually occurred at the exact peak of a huge bull market. This incredible sell signal, however, was also preceded by five other reversal days that occurred far earlier in the advance. Anyone who might have traded this market based

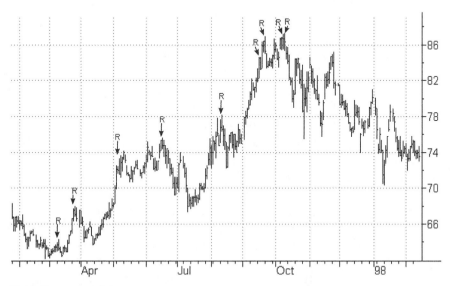

Note: R = reversal day.

FIGURE 5.7 Reversal days—the signal that cried "bear:" Atlantic Richfield. Chart created with TradeStation® by Omega Research, Inc.

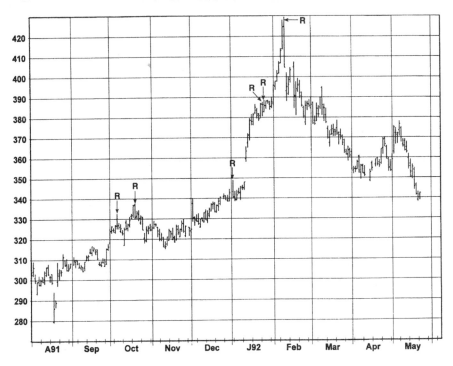

Note: R = reversal day.

FIGURE 5.8   Reversal days—the signal that cried "bear:" July 1992 wheat.

on reversal day signals would probably have thrown in the towel well before the valid signal finally materialized.

In the examples just provided, at least a reversal day signal occurred at or near the actual high. Frequently, however, an uptrend will witness a number of reversal highs that prove to be false signals and then fail to register a reversal high near the actual top. It can be said that reversal high days successfully call 100 out of every 10 highs. In other words, reversal days provide occasional excellent signals, but far more frequent false signals.

In my opinion, the standard definition of reversal days is so prone to generating false signals that it is worthless as a trading indicator. The problem with the standard definition is that merely requiring a close below the prior day's close is much too weak a condition. Instead, I suggest defining a reversal high day as a day that witnesses a new high in an upmove and then reverses to close below the preceding day's *low*. (If desired, the condition can be made even stronger by requiring that the close be below the low of the prior two days.) This more restrictive definition will greatly reduce the number of false reversal signals, but it will also knock out some valid signals. For example, this revised definition would have eliminated all but two false signals in Figure 5.7; unfortunately, it would also have excluded the best signals at the market's peak. In Figure 5.8, however, the more restrictive definition for a reversal day would have avoided all five premature reversal day signals, while leaving the single valid signal intact.

A reversal day may sound somewhat similar to a spike day, but the two patterns are not equivalent. A spike day will not necessarily be a reversal day, and a reversal day will not necessarily be a spike day. For example, a spike high day may not witness a close that is below the previous day's low (or even below the previous day's close—as specified by the standard definition), even if the close is at the day's low. As an example of the reverse case, a reversal high day may not significantly exceed the prior day's high, as required by the spike high definition, or exceed to the subsequent day's high at all, since the subsequent day's price action is not part of the reversal day definition. Also, it is possible that a reversal day's close may not be near the low, a standard characteristic of a spike day, even if it is below the previous day's close.

Occasionally, a day will be both a reversal day and a spike day. Such days are far more significant than days that are only reversal days. An alternative to using the more restrictive definition for a reversal day is using the standard definition, but requiring that the day also fulfill spike day conditions. (Although a day that met both the strong reversal day condition and the spike day conditions would be most meaningful of all, such days are fairly rare.) Figure 5.9 provides an example of a day that met both spike and reversal low day conditions. After plunging downward, the stock closed near its high for the day, marking the end of a significant correction within a long-standing uptrend (not pictured), and initiating a quick rebound in prices.

Thrust Days

An *upthrust day* is a day in which the close is above the previous day's high. A *downthrust day* is a day in which the close is below the previous day's low. The significance of thrust days is tied to the concept that the close is by far the most important price of the day. A single thrust day is not particularly meaningful, since thrust days are quite common. However, a series of upthrust days (not necessarily consecutive) reflects pronounced strength. Similarly, a series of downthrust days reflects pronounced market weakness.

During bull markets upthrust days significantly outnumber downthrust days. See, for example, the January–February period in Figure 5.10. Conversely, in bear markets downthrust days significantly outnumber

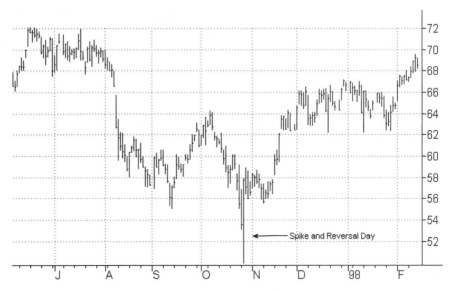

FIGURE 5.9 Spike reversal day: Coca-Cola.
Chart created with TradeStation® by Omega Research, Inc.

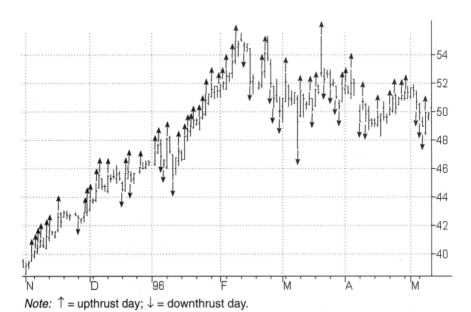

Note: ↑ = upthrust day; ↓ = downthrust day.

FIGURE 5.10 Upthrust and downthrust days in bull market: Rockwell Intl.
Chart created with TradeStation® by Omega Research, Inc.

upthrust days. See, for example, Figure 5.11 (notice, however, the prevalence of upthrust days during the countertrend upswings that occasionally interrupt the downtrend). And, as should come as no surprise, in sideways markets, upthrust and downthrust days tend to be in rough balance. See, for example, the February to May period in Figure 5.10. (A more powerful version of the thrust day, called a *run day*, is defined in the Appendix.)

Wide-Ranging Days

A *wide-ranging day* is exactly what it sounds like: a daily price bar that is significantly bigger than the days preceding it. This is another way of describing a day whose volatility significantly exceeds the average volatility of recent trading days. Wide-ranging days are easy to understand and see on a chart, but they also can be defined mathematically. For example, a wide-ranging day might be defined as a day whose range is more than two times the average range of the preceding N bars. The Appendix provides a specific formula for defining wide-ranging days.

Wide-ranging days can have special significance. For example, a wide-ranging day with a strong close that materializes after an extended decline is often a signal of an upside trend reversal. Figures 5.12 and 5.13

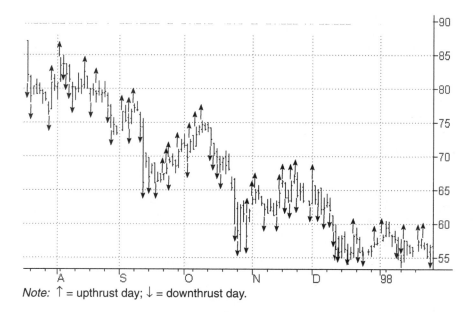

Note: ↑ = upthrust day; ↓ = downthrust day.

FIGURE 5.11 Upthrust and downthrust days in bear market: Motorola. Chart created with TradeStation® by Omega Research, Inc.

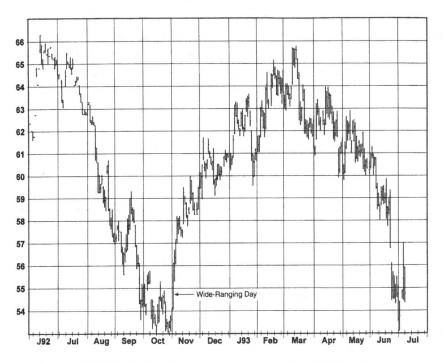

FIGURE 5.12 Wide-ranging up day: July 1993 cotton.

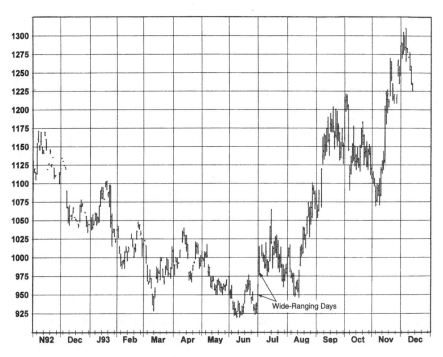

FIGURE 5.13 Wide-ranging up days: December 1993 cocoa.

provide examples of wide-ranging up days that materialized following extended declines and heralded major advances. In Figure 5.13 there are actually two back-to-back wide-ranging days that developed just above the low of the prior bear market.

Similarly, a wide-ranging day with a weak close that occurs after a major advance can often signal a downside trend reversal. Figures 5.14 and 5.15 show wide-ranging down days that occurred near the peaks of prior major advances (notice that the second wide-ranging day with a weak close in Figure 5.14 occurred after a downtrend was established and was followed by a brief counter-trend upswing). Such huge wide-ranging days should be viewed as serious warning flags that a previous major trend has been reversed. Figure 5.16 shows an incredible succession of four wide-ranging days that retraced the equivalent of four months of prior upward movement. The first of these days emerged fairly close to what effectively was the top of a seven-year bull market.

CONTINUATION PATTERNS

Continuation patterns are various types of congestion phases that materialize within long-term trends. As the name implies, a continuation pattern is expected to be resolved by a price swing in the same direction that preceded its formation.

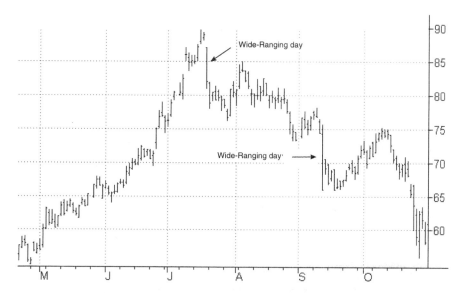

FIGURE 5.14 Wide-ranging down days: Motorola.
Chart created with TradeStation® by Omega Research, Inc.

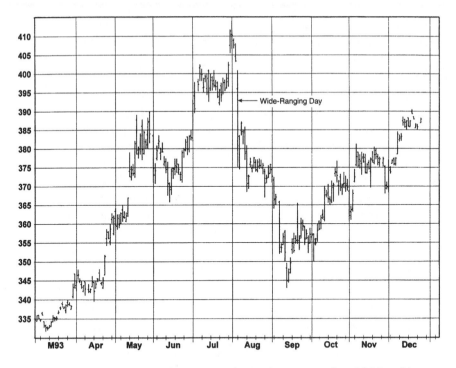

FIGURE 5.15 Wide-ranging down day: December 1993 gold.

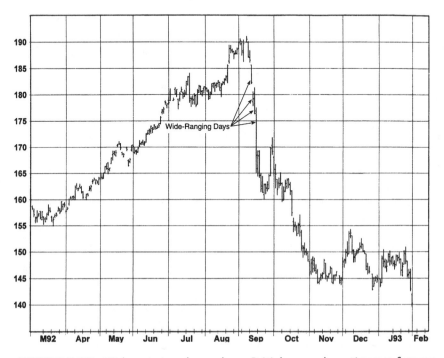

FIGURE 5.16 Wide-ranging down days: British pound continuous futures.

Triangles

There are three basic types of *triangle* patterns: symmetrical (see Figures 5.17 and 5.18), ascending (see Figures 5.19 and 5.20), and descending (see Figures 5.21 and 5.22). A symmetrical triangle is usually followed by a continuation of the trend that preceded it, as in Figures 5.17 and 5.18. Conventional chart wisdom suggests that nonsymmetrical triangles will yield to a trend in the direction of the slope of the hypotenuse, as is the case in Figures 5.19–5.22. However, the direction of the breakout from a triangle formation is more important than the type. For example, although the July–September congestion pattern in Figure 5.23 is a descending triangle, the breakout is on the upside—the same direction the triangle was entered.

Flags and Pennants

Flags and *pennants* are narrow-band, short-duration (e.g., one to three weeks) congestion phases within trends. The formation is called a flag when it is enclosed by parallel lines and a pennant when the lines converge. Figures 5.24 and 5.25 illustrate both types of patterns. Pennants may appear to be similar to triangles, but they differ in terms of time: the triangle has a longer duration.

Flags and pennants typically represent pauses in a major trend. In

FIGURE 5.17 Symmetrical triangle: Delta Air Lines.

FIGURE 5.18 Symmetrical triangle: Swiss franc continuous futures.

FIGURE 5.19 Ascending triangle: September 1992 Eurodollar.

FIGURE 5.20 Ascending triangle: October 1992 sugar.

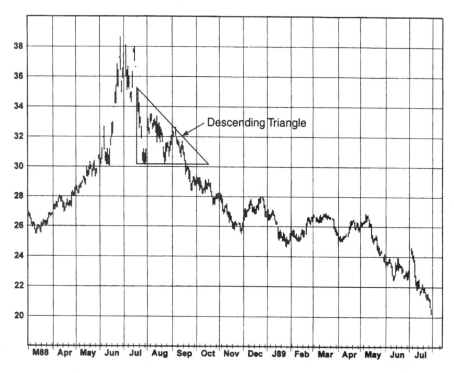

FIGURE 5.21 Descending triangle: soybean oil continuous futures.

FIGURE 5.22 Descending triangle: soybean meal continuous futures.

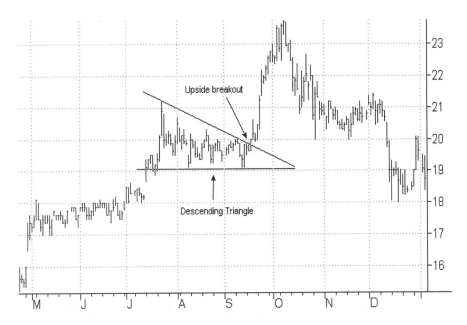

FIGURE 5.23 Descending triangle with upside breakout: Host Marriott Corp. Chart created with TradeStation® by Omega Research, Inc.

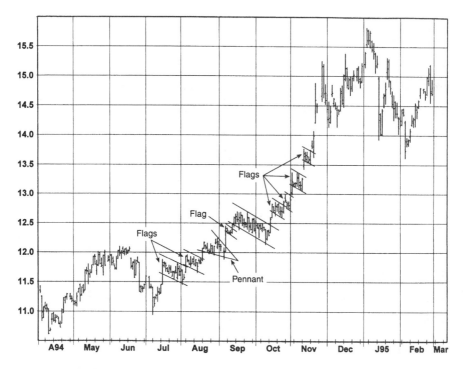

FIGURE 5.24 Flags and pennants: March 1995 sugar.

other words, these patterns are usually followed by price swings in the same direction as the price swings that preceded their formation.

A breakout from a flag or pennant can be viewed as a confirmation that the trend is continuing and a trading signal in the direction of the trend. Since breakouts are usually in the direction of the main trend, however, I prefer to enter positions during the formation of the flag or pennant, anticipating the probable direction of the breakout. This approach allows for more advantageous trade entries without a significant deterioration in the percentage of correct trades, since reversals following breakouts from flags and pennants are about as common as breakouts in the counter-to-anticipated direction. Following a breakout from a flag or pennant, the opposite extreme of the formation can be used as an approximate *stop-loss* point.

A significant penetration of a flag or pennant in the opposite-to-anticipated direction—that is, counter to the main trend—can be viewed as a signal of a potential trend reversal. For example, in Figure 5.25 note that after a long string of flags and pennants that were resolved by breakouts in the direction of the main trend, the opposite direction penetration of the flag formed in June led to a sharp rally. Flags and pennants typically point

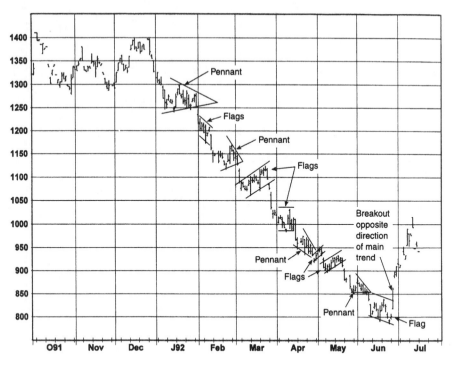

FIGURE 5.25 Flags and pennants: July 1992 cocoa.

in the opposite direction of the main trend, as is the case with the majority of flags and pennants in Figure 5.24. In my experience, however, I have not found any significant difference in reliability between flags and pennants that point in the same direction as the main trend as opposed to the more usual opposite slope.

Flags or pennants that form near the top or just above a trading range can be particularly potent bullish signals. In the case where a flag or pennant forms near the top of a trading range, it indicates that the market is not backing off despite having reached a major resistance area—the top of the range. Such price action has bullish implications and suggests that the market is gathering strength for an eventual upside breakout. In the case where the flag or pennant forms above the trading range, it indicates that prices are holding above a breakout point, thereby lending strong confirmation to the breakout. Generally speaking, the more extended the trading range, the greater the potential significance of a flag or pennant that forms near or above its top. Figures 5.26 and 5.27 provide two examples of flags or pennants that

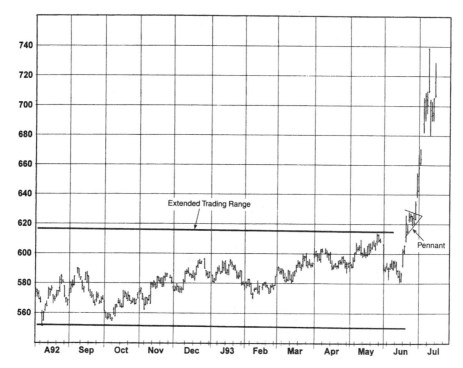

FIGURE 5.26 Pennant above top of trading range as bullish signal: July 1993 soybeans.

materialized near the top or above trading ranges and proved to be precursors of explosive advances.

For similar reasons, flags or pennants that form near the bottom or just below trading ranges are particularly bearish patterns. Figures 5.28 and 5.29 provide two examples of flags or pennants that materialized near the bottom or below trading ranges and proved to be harbingers of steep price declines.

TOP AND BOTTOM FORMATIONS

V Tops and Bottoms

The V formation is a turn-on-a-dime type of top (see Figure 5.30) or bottom pattern (see Figure 5.31). One problem with a *V top* or *V bottom* is that it is frequently difficult to distinguish from a sharp correction unless accompanied by other technical indicators (e.g., prominent spike, signifi-

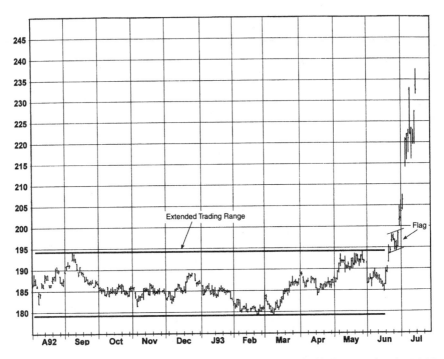

FIGURE 5.27 Flag above top of trading range as bullish signal: July 1993 soybean meal.

FIGURE 5.28 Flag near bottom of trading range as bearish signal: June 1994 Eurodollar.

FIGURE 5.29 Flag below bottom of trading range as bearish signal: November 1994 natural gas.

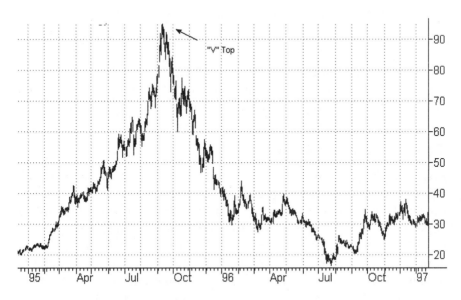

FIGURE 5.30 "V" top: Micron Technology.
Chart created with TradeStation® by Omega Research, Inc.

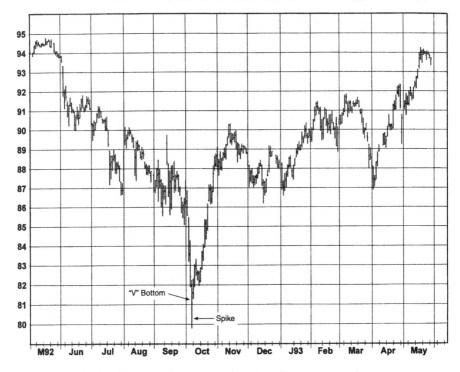

FIGURE 5.31 V bottom: Italian bond continuous futures.

cant reversal day, wide gap, wide-ranging day). The V bottom in Figure 5.31 does contain such a clue—an extreme spike—whereas the V top in Figure 5.30 is unaccompanied by any other evidence of a trend reversal.

Double Tops and Bottoms

Double tops and *double bottoms* are exactly what their names imply. Of course, the two tops (or bottoms) that make up the pattern need not be exactly the same, only in the same general price vicinity. Double tops and bottoms that materialize after large price moves should be viewed as strong indicators of a major trend reversal. Figure 5.32 illustrates a major double top in the deutsche mark. (Continuous futures are used for all of the futures charts illustrating double tops and bottoms because the liquid trading period for most individual contracts is not sufficiently long to display the time span encompassing these patterns and the preceding and succeeding trends.)

A double top (or bottom) is considered completed when prices move below (or above) the reaction low (or high) between the two tops

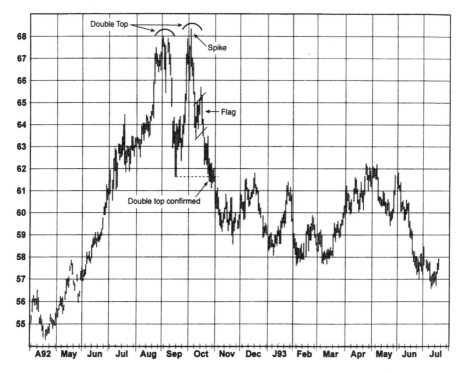

FIGURE 5.32 Double top: deutsche mark continuous futures.

(or bottoms) of the formation. When the intervening reaction is very deep, as in Figure 5.32, it is impractical to wait for such an "official" confirmation, and the trader may have to anticipate that the pattern has formed based on other evidence. For example, in Figure 5.32 the confirmation of the double top does not occur until the market has surrendered nearly half of the entire April–August advance. However, the spike high that developed at the second top and the flag pattern that formed after the initial downswing from that high implied that the next price swing would also be down. Based on these clues, a trader could have reasonably concluded that a double top was in place, even though the pattern had not yet been completed in terms of the standard definition.

Figure 5.33 depicts the double top that capped the imposing bull market in the Australian 10-year bond in the early 1990s. Note that a weekly chart is used in order to show the full extent of the prolonged advance that preceded this formation. This chart provides a perfect example of the double top (or bottom) as a major trend transition pattern. In this instance, the pullback between the two tops is very shallow, and as a

FIGURE 5.33 Double top: Australian 10-year bond weekly continuous futures.

result, in sharp contrast to Figure 5.32, the double-top pattern is confirmed very close to the actual peak.

Figures 5.34 illustrates a double-bottom pattern. Figure 5.35 shows a single chart containing both a double bottom and a double top. Top and bottom formations with more repetitions (e.g., *triple top* or *triple bottom*) occur rather infrequently, but would be interpreted in the same fashion. Figure 5.36 displays a triple bottom, with all three lows nearly identical. Figure 5.37 provides an example of a triple top.

Head and Shoulders

The *head and shoulders* is one of the best-known chart formations. The head-and-shoulders top is a three-part formation in which the middle high is above the high points on either side (see Figure 5.38). Similarly, the head-and-shoulders bottom is a three-part formation in which the middle low is below the low point on either side (see Figure 5.39). Perhaps one of the most common mistakes made by novice chartists is the premature anticipation of the head-and-shoulders formation. The head

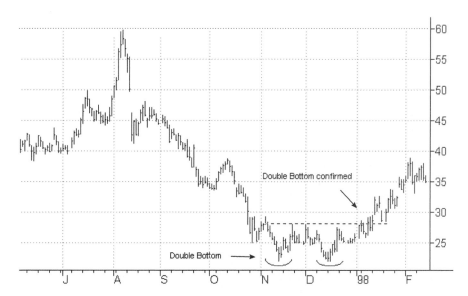

FIGURE 5.34 Double bottom: Micron Technology.
Chart created with TradeStation® by Omega Research, Inc.

FIGURE 5.35 Double top and double bottom: Japanese yen continuous futures.

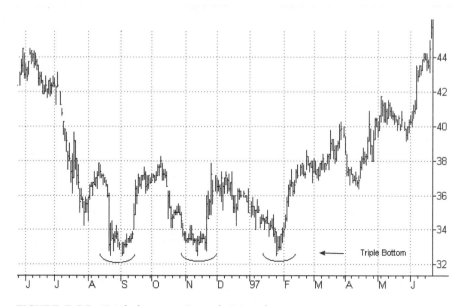

FIGURE 5.36 Triple bottom: Bausch & Lomb.
Chart created with TradeStation® by Omega Research, Inc.

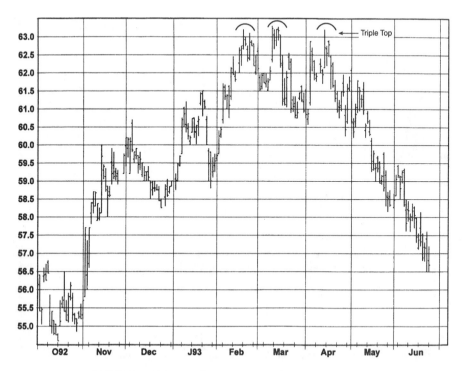

FIGURE 5.37 Triple top: December 1993 cotton.

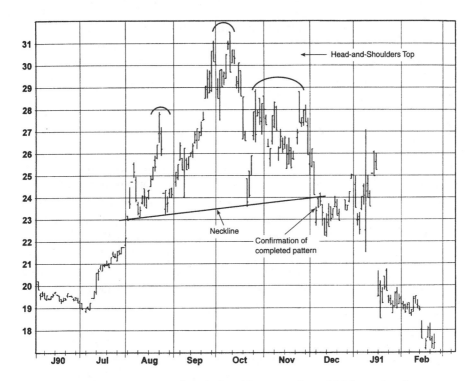

FIGURE 5.38 Head-and-shoulders top: June 1991 crude oil.

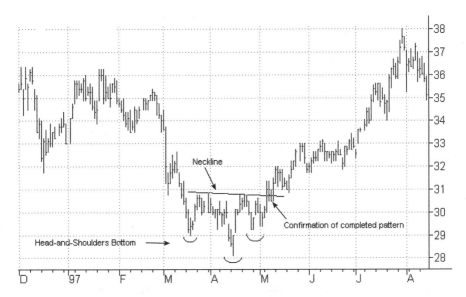

FIGURE 5.39 Head-and-shoulders bottom: Chrysler.
Chart created with TradeStation® by Omega Research, Inc.

and shoulders is not considered complete until the *neckline* is penetrated (see Figures 5.38 and 5.39). Furthermore, a valid head and shoulders is formed only after a major price move has occurred. Patterns that bear the shape of a head-and-shoulders formation but lack this requirement can be misleading.

Rounded Tops and Bottoms

Rounded tops and *rounded bottoms* (also called saucers) occur some-what infrequently, but are among the most reliable top and bottom formations. Figure 5.40 shows a continuous futures chart with a rounding top that marked the transition between a major uptrend and an even more imposing downtrend. Ideally, the pattern would not contain any jags, as this chart does; however, I consider the main criterion to be whether the outer perimeter conforms to a rounding shape, which it does. Figure 5.41 depicts a rounding top pattern in a stock chart. Figures 5.42 and 5.43 provide examples of rounding bottom formations.

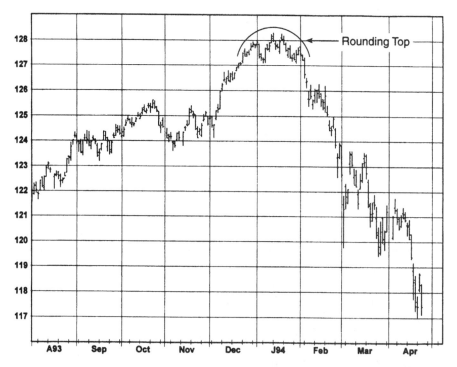

FIGURE 5.40 Rounding top: Matif notional bond continuous futures.

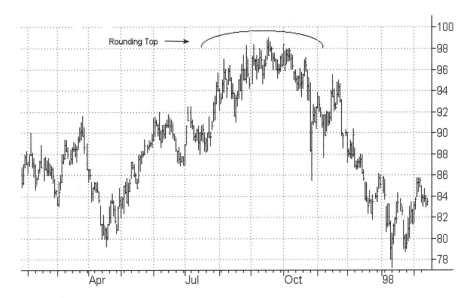

FIGURE 5.41 Rounding top: Amoco.
Chart created with TradeStation® by Omega Research, Inc.

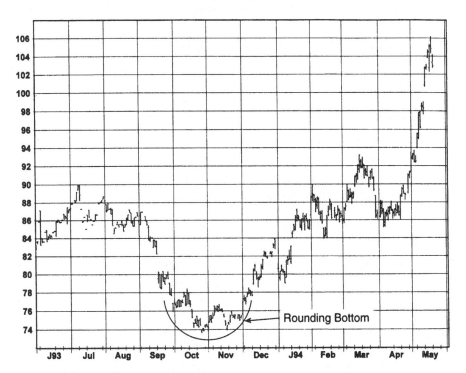

FIGURE 5.42 Rounding bottom: May 1994 copper.

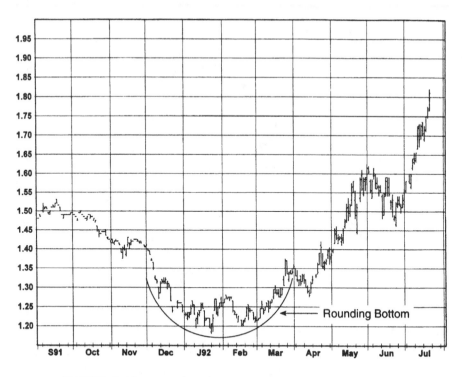

FIGURE 5.43 Rounding bottom: August 1992 natural gas.

Triangles

Triangles, which are among the most common continuation patterns, can be top and bottom formations as well. Figure 5.44 illustrates a triangle top. As in the case of the continuation pattern, the key consideration is the direction of the breakout from the triangle.

Wedges

In a rising *wedge*, prices edge steadily higher in a converging pattern (see Figure 5.45). The inability of prices to accelerate on the upside despite continued probes into new high ground suggests the existence of strong scale-up selling pressure. A sell signal occurs when prices break below the wedge line. Figure 5.46 provides an example of a declining wedge. Wedge patterns can sometimes take years to complete. Figure 5.47 depicts a multiyear declining wedge in continuous gold futures.

FIGURE 5.44 Triangle top: Intel.
Chart created with TradeStation® by Omega Research, Inc.

FIGURE 5.45 Rising wedge: Pepsico.
Chart created with TradeStation® by Omega Research, Inc.

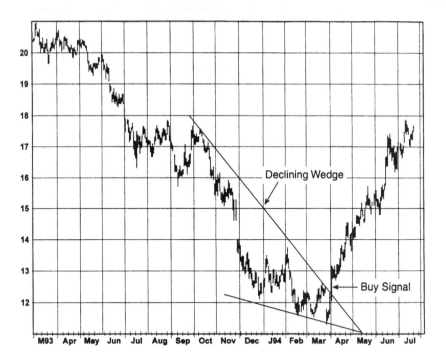

FIGURE 5.46 Declining wedge: crude oil continuous futures.

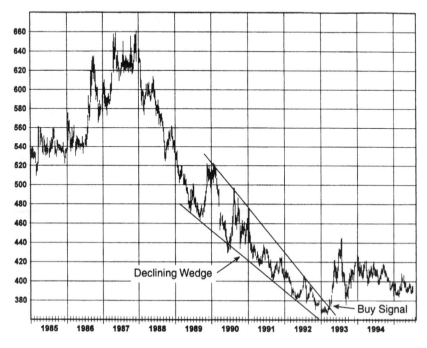

FIGURE 5.47 Multiyear declining wedge: gold weekly continuous futures.

Island Reversals

A relative of spike days and reversal days, an *island top* is formed when prices gap higher after an extended advance, trade one or more days leaving the gap open, and then gap lower. Figure 5.48 shows an island top in which the "island" portion of the formation consists of a single day, while Figure 5.49 illustrates an island top in which the market traded above the initial gap for several days before gapping lower. Figure 5.50 depicts an *island bottom*. Sometimes the market can trade for several weeks before a second gap in the opposite direction completes the formation (see, for example, the island top in Figure 5.51).

The sequence of a climactic gap up (or down) without any follow-through and a subsequent gap in the opposite direction is a potent combination. Island reversals can often signal major trend transitions and should be given significant weight unless the gap is eventually filled.

An island reversal signal would remain in force as long as the more recent gap of the formation is not filled. It should be noted that false is-

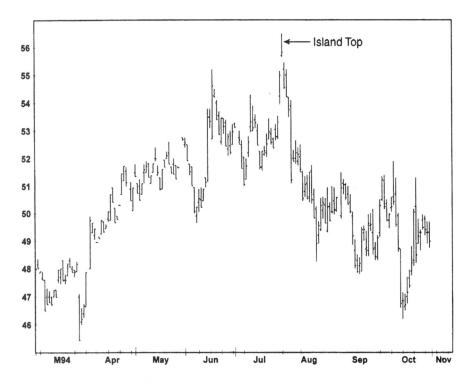

FIGURE 5.48 Island top: November 1994 heating oil.

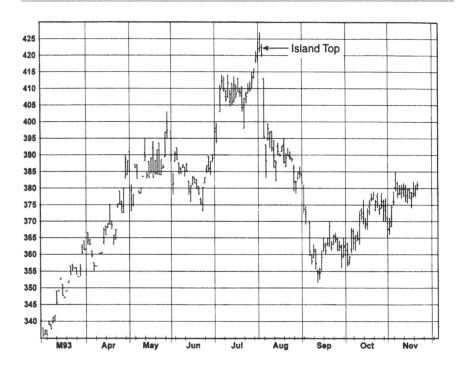

FIGURE 5.49   Island top: January 1994 platinum.

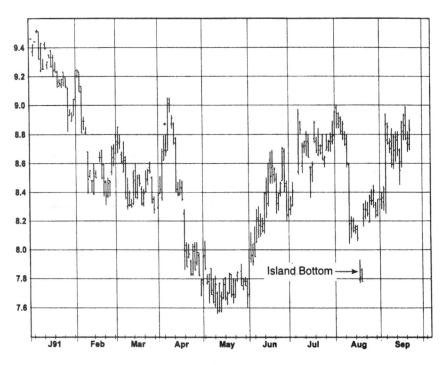

FIGURE 5.50   Island bottom: March 1992 sugar.

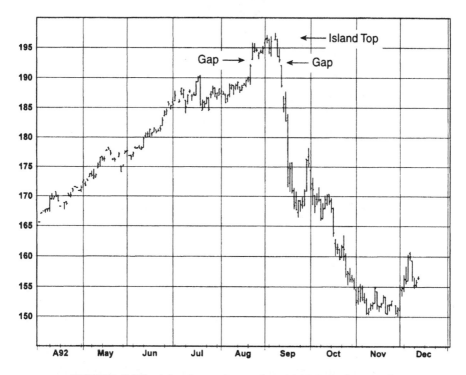

FIGURE 5.51   Island top: December 1992 British pound.

land reversal signals are common—that is, island reversals are often filled within the first few days of their formation. Consequently, it is usually a good idea to wait at least three to five days after the island reversal's initial formation before concluding that it is a valid reversal signal. The trade-off, however, is that such a wait for confirmation will often result in a worse entry level when the island reversal signal is valid.

Chapter

Oscillators

I know millions of things that won't work. I've certainly learned a lot.
—Thomas A. Edison

A long with chart analysis, traders commonly use a variety of price-based mathematical formulas—called technical indicators—to evaluate price activity and make trading decisions. Among the most popular indicators are those tools loosely referred to as *oscillators*, a group that includes the relative strength index (RSI), stochastics, moving average convergence-divergence (MACD), momentum, and rate of change (ROC), among others. Perhaps because they are most often used as countertrend indicators (to identify shorter-term price reversal points rather than longer-term trends) oscillators naturally appeal to many traders' contrarian inclinations. Figure 6.1 shows the RSI and stochastic below a daily stock chart.

OSCILLATORS AND MOMENTUM

While the arcane names and imposing formulas of many oscillators may initially seem confusing, virtually all these indicators are based on the concept of *momentum*, which, not surprisingly, refers to the rate (or speed) at which prices change.

The significance of momentum has two major components. First, healthy price trends tend to exhibit strong momentum, while weakening trends often have stagnant or decreasing momentum (alerting a trader to a possible trend reversal or correction). Consider a stock that gains a half point one day, one point the next, two points the day after that, three more the following day, and four points the next. Then consider a stock

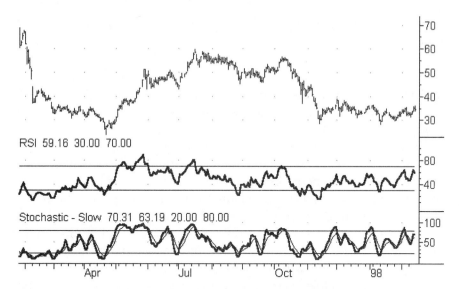

FIGURE 6.1 Relative strength index and slow stochastics: 3Com Corp. Chart created with TradeStation® by Omega Research, Inc.

that gains two points one day, loses a point the next day, gains a half-point each of the next two days, and gains a quarter point the day after that. While both stocks have risen over the five-day period, the first stock is obviously moving with much greater force—that is, showing greater momentum—than the second stock.

Second, momentum indicators also highlight shorter-term market extremes or exhaustion points referred to as *overbought* or *oversold* levels. The logic is that extremely strong, rapid price moves are not indefinitely sustainable; when a market rises or falls a great deal over a relatively short time period (like the first stock example in the preceding paragraph), prices will frequently reverse, at least temporarily. Even the strongest of trends is punctuated by retracements of varying degrees. Momentum oscillators are designed to capture such turning points.

BASIC OSCILLATORS

Momentum can be derived from price any number of ways. The most simple calculation, and the one that bears the name *momentum*, is simply the difference between today's price (the closing price is generally used) and the price N days ago. For example, the 10-day momentum would be today's close minus the close 10 days ago. An equivalent calculation, usually referred to as *rate of change* (ROC), is today's price divided by the price N days ago.

Figure 6.2 shows 10-day momentum and ROC indicators below a stock chart. Except for the difference in scale, the indicators are virtually identical. Both indicators have a horizontal median, called the equilibrium line. When indicator values are above the equilibrium line, the current price is higher than the price 10 days earlier; when indicator values are below this line, the current price is lower than the price 10 days earlier. When the indicator is above the equilibrium line and rising, prices are advancing with increasing momentum; when the indicator is below the line and dropping, prices are falling with increasing momentum. Extreme indicator readings above the equilibrium line represent overbought levels, while extreme indicator readings below the equilibrium line are oversold levels. Note that some (but not all!) of these indicator peaks and troughs correspond to at least short-term price reversals. (Later, we will examine ways to define overbought and oversold levels.) Notice also how trend affects the oscillators: the pronounced oversold readings and lack of overbought readings during the January–April 1997 downtrend and the opposite conditions during the uptrend that followed.

As with moving averages, the number of days used in an oscillator calculation determines how sensitive the indicator will be. For example, a

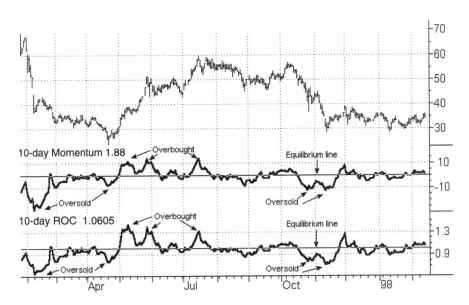

FIGURE 6.2 Overbought and oversold indications in momentum and rate of change: 3Com Corp.
Chart created with TradeStation® by Omega Research, Inc.

5-day momentum study will more closely track short-term market fluctuations than a 20-day momentum study. Similarly, the reversal portended by a 5-day oscillator will generally be proportionally smaller to that portended by a 20-day oscillator. Figure 6.3 shows that the 5-day momentum study reflects more of the smaller market swings, while the 20-day study mostly reflects the major turning points.

Moving averages can also be used to construct momentum oscillators. Figure 6.4 shows price superimposed with a 20-day moving average, and below the price series, an oscillator constructed by subtracting the moving average from price. As price rises and falls, it moves above and below the average. The faster price moves above or below the average, the greater the momentum being displayed; the farther price is from the average, the more extended (overbought or oversold) the price move. (Longer moving averages will reflect more significant trends; oscillators based on longer averages will reflect longer-term price swings.) Note that the equilibrium line ("0") represents identical price and moving average values. When the oscillator crosses above and below this line, it is equivalent to price crossing above and below the moving average.

A similar oscillator to the one just described is the *price oscillator*, which, instead of subtracting a moving average from price, subtracts a longer-term moving average from a shorter-term moving average. Figure

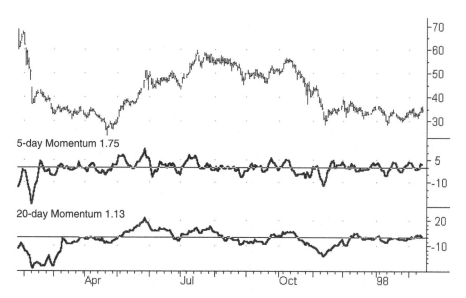

FIGURE 6.3 Comparison of 5-day and 20-day momentum indicators: 3Com Corp.
Chart created with TradeStation® by Omega Research, Inc.

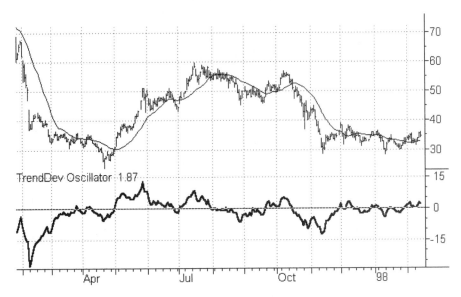

FIGURE 6.4 Oscillator resulting from subtracting moving average from price: 3Com Corp.
Chart created with TradeStation® by Omega Research, Inc.

6.5 shows a price series with 10- and 20-day moving averages and below it the oscillator that results from subtracting the 20-day average from the 10-day average. The price oscillator is essentially an alternate depiction of the basic moving average crossover system described in Chapter 14. The arrows on the chart indicate points where the shorter average crosses above or below the longer average. These crossover points correspond to where the price oscillator crosses above and below its equilibrium line. Similar to the relationship between momentum and rate of change, moving average–based oscillators can also be calculated by division instead of subtraction (i.e., dividing price by a moving average, or dividing a shorter-term average by a longer-term average). The resulting indicators are equivalent.

The well-known *moving average convergence-divergence* (MACD) indicator is a unique version of the price oscillator just described. It takes the difference between two exponential moving averages (see the Appendix for definition) of specific length—12 days and 26 days—and then calculates a 9-day moving average of this difference (see Figure 6.6) called the *signal line*. A basic MACD trading signal is to buy when the primary MACD line moves above the 9-day signal line and sell when it crosses below the 9-day signal line, in much the same fashion as a moving average crossover. The arrows in Figure 6.6 indicate the buy and sell signals that would have been generated using this technique. (The histogram

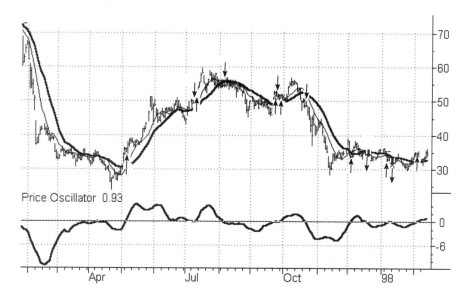

FIGURE 6.5 Comparison of moving average crossover and price oscillator: 3Com Corp.
Chart created with TradeStation® by Omega Research, Inc.

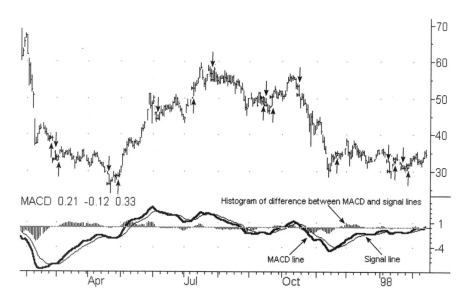

FIGURE 6.6 Moving average convergence divergence indicator: 3Com Corp.
Chart created with TradeStation® by Omega Research, Inc.

is simply the difference between the primary MACD line and the signal line, and is included to highlight crossovers of the two.) To help filter out low-probability trades, overbought and oversold levels could also be established and only the crossovers that occurred in these zones used as trade signals. A price oscillator that used 12- and 26-day moving averages would look much the same as the MACD except for the presence of the 9-day signal line.

One of the most significant aspects of Figures 6.1–6.5 is the similarity between the different oscillators despite the variety of calculations used to construct them (the use of the same price series for all these examples is intended to underscore this point). Not surprisingly, almost all popular oscillators are variations on these simple themes.

Overbought, Oversold, and Divergence

Indicators like momentum, rate-of-change, the price oscillator, and the MACD are "unbounded" studies, that is, they have no absolute high or low boundaries. Overbought and oversold zones, however, can be established simply by picking levels that isolate more extreme oscillator values. There are no hard-and-fast rules; a common guideline is to capture the highest and lowest 10% of oscillator readings. Reviewing past peaks and troughs can provide an indication of appropriate levels. Figure 6.7 shows the 10-day momentum and ROC studies from Figure 6.2 with overbought and oversold lines drawn to isolate the most significant oscillator peaks and troughs. Unfortunately, there is no guarantee that overbought or oversold levels set today will be appropriate for market conditions a month from now.

Overbought and oversold signals represent potential selling and buying opportunities, respectively. Accordingly, they can be used to establish positions in anticipation of a new trend, or to liquidate, reduce, or protect existing positions. For example, an oscillator moving above its overbought level might lead a trader to (1) go short in anticipation of a downturn in prices, (2) liquidate an existing long position, (3) liquidate part of a long position, or (4) move a stop order closer to the market to protect profits. The precise timing of the trade is another matter. Possibilities include (1) when the oscillator first penetrates an extreme level, (2) after it penetrates an extreme level and reverses by a specified amount, (3) only after it exits the extreme zone, or (4) only when a price pattern confirms a reversal. The last technique is probably the most prudent, for reasons that will be made clear in a moment.

Indicators like the RSI and stochastics (see the Appendix for the formulas) are "normalized" oscillators; that is, they have fixed upper and

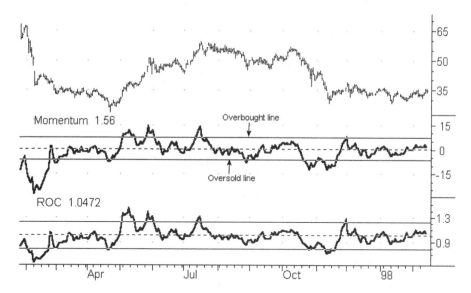

FIGURE 6.7 Overbought and oversold lines in momentum and rate of change indicators: 3Com Corp.
Chart created with TradeStation® by Omega Research, Inc.

lower boundaries. The RSI and stochastics, for example, both range between 0 and 100. Overbought and oversold levels for such indicators are commonly set equidistant from the upper and lower limits—for example, 70 and 30 or 80 and 20 (although this is not required, and would even be inappropriate in strongly trending markets; see below). Figure 6.1 compares the 10-day RSI and stochastic. The additional line on the stochastic is a 3-day moving average of the basic stochastic, similar to the signal line of the MACD. The RSI has overbought and oversold levels of 70 and 30, respectively, while the stochastic uses levels of 80 and 20. Although the developers of these indicators suggest a variety of applications for these oscillators, the fundamental information they convey is identical to that of the other indicators discussed in this chapter: Overbought levels are assumed to represent selling opportunities, and oversold levels are assumed to represent buying opportunities.

Besides overbought and oversold levels, the other notable countertrend oscillator signal is referred to as *divergence*, which describes the phenomenon of momentum moving in the opposite direction of price. As mentioned earlier, waning momentum often signals a dying trend and a possible reversal or correction. A *classic divergence* refers to a higher price high accompanied by a lower oscillator high, or a lower price low accompanied by a higher oscillator low. The implication is that the market has posted a new high (or low), but momentum, by failing to confirm the price move with a new high (or low) of its own, is revealing trend vulnerability. For example, every indicator in Figures 6.1–6.7—with the exception of the stochastic in Figure 6.1—shows a classic divergence between the February 1997 price low and the lower April 1997 price low: The April indicator lows are higher than the February indicator lows.

The traditional response to a divergence in a rising market would be to establish a short position in anticipation of a new downtrend, or liquidate (or reduce) an open long position as a protective measure. For example, Figure 6.8 shows an extended uptrend on a weekly stock chart. Below the price chart is a 10-day RSI. First consider points A, B, C, and D, which mark relative price highs and their corresponding RSI peaks. While price posts consecutive higher relative highs from November 1996 to October 1997, the corresponding oscillator highs are actually lower—momentum has diverged from price, suggesting the uptrend is losing steam (compare the oscillator during this period to its behavior in the March–October 1995 advance). Classic divergences in uptrends (as in this example) are called *bearish divergences* because they portend a downturn in prices; classic divergences in downtrends are called *bullish divergences* because they portend an upturn in prices.

Unfortunately, divergences rarely occur only between the penultimate and final peaks in an advance, or the last two lows in a downtrend.

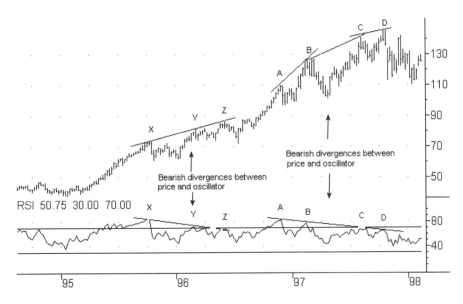

FIGURE 6.8 Repeated false divergence signals in trending market: Citicorp. Chart created with TradeStation® by Omega Research, Inc.

There are frequently multiple divergences, as there are in this example between A and B, B and C, and C and D. A trader who established a short position based on the first divergence in this series (between points A and B), for example, would have entered the market prematurely and seen the market, after a brief correction, continue to climb. Furthermore, the market posted multiple divergences much earlier in the uptrend at points X, Y, and Z. Traders selling into these classic divergences would have entered the market even more prematurely.

Another weakness Figure 6.8 highlights is the tendency for oscillators to become skewed in the direction of the prevailing trend. Throughout the period shown on the chart, the oscillator posted repeated and sustained overbought signals without registering a single oversold signal. As a result, the oscillator produced many false sell signals without producing any buy signals, although the latter would have been more useful for traders seeking entry points to the existing trend. Because of this tendency, it is necessary to adjust overbought and oversold levels to compensate for trend—in this case, raising them to capture more of the oversold signals and exclude more of the overbought signals.

CONCLUSION

While the traditional countertrend approach of selling when the oscillator is overbought and buying when the oscillator is oversold may provide excellent entry points in trading ranges, it is a recipe for disaster in trending markets, as the previous example shows. Unfortunately, however, it is impossible to know when a trend will end and a trading range will begin. Unless stops are used to limit risk, countertrend oscillator signals can lead to large and repeated losses.

Because of these limitations, oscillator signals are often used as "trading alerts," warnings of *possible* price developments. Positions are established only when price confirms a reversal. For example, when an oscillator moves above its overbought threshold, it alerts the trader the market is overextended and may reverse. The trader would then look for a definitive price signal before initiating a position.

Is Chart Analysis Still Valid?

I always laugh at people who say, "I've never met a rich technician." I love that! It is such an arrogant, nonsensical response. I used fundamentals for nine years and got rich as a technician.

—Marty Schwartz

Most traders who have never used chart analysis (and even some who have) are quite skeptical about this approach. Some of the commonly raised objections include: "How can such a simple analytical approach work?" "Since key chart points are hardly a secret, won't floor traders sometimes push the market enough to trigger chart stops artificially?" "Even if chart analysis worked before it was detailed in scores of books, isn't the method too well publicized to still be effective?"

Although the points raised by these questions are basically valid, a number of factors explain why chart analysis remains an effective trading approach:

1. *Risk Control.* Trading success does not depend on being right more than half the time, or for that matter, even half the time, as long as losses are rigidly controlled and profitable trades are permitted to run their course. For example, consider a trader who in March 1991 assumes that September 1992 Eurodollars have entered another trading range (see Figure 7.1) and decides to trade in the direction of any subsequent closing breakout. Figure 7.2 indicates the initial trade signals and liquidation points that would have been realized as a result of this strategy. (The implicit assumption is that stops are placed at the midpoint of the

FIGURE 7.1 Trading range market: September 1992 Eurodollar.

trading range; the relevant considerations in choosing stop points are discussed in detail in Chapter 9.) As Figure 7.2 shows, the first two trades would have resulted in immediate losses. Figure 7.3, however, illustrates that the third signal proved to be the real thing, indicating a long position in time to benefit from a major price advance that far exceeded the combined price swings on the prior two adverse trades. (Note that the relevant trading range is redefined—that is, widened—after each of the false breakouts.)

Although two out of three trades were losers, on balance the trader would have realized a large net profit. The key point is that a disciplined adherence to risk control principles is an essential ingredient in the successful application of chart analysis to trading.

2. *Confirmation Conditions.* Chart analysis can be made much more effective by requiring confirmation conditions for trade entry, rather than blindly following all technical signals. There is a natural trade-off in the choice of confirmation rules: The

FIGURE 7.2 False breakout signals: September 1992 Eurodollar.

less restrictive the conditions, the greater the number of false signals; the more restrictive the conditions, the greater the surrendered profit potential due to late entry. Some of the key methods that can be used to construct confirmation conditions might include the following: time delays, minimum percent penetration, and specific chart patterns (e.g., trade must be confirmed by two subsequent thrust days in the direction of signal).

There is no such thing as a best set of confirmation conditions. In any list of tested alternatives, the indicated best strategy will vary from market to market as well as over time. Thus, the ultimate choice of confirmation rules will depend upon the trader's analysis and experience. In fact, the specific choice of confirmation conditions is one of the pivotal ways in which chart analysis is individualized.

As an illustration of how confirmation conditions might be used, consider the following set of rules:

a. Wait three days after signal is received.

b. For a buy signal, enter trade if the close is above the high since the signal was received, or on the first subsequent day fulfill-

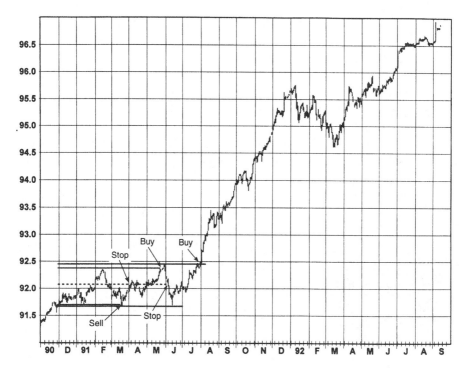

FIGURE 7.3 Winning breakout signal after two false signals: September 1992 Eurodollar.

ing this condition. An analogous condition would apply to sell signals.

These rules would have filtered out the losing March and May signals in Figures 7.2, while only modestly delaying the entry point for the subsequent highly profitable buy signal. Of course, one could also construct examples in which the use of confirmation conditions is detrimental to the trading results. However, the key point is that the use of confirmation rules is one of the primary means of transforming classical chart concepts into a more powerful trading approach.

3. *Putting Chart Patterns in Context.* Chart analysis is more than just the recognition and interpretation of individual patterns. One of the earmarks of the successful chart trader is an ability to synthesize the various components of the overall picture. For example, the trader who recognizes just a trading range in September 1992 Eurodollars (see Figure 7.1) would treat upside and downside breakouts equivalently. However, the more experienced chartist will also consider the broader picture. For ex-

ample, by examining the long-term weekly continuous futures chart in early 1991 (see Figure 7.4), the analyst could have noted that the market had just formed a flag pattern near the top of a five-year trading range. This extremely bullish long-term chart picture would have strongly cautioned against accepting any apparent sell signals on the daily chart. Such a more comprehensive chart analysis could therefore have helped the analyst avert the false sell signal in March (see Figure 7.2) and adopt a much more aggressive trading stance from the long side than would have been warranted if the situation were viewed as just another trading range.

While the preceding example benefits from hindsight, it illustrates the multifaceted analytical process of the experienced chart trader. It should be clear that the skill and subjectivity implied in this approach place chart analysis in the realm of an art that cannot be mimicked by merely following a set of textbook rules. This is a crucial point in understanding how the chartist approach can remain valid despite widespread publicity.

4. *Knowledge of Fundamentals.* Assuming some skill in fundamental forecasting (i.e., a better than 50–50 accuracy rate), chart analysis can be combined with fundamental projections to provide a more effective approach. Specifically, if the long-term fundamental forecast indicates the probability of much higher (lower) prices, only bullish (bearish) chart signals would be accepted. If the fundamental projection was neutral, both buy and sell signals would be accepted. Thus, the chart analyst who is also a competent fundamental analyst would have a decided edge over the majority of traders basing their trading decisions solely on chart-oriented input.

5. *Using Failed Signals.* The failure of a market to follow through in the direction of a key chart signal is a crucial item of information often overlooked by novice chartists. Recognizing and acting on these situations can greatly enhance the effectiveness of the chartist approach. This subject is discussed in detail in Chapter 11, "The Most Important Rule in Chart Analysis."

In conclusion, the skeptics are probably correct in claiming that a Pavlovian response to chart signals will not lead to trading success. However, this in no way contradicts the contention that a more sophisticated utilization of charts, as suggested by the cited factors, can indeed provide

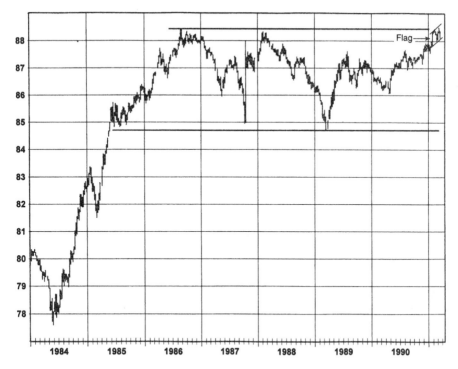

FIGURE 7.4 Long-term chart as part of comprehensive analysis: Eurodollar continuous futures.

the core of an effective trading plan. In any case, chart analysis remains a highly individualistic approach, with success or failure critically dependent on the trader's skill and experience. It would be unreasonable to expect to play the violin well without some degree of practice and innate talent. Chart analysis is no different.

PART TWO

TRADING ISSUES

Chapter

Midtrend Entry
and Pyramiding

Nobody can catch all the fluctuations.

—Edwin Lefèvre

For many reasons, a trader may find herself considering whether to enter a new position after the market has already witnessed a substantial price move. Some examples: (1) she was not previously following the market; (2) in an effort to get a better price, she futilely waited for a price correction that never developed; (3) she was previously skeptical of the sustainability of the trend, but has now changed her opinion. Faced with such a situation, many traders will be extremely reluctant to trade the market.

Consider a chart-oriented trader examining the coffee market in mid-May 1994 (see Figure 8.1) after not having participated in the sharp price advance prior to that time. She would note that the market had penetrated the upside of a prior yearlong trading range, with prices remaining in new high ground for two weeks—a very bullish chart configuration. In addition, she would note that prices had just formed a flag pattern after an up move—price action indicative of another imminent upswing. However, observing that prices had already advanced over 35% since the April low set less than one month earlier, she might be reluctant to enter a new long position belatedly, reasoning that the market was overextended.

Figure 8.2 vividly illustrates the folly of this conclusion. Incredibly, as of mid-May 1994, coffee prices had completed only about one-fifth of their ultimate advance. Moreover, the remaining four-fifths of the price rise was achieved in a mere two months. The moral of this tale is provided

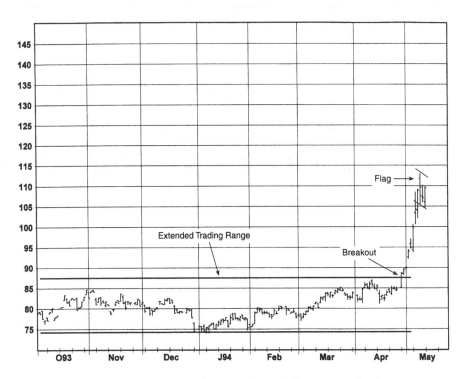

FIGURE 8.1 Missed price move? (July 1994 coffee).

by an observation in *Reminiscences of a Stock Operator* by Edwin Lefèvre: "[Prices] are never too high to begin buying or too low to begin selling."

The key question is how one enters the market in the midst of a major trend. Pauses or corrections in a trend offer opportunities to enter a market in preparation for a possible resumption of the trend. The goals in implementing a midtrend position are the same as those for initiating any position: favorable timing of entry and risk control. The following are a few key strategies that could be employed to achieve these objectives:

1. *Percent Retracement.* This approach attempts to capitalize on the natural tendency of a market to partially retrace prior price swings. Generally speaking, one might initiate the position anytime the market retraces a given percentage of the price swing from the last relative low or relative high. A reasonable choice for this percentage would be a figure in the 35–65% range. A price in the proximity of the relative low or relative high could be used as a stop point on the position. Figure 8.3 highlights two entry

FIGURE 8.2 How it turned out (July 1994 coffee).

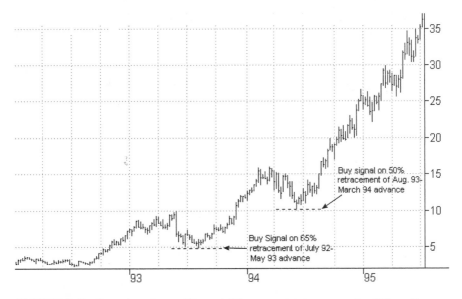

FIGURE 8.3 Buy signals on 65- and 50-percent retracements: 3Com Corp. Chart created with TradeStation® by Omega Research, Inc.

points using this approach, with a retracement level of 65% in the first instance and 50% in the second. The main advantage of this method is that it is capable of providing superior entry points (as was the case in the chosen illustration). However, it is also subject to a major disadvantage: Frequently, the necessary retracement condition may not be fulfilled until the trend has carried much further, or possibly even reversed.

2. *Reversal of Minor Reaction.* This approach is based on waiting for a minor reaction to materialize and then entering on the first signs of a resumption of the major trend. Of course, the precise method would depend on how a reaction and trend resumption were defined. The choices are virtually limitless. For illustration purposes, we will provide one possible set of definitions. A minor reaction in an uptrend could be defined as a N-day low (a new low that is lower than the lowest low of the previous N days); the resumption of the trend could be a close higher than the most recent X-day high. The circumstances would be reversed in a downtrend. For example, a minor reaction in a downtrend could be defined as a new eight-day (relative) high; a sell signal would occur when price closes below the most recent four-day (relative) low. (The relative high would be used as a protective stop level.) Larger or smaller values of N and X would change the sensitivity of the approach. For example, changing the trend resumption requirement to a close below the seven-day low would probably remove some false signals at a cost of delaying trend reentry. Figure 8.4 shows the sell signals in a downtrend using a 10-day relative high to define a reaction and a close below the three-day low to define a trend resumption. (A related, but more sophisticated technique, is described in the Appendix.)

3. *Continuation Pattern and Trading Range Breakouts.* The use of continuation patterns and trading ranges for entry signals was discussed in Chapter 5. Since to some extent chart patterns are in the eye of the beholder, this approach will reflect a degree of subjectivity. Figure 8.5 offers one interpretation of continuation patterns (implicit assumption: at least five trading days are required to form a continuation pattern), and the corresponding buy points based on closes above these consolidations. It should be noted, however, that once a trend is considered established, it is not absolutely necessary to wait for penetrations of continuation patterns as confirmation of trade entry signals. By definition, these patterns are expected to be resolved by price swings in the

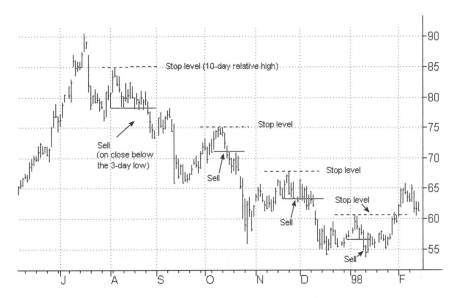

FIGURE 8.4 Reversal of minor reaction: Motorola.
Chart created with TradeStation® by Omega Research, Inc.

same direction as the price moves that preceded their formation. Thus, for example, in an uptrend, long positions could be established within consolidation patterns based on an expectation of an eventual upside breakout. The low prices in the patterns depicted in Figure 8.5 could be used as reference points for the placement of protective stops.

4. *Reaction to Long-Term Moving Average.* Price retracements to a moving average of the price series can be viewed as signals that the reaction to the main trend is near an end. Specifically, if a trader believed that an uptrend was in place, long positions could be entered anytime prices declined to or below a specified moving average. Similarly, if a downtrend was believed to be in effect, short positions could be initiated on rallies above the moving average. Figure 8.6, which superimposes a 40-day moving average over a stock chart, provides an illustration of this approach. Assume that a trader decided that the stock had entered an uptrend. Price pullbacks below the 40-day moving average could be used as entry signals for long positions. The arrows in Figure 8.6 indicate the potential buy entry points based on this approach.

In Chapter 14, we see how crossovers of moving averages can be used as trend-reversal signals. In the application just described,

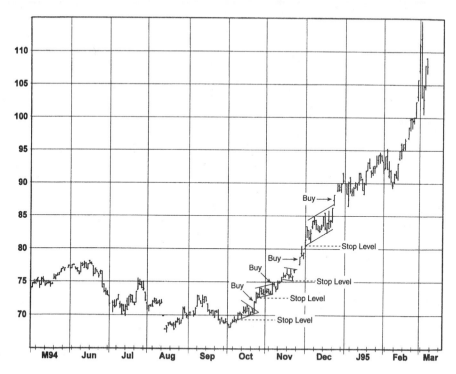

FIGURE 8.5 Continuation pattern breakouts as entry signals: March 1995 cotton.

we have used moving average crossover points to signal countertrend trade entry signals. There is no contradiction. When moving average crossovers are employed for generating trend-reversal
signals, typically, two moving averages are used so that the
smoothing of both data series will reduce false trend-reversal
signals. In the method just detailed, we deliberately defined
crossover points based on the price series itself (which is more
sensitive than a moving average since it contains no smoothing
of the data) and one moving average. In other words, we would
use more sensitive definitions of moving average crossovers for
countertrend applications than we would for trend-identification
applications. Similarly, the reversal of a minor reaction technique outlined in strategy #2 (above) is similar to the breakout
system described in Chapter 17. Again, the number of days
(three) used in the example to define a trend resumption is
much smaller, and thus more sensitive, than would typically be
used in a trend-following system.

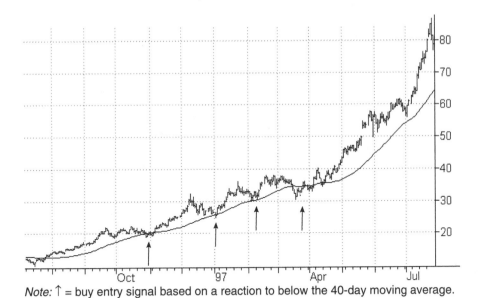

Note: ↑ = buy entry signal based on a reaction to below the 40-day moving average.

FIGURE 8.6 Reaction to long-term moving average: Dell Computer.
Chart created with TradeStation® by Omega Research, Inc.

It should be noted that the problem of midtrend entry is identical to the problem of *pyramiding*, the process of adding new positions to an existing open trade (i.e., initially buying a stock at $30 and then purchasing additional lots at $35, $45, and so on, as the market continues to rise). Both transactions involve implementing a position after the market has already witnessed a substantial move in a given direction. Consequently, the strategies discussed in this chapter for a midtrend entry could also be applied to the timing of pyramid positions. A few additional guidelines are necessary for pyramiding. First, one should not add to any existing position unless the last unit placed shows a profit. Second, one should not add to an existing position if the intended stop point would imply a net loss for the entire position. Third, pyramid units should be no greater than the base (initial) position size.

Choosing Stop-Loss Points

It was the same with all. They would not take a small loss at first but had held on, in the hope of a recovery that would "let them out even." And prices had sunk and sunk until the loss was so great that it seemed only proper to hold on, if need be a year, for sooner or later prices must come back. But the break "shook them out," and prices just went so much lower because so many people had to sell, whether they would or not.

—Edwin Lefèvre

The success of chart-oriented trading is critically dependent on the effective control of losses. As mentioned in Chapter 7, it is not necessary to be right half the time; what is necessary is limiting losses on bad trades sufficiently so that winning trades are substantial enough to return a profit. Accordingly, a precise *stop-loss* liquidation point should be determined before initiating a trade. The most disciplined approach would be to enter a *good-till-canceled* (GTC) stop order at the same time the trade is implemented. However, if the trader knows he can trust himself, he could predetermine the stop point and then enter a day order at any time this price is within the permissible daily limit.

How should stop points be determined? A basic principle is that the position should be liquidated at or before the point at which price movement causes a transition in the technical picture. For example, assume a trader decides to buy the stock in Figure 9.1 after the April 1995 upside breakout has remained intact for five bars (weeks). In this case, the protective sell stop should be placed no lower than the lower boundary of the April 1994–April 1995 trading range, since the realiza-

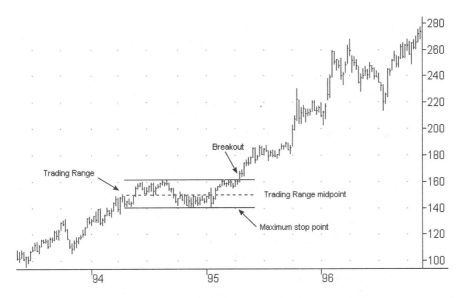

FIGURE 9.1 Stop placement following trading range breakout: Wells Fargo. Chart created with TradeStation® by Omega Research, Inc.

tion of such a price would totally transform the chart picture. Some of the technical reference points commonly used for placing protective stops include:

1. *Trend Lines.* A sell stop can be placed below an uptrend line; a buy stop can be placed above a downtrend line. One advantage of this approach is that the penetration of a trend line will usually be one of the first technical signals in a trend reversal. Thus, this type of stop point will strongly limit the magnitude of the loss or surrendered open profits. However, this attribute comes at a steep price: Trend line penetrations are prone to false signals. As discussed in Chapter 3, it is common for trend lines to be redefined in the course of a bull or bear market.

2. *Trading Range.* As illustrated in the preceding stock example, the opposite side of a trading range can be used as a stop point. Frequently, the stop can be placed closer (particularly in the case of broader trading ranges) because if the breakout is a valid signal, prices should not retreat too deeply into the range. Thus, the stop might be placed somewhere in the zone between the midpoint and the more distant boundary of the range (see the dashed line representing the midpoint of the trading range in Figure 9.1). The near end of the trading range, however, would not be a

meaningful stop point. In fact, retracements to this area are so common that many traders prefer to wait for such a reaction before initiating a position. (The advisability of this delayed entry strategy following breakouts is a matter of personal choice: In many instances it will provide better fills, but it will also cause the trader to miss some major moves.)

3. *Flags and Pennants.* After a breakout in one direction of a flag or pennant formation, the return to the opposite end (or some point beyond) can be used as a signal of a price reversal, and by implication a point for placing stops. For example, in Figure 9.2 the dashed line marks the stop level indicated by the lower boundary of a flag. After the upside breakout of the flag, a penetration of this level would imply a reversal of the current uptrend and require liquidation of the long position.

4. *Wide-Ranging Days.* Similar to flags and pennants, after a breakout in one direction, the return to the opposite end can be used as a signal of a price reversal, and hence a point for placing stops. For example, in Figure 9.3 note how the return of prices back to below the *true low* (see Appendix) of the wide-ranging up day formed in mid-September (after initially trading above this pattern) led to a major price collapse.

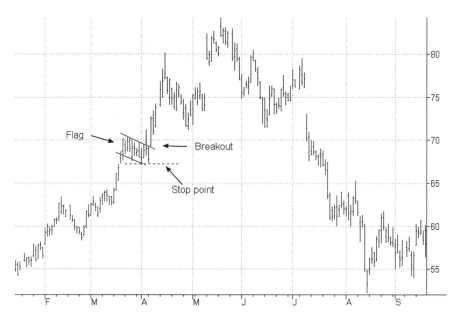

FIGURE 9.2 Stop placement following flag pattern breakout: DuPont. Chart created with TradeStation® by Omega Research, Inc.

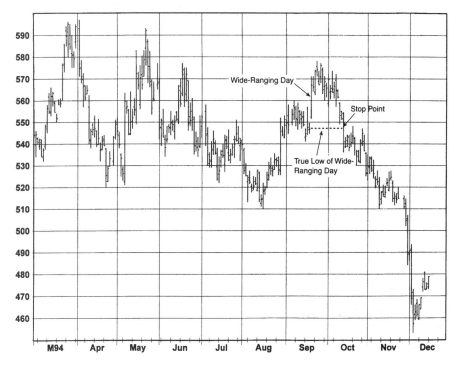

FIGURE 9.3 Stop placement following wide-ranging day breakout: December 1994 silver.

5. *Relative Highs and Relative Lows.* If the implied risk is not too great, the most recent relative high or relative low can be used as a stop point.* For example, assume a trader initiated a long position in response to the early January 1998 confirmation of the double bottom shown in Figure 9.4. In this case, both the November and December 1997 lows implied essentially the same stop level. A drop below this level would negate the validity of a long position.

Sometimes the risk implied by even the closest technically significant points may be excessive. In this case, the trader may decide to use a *money stop*—that is, a protective stop-loss point with no technical significance

---

*The specific definition of a relative low (relative high) is somewhat arbitrary. (The following description is in terms of the relative low, but analogous commentary would apply to the relative high.) The general definition of a relative low is a day whose low is below the lows of the preceding and succeeding N days. The specific definition of a relative low will depend on the choice of N. A reasonable range for N is between 5 and 15.

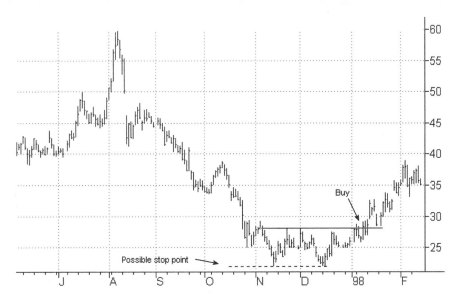

FIGURE 9.4 Stop placement at relative lows: Micron Technology.
Chart created with TradeStation® by Omega Research, Inc.

that is determined by the desired dollar risk level. For example, consider
the plight of a trader in early April 1993 who after the swift, steep March
1993 price break is convinced that the lumber market has witnessed a
major top (see Figure 9.5). The closest meaningful stop point—the contract high (which is the nearest relative high)—would imply a risk of
nearly $15,000 per contract (assuming entry at the midpoint of the April
trading range)! Although risk can sometimes be reduced if the trader
waits for a reaction before entering the market, such a retracement may
not occur until the market moves substantially lower. Thus, in a situation in which the nearest meaningful stop point implies a very large risk,
a market order accompanied by a money stop may represent the most viable trading approach.

     Stops should be used not only to limit losses but also to protect prof-
its. In the case of a long position, the stop should be raised intermittently
as the market rises. Similarly, in a declining market, the stop should be
lowered as the market declines. This type of stop is called a *trailing stop.*

     Figure 9.6 illustrates the use of a trailing stop. Assume a trader im-
plements a long position on the November upside gap above the September–November trading range, with a stop-loss liquidation plan keyed to
relative lows. Specifically, the trader plans to liquidate the long position
following a close below the most recent relative low with the reference
point being revised each time the market moves to new high ground. (Of

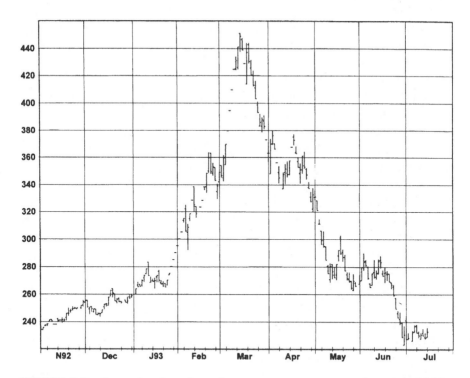

FIGURE 9.5 Example of market where money stop appropriate: July 1993 lumber.

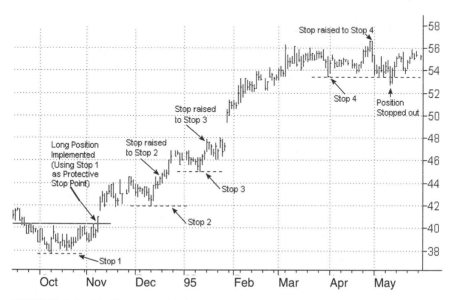

FIGURE 9.6 Trailing stop: Walt Disney.
Chart created with TradeStation® by Omega Research, Inc.

course, the stop condition may often be more restrictive. For example, the trader might require a specified number of closes below a previous low, or a minimum penetration of that low to activate the stop.) Thus, the initial stop-loss point would be a close below the October low (stop 1). (In this example, a relative low is defined as the lowest low of the past 10 days.) Following the December rally to new highs, the stop-loss reference point would be raised to the December low (stop 2). In similar fashion the stop reference points would be raised successively to the levels indicated by stop 3 and stop 4. The positions would be stopped out on the decline below stop 4 in May. Alternately, a trailing stop could follow a position by a fixed dollar, percentage, or point value. This technique, however, has the same implications as the simple money stop described earlier: It keeps risk at a known level and frees the trader from overly risky stop points based on chart patterns, but may also liquidate a trade when there is no technical reason for doing so.

As a general rule, stops should only be changed in order to reduce risk. Some traders who can't stand the thought of getting stopped out at the bottom of a move (or at the top if short) may be diligent in placing a GTC stop order upon initiating the position, but then cancel the order when the market gets within range. This type of order has been derisively, albeit appropriately, referred to as a CIC (cancel if close) order. Revising the stop to allow greater risk defeats the entire purpose of the stop.

Setting Objectives and Other Position Exit Criteria

It never was my thinking that made the big money for me. It was always my sitting. Got that? My sitting tight! It is no trick at all to be right on the market.

—Edwin Lefèvre

A trade is like the army—getting in is a lot easier than getting out. Provided the trader is adhering to risk control principles, a losing trade presents little ambiguity; that is, liquidation would be indicated by a predetermined stop point. However, the profitable trade presents a problem (albeit a desirable one). How should the trader decide when to take profits? Myriad solutions have been proposed for this dilemma. The following sections explore some of the primary approaches.

CHART-BASED OBJECTIVES

Many chart patterns are believed to provide clues regarding the magnitude of the potential price move. For example, conventional chart wisdom suggests that once prices penetrate the neckline of a head-and-shoulders formation, the ensuing price move will at least equal the distance from the top (or bottom) of the head to the neckline. As another example, many point-and-figure chartists claim that the number of columns that compose a trading range provides an indication of the potential number of boxes in a subsequent trend. (See Chapter 2 for an explanation of point and figure charting.) Generally speaking, chart patterns are probably considerably less reliable as indicators of price objectives than as trade signals.

MEASURED MOVE

This method is the essence of simplicity. The underlying premise is that markets will move in approximately equal-size price swings. Thus, if a market rallies 30 cents and then reacts, the implication is that the rally from the reaction low will approximate 30 cents. Although the measured move concept is so simple that it strains credibility, the approach offers reasonable guidelines more frequently than one might expect. When two or more of these objectives nearly coincide, it tends to enhance the reliability of the price area as an important objective zone.

Figure 10.1 depicts a number of measured move objectives based on both smaller and broader price swings, denoting the former with a number suffix (e.g., MM1), and the latter with a letter suffix (e.g., MMA). Most of these objectives proved to be surprisingly accurate. For example, the initial rally of $2^{11}/_{16}$ (price swing "1") in July–August 1994 provided a price objective at MM1. After retracing approximately a point over the next five weeks, the market rallied $2^{9}/_{16}$ in October–November, only $^2/_{16}$ away from

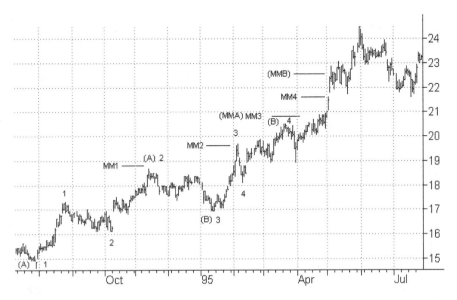

FIGURE 10.1 Measured moves: Pepsico.
Chart created with TradeStation® by Omega Research, Inc.

this target. Similarly, price swing "2" defined a measured move objective that almost precisely matched the early February high. Sometimes more than one measured move objective can coincide in the same approximate price area. Note particularly measured move objectives MM3 and MMA, which both were closely in line with the March relative high. Only MM4, which coincided with the early May gap, was significantly off-target.

Since price swings often span several futures contracts, it is useful to apply the measured move technique to longer-term price charts that link several contracts. Generally speaking, continuous futures charts are more appropriate than nearest futures charts for measured move analysis because, as was noted in Chapter 2, continuous futures accurately reflect price swings, whereas nearest futures do not.

Figure 10.2 shows the application of the measured move approach to a corn continuous futures chart. This chart reflects a multitude of surprisingly accurate measured move targets. The measured move objective implied by the initial downswing from the January 1994 market top (MM1) almost exactly coincided with the actual March 1994 relative low. Although the measured move objective implied by the February–early

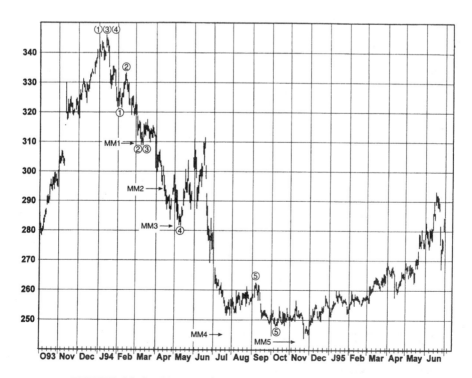

FIGURE 10.2 Measured moves: corn continuous futures.

March downswing (MM2) proved a bit wide of the actual May low, the measured move objective indicated by the entire decline from the January 1994 top to the March relative low (MM3) was near perfect in projecting the actual May low. Particularly striking was the fact that the very major measured move objective implied by the entire decline from the January 1994 top to the May 1994 low (MM4) almost exactly projected the November 1994 bottom. Moreover, the September–early October downswing provided a similar reinforcing measured move objective (MM5). Together, these two measured move objectives provided strong evidence that the market was near a major bottom in late November 1994.

As was seen in this corn chart example, there often will be more than one measured move objective for the same projected low or high. This will occur when there is more than one relevant price swing for deriving a measured move objective. When two or more of these objectives nearly coincide, it tends to enhance the reliability of the projected price area as an important target zone.

Figure 10.3 provides a perfect example of multiple near-coinciding

FIGURE 10.3 Concentration of measured move targets: October 1994 crude oil.

measured move price targets. As can be seen, the measured move objectives implied by the late March to late May advance (MM1), the June upswing (MM2), and the late-June to mid-July upmove (MM3) all approximately coincided just below the actual market top formed in August.

SUPPORT AND RESISTANCE LEVELS

Points near support levels provide a reasonable choice for setting initial objectives on short positions. For example, the indicated objective zone in Figure 10.4 is based on support anticipated in the area of two prior relative highs. Similarly, prices near resistance levels can be used for setting initial objectives on long positions. For example, the indicated objective level in Figure 10.5 is based on resistance implied by a prior significant high.

Generally speaking, support and resistance levels usually represent only temporary rather than major objectives. Consequently, in using this

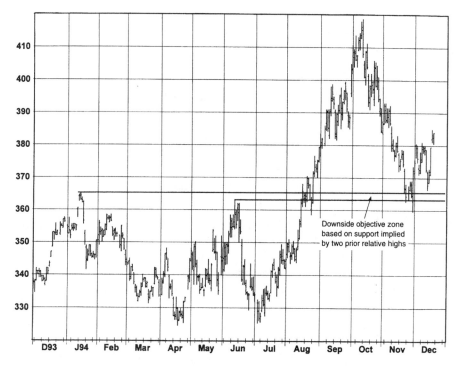

FIGURE 10.4 Downside objective at support zone: December 1994 wheat.

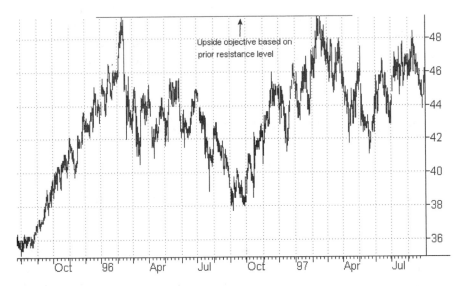

FIGURE 10.5 Upside objective at resistance level based on prior significant high: GTE Corp.
Chart created with TradeStation® by Omega Research, Inc.

approach, it is advisable to seek to reenter the position at a better price if a reaction does develop.

OVERBOUGHT/OVERSOLD INDICATORS

Overbought/oversold indicators are various technical measures, sometimes referred to as oscillators, intended to reflect when prices have risen or fallen too sharply and are thus vulnerable to a reaction. These indicators were described in detail in Chapter 6. Figure 10.6 illustrates the relative strength index (RSI), which has a range of values between 0 and 100. Based on the standard interpretation, levels above 70 suggest an overbought condition, while levels below 30 suggest an oversold condition.

The choice of specific overbought/oversold boundaries is a subjective one. For example, instead of 70 and 30, one might use 75 and 25, or 80 and 20. The more extreme the selected threshold levels, the closer the overbought/oversold signals will be to market turning points, but the greater the number of such points that will be missed.

The buy arrows in Figure 10.6 denote points at which the RSI

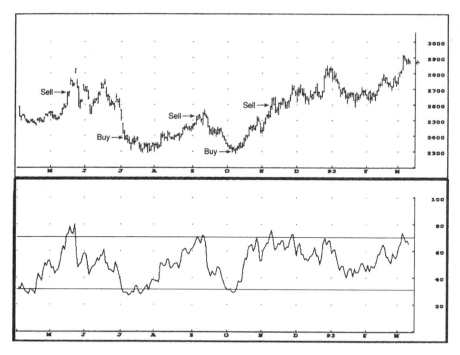

FIGURE 10.6 Relative strength index in trading range market: March 1995 soybean oil.

crosses below 30—that is, reaches an oversold condition that can be viewed as a signal to liquidate short positions. The sell arrows in Figure 10.6 denote points at which the RSI crosses above 70—that is, reaches an overbought condition that can be viewed as a signal to liquidate long positions.

On balance, the overbought/oversold signals in Figure 10.6 provide reasonably good position liquidation signals. This example hints at both the attributes and the drawbacks of using overbought/oversold indicators as liquidation signals. The approach will usually work well when the market is in a trading range, but will fail miserably during strong trending phases.

In Figure 10.6, the overbought/oversold signals work on balance because the illustrated market remains predominantly in a trading range pattern. Figure 10.7 illustrates the application of RSI overbought/oversold signals in a market dominated by a trend. Again, while the signals in the October 1995 to January 1996 broad trading range are useful, the repeated sell signals in the preceding nine-month rally highlight the limitations of this technique in a trending market.

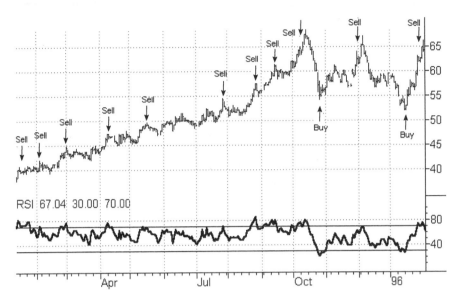

FIGURE 10.7 Relative strength index in trending market: Household International.
Chart created with TradeStation® by Omega Research, Inc.

CONTRARY OPINION

The theory of *contrary opinion* suggests that whenever a large majority of speculators are bullish, those who want to be long are already long. Consequently, there will be a paucity of potential new buyers, and the market will be vulnerable to a downside reaction. An analogous interpretation would apply when the majority of traders are bearish. Contrary opinion measures are based either on surveys of recommendations contained in market letters or on trader surveys, and implicitly assume that these opinions represent a reasonable proxy for overall market sentiment. The overbought and oversold thresholds in contrary opinion indexes will vary with the source.

Although contrary opinion is undoubtedly a sound theoretical concept, the Achilles' heel of this approach is the difficulty of measuring market sentiment accurately. Contrary opinion measures provided by existing services have frequently signaled major turning points. On the other hand, it is also not unusual for a contrary opinion index to stay high while the market continues to climb, or to stay low as the market continues to slide. On balance, this method provides useful information as long as it is not used as the sole trading guideline.

TRAILING STOPS

The use of trailing stops may be among the least glamorous, but most sensible, methods of determining a trade exit point. Although one will never sell the high or buy the low using this method, the approach comes closest to the ideal of permitting a profitable trade to run its course. Trailing stops were detailed in Chapter 9.

CHANGE OF MARKET OPINION

This is another approach with very little flash, but lots of common sense. In this case, the trader sets no predetermined objectives at all, but rather maintains the position until market opinion changes to at least neutral.

The Most
Important Rule in
Chart Analysis

The market is like a flu virus—as soon as you think you have it pegged, it mutates into something else.

—Wayne H. Wagner

FAILED SIGNALS

A *failed signal* is among the most reliable of all chart signals. When a market fails to follow through in the direction of a chart signal, it very strongly suggests the possibility of a significant move in the opposite direction. For example, in Figure 11.1 note how the market abruptly reversed course after breaking out above the June–July consolidation. If the upside penetration signal were valid, the market should not have retreated back to the lower portion of the consolidation and certainly not below its lower boundary. The fact that such a retracement occurs almost immediately following the breakout strongly suggests a *bull trap*. Such price action is consistent with the market's rising just enough to activate stop orders lying beyond the boundary of the range, but uncovering no additional buying support after the breakout—an indication of a very weak underlying technical picture. In effect, the immediate failure of the apparent buy signal can be viewed as a strong indication that the market should be sold.

Now that we have established the critical importance of failed signals, the following sections detail various types of failed signals, along with interpretation and trading guidelines.

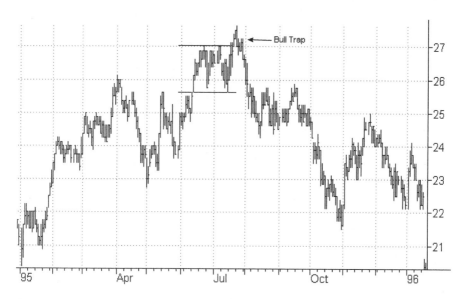

FIGURE 11.1 Bull trap: Wal-Mart Stores Inc.
Chart created with TradeStation® by Omega Research, Inc.

BULL AND BEAR TRAPS

Bull and *bear traps* are major breakouts that are soon followed by abrupt, sharp price reversals, in stark contrast to the price continuation patterns that are expected to follow breakouts. In my experience, this type of counter-to-anticipated price action is among the most reliable indicators of major tops and bottoms. An example of a bull trap was provided in the previous section (Figure 11.1). Another classic example of a bull trap was the October 1993 peak of a six-year bull market in T-bonds (see Figure 11.2). Note that the mid-October upside breakout to new record highs above the prior seven-week trading range was immediately followed by a steep price break.

Analogous to the bull trap, in the case of a bear trap the market falls just enough to trigger resting stops below the low end of a trading range, but fails to uncover any additional selling pressure after the breakout—an indication of substantial underlying strength. In effect, the immediate failure of a sell signal can be viewed as a signal that the market should be bought.

Figure 11.3, which depicts the culmination of a six-year downtrend in the silver market, provides a classic example of a bear trap. In February 1993 the market witnessed a sharp two-day plunge below both the prior very narrow three-month trading range and a broader

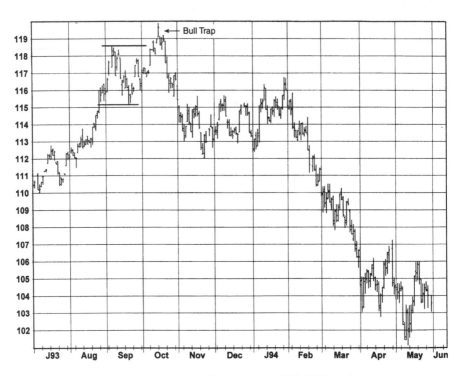

FIGURE 11.2 Bull trap: June 1994 T-bond.

FIGURE 11.3 Bear trap: July 1993 silver.

six-month trading range. Instead of continuing lower, prices held in midair, initially moving sideways and eventually rebounding back into the trading range. This price action proved to be a precursor of a dramatic rally.

How much of a pullback is required to indicate that a bull or bear trap has occurred? The following are several possible confirmation conditions:

> *Initial Price Confirmation.* A price retracement to the median of the consolidation that preceded the breakout.
>
> *Strong Price Confirmation.* A price retracement to the more distant boundary (lower for bull trap; upper for bear trap) of the consolidation that preceded the breakout.
>
> *Time Confirmation.* The failure of the market to return to the extreme price witnessed following the breakout within a specified amount of time (e.g., four weeks).

The trade-off between initial and strong price confirmations is that the former will provide better entry levels in trading bull and bear traps, whereas the latter will provide more reliable signals. The time confirmation condition can be used on its own or in conjunction with the two price confirmation conditions. Figures 11.4 and 11.5 repeat Figures 11.2 and 11.3 adding each of the three confirmation conditions (the time confirmation condition is assumed to be four weeks). Note that the time confirmation can occur after both price confirmation conditions (as is the case in Figure 11.4), before both price confirmation conditions (as is the case in Figure 11.5), or at any point between.

A bull trap signal would be invalidated if the market returned to the breakout high. Similarly, a bear trap signal would be invalidated if the market returned to the breakout low. More sensitive conditions could be used to invalidate bull or bear trap signals once the market has moved sufficiently in the direction of the signal or a specified amount of time has elapsed. An example of such a condition would be the return of prices to the opposite boundary of a consolidation once a strong price confirmation signal was received (e.g., in the case of a bull trap, a return to the top of the consolidation after prices broke to below the low end of the consolidation).

If the selected invalidation condition does not occur, a trade implemented on a bull or bear trap signal would be held until a price objective or other trade liquidation condition was met or until there was evidence of an opposite direction trend reversal.

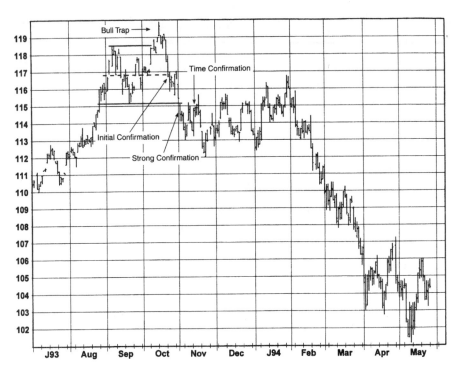

FIGURE 11.4 Bull trap confirmation conditions: June 1994 T-bond.

FIGURE 11.5 Bear trap confirmation conditions: July 1993 silver.

FALSE TREND LINE BREAKOUTS

As was discussed in Chapter 3, trend lines are particularly prone to false breakouts. Such false breakouts can be used as signals for trading in the direction opposite to the breakout. In fact, in my opinion, false trend breakout signals are considerably more reliable than conventional trend breakout signals. In the case of a downtrend, a false trend breakout would be confirmed if the market witnessed a specified number of closes (e.g., two, three) below the trend line following an upside breakout. Similarly, in the case of an uptrend, a false trend breakout would be confirmed if the market witnessed a specified number of closes above the trend line following a downside breakout.

Figure 11.6 provides an example of a false breakout of an uptrend line. Note that the September downside breakout of the uptrend line defined by four prior relative lows was soon followed by a break above the line. The indicated failure signal is based on an assumed requirement of two closes above the line for confirmation. Additional trend line penetrations occurred in October 1997 and January 1998. The slight October penetration, however, did not close below the trend line, discounting its importance as a false trend line breakout.

It is quite possible for a chart to yield several successive false trend

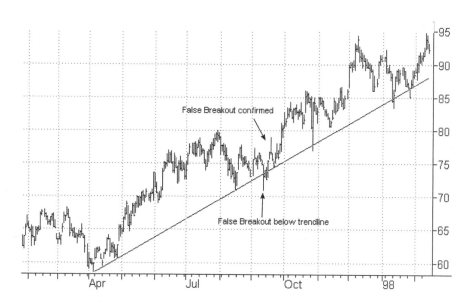

False Breakout confirmed

False Breakout below trendline

FIGURE 11.6 False breakout of uptrend line: Allstate Corp.
Chart created with TradeStation® by Omega Research, Inc.

breakout signals in the process of the trend line (I) being repeatedly rede-fined. In Figure 11.7 the initial upside penetration of the prevailing down-trend line (I) occurred in mid-December. Prices quickly retreated back below the line, with the indicated failure signal assumed to be triggered by the second close below the line. Another false breakout occurred several weeks later, based on the redefined trend line using the December relative high (trend line II). Once again prices quickly retreated below the down-trend line, yielding another false trend breakout signal. The redrawn trend line incorporating the January relative high (trend line III) was briefly penetrated on the upside in March, leading to a third false trend breakout.

FILLED GAPS

As was detailed in Chapter 5, gaps are normally considered patterns that presage a continuation of the trend in the direction of the gap. When a gap is filled, such a development qualifies the original gap as a failed sig-

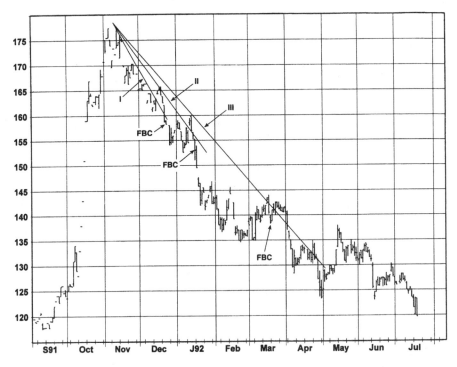

Note: FBC = false breakout confirmed (i.e., two closes below trend line).

FIGURE 11.7 Multiple false breakouts of downtrend lines: July 1992 FCOJ.

nal. The significance of filled gaps is enhanced if the following additional characteristics apply:

✔ The filled gap is particularly wide.

✔ The filled gap is a breakaway gap.

✔ Two or more consecutive gaps are filled.

Although typically a gap is considered filled if the intraday price reaches the high (or low, in the case of a downside gap) of the day prior to the gap, I prefer a more rigid definition requiring a close below (above, in the case of a downside gap) the close on the day prior to the gap day. This more restrictive definition will reduce the number of times a prior gap is interpreted as a failed signal when such a conclusion ultimately proves unwarranted, at the expense of signaling such an event slightly later in cases where it is the correct call.

In Figure 11.8 a breakaway upside gap is filled about one week later. Interestingly, the gap is filled on a wide-ranging day, which is itself a signal that a downside reversal may have occurred. These patterns presaged

FIGURE 11.8 Filled upside gap: March 1991 sugar.

an extended price slide in sugar futures. In Figure 11.9 an upside gap that formed one day before the extreme high of the bull market was filled two days later, providing a very early signal of what proved to be a major trend reversal. Fig. 11.10 shows a huge upside gap in August 1997 that was nearly filled six days later by an abrupt downside swing. The market then traded sideways for two months before finally filling the gap completely in October 1997, at which point prices continued to descend.

Figures 11.11 and 11.12 provide examples of downside filled gaps as failed signals. In Figure 11.11 a wide downside gap to a new low is filled only two days later (one day after the low), providing an extremely early signal of what ultimately proved to be a very major trend reversal. (Another instance of a downside gap being filled occurred just under three months later.) Figure 11.12 provides an example of two consecutive downside gaps being filled. Although this price action accurately signaled that a major bottom had been established, note that prices first retreated before beginning a sustained advance. The implied lesson is that even valid indications of a failed signal may first witness a price correction before the anticipated price move materializes. In the case of downside gaps, the failed signal can be

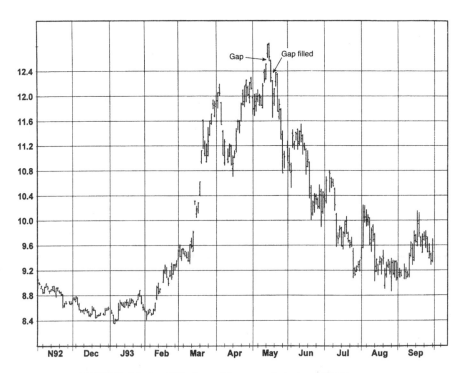

FIGURE 11.9 Filled upside gap: October 1993 sugar.

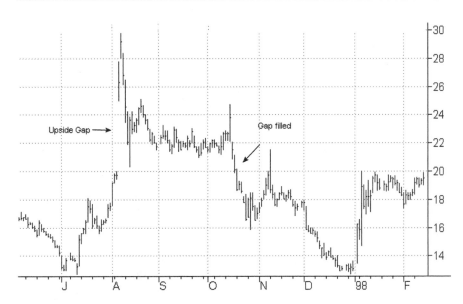

FIGURE 11.10 Filled upside gap: Apple Computer.
Chart created with TradeStation® by Omega Research, Inc.

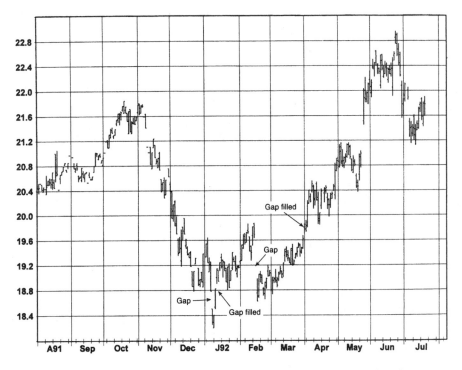

FIGURE 11.11 Filled downside gaps: August 1992 crude oil.

FIGURE 11.12   Filled downside gaps: March 1995 cotton.

considered to remain in force as long as prices do not close below the gap, or lowest gap if there is more than one. (Similarly, in the case of upside gaps, the failed signal can be considered to remain in force as long as prices do not close above the gap, or highest gap if there is more than one.)

RETURN TO SPIKE EXTREMES

As was detailed in Chapter 5, price spikes frequently occur at important price reversals. Consequently, the return of prices to a prior spike extreme can be viewed as transforming the original spike into a failed signal. The more extreme the spike (i.e., the greater the magnitude by which the spike high exceeds the highs on the prior and subsequent days or the spike low falls below the lows on the prior and subsequent days), the greater the significance of its penetration. The significance of such failed signals is also enhanced if at least several weeks, and preferably several months, have elapsed since the original spike.

In Figure 11.13 the return to the July spike high four months later led to a substantial extension on the upside. Figure 11.14 provides an

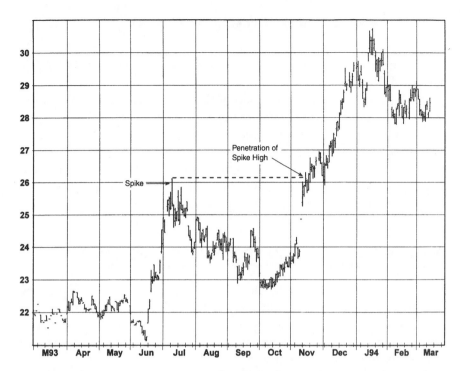

FIGURE 11.13 Penetration of spike high: March 1994 soybean oil.

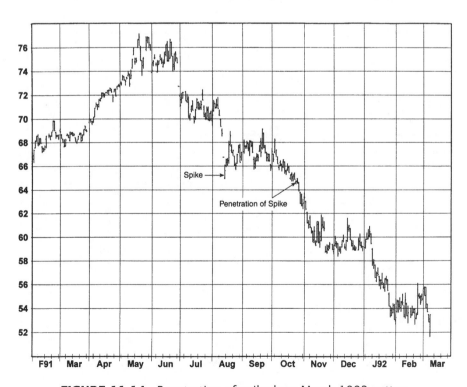

FIGURE 11.14 Penetration of spike low: March 1992 cotton.

163

example of the penetration of a downside spike, with prices sliding sharply following this event.

In Figure 11.15 the penetration of the July spike high a little over a month later leads to the anticipated further advance. Note, however, that the penetration of the October spike low several months later proves misleading—a *failed* failed signal, so to speak. Generally speaking, a close beyond the opposite extreme of the spike can be viewed as negating the failed signal. In this case, the market closed above the high of the spike low day four days after the spike was penetrated.

RETURN TO WIDE-RANGING DAY EXTREMES

As was explained in Chapter 5, wide-ranging days with particularly strong or weak closes tend to lead to price extensions in the same direction. Consequently, the close above the high price of a downside wide-ranging day or below the low price of an upside wide-ranging day can be viewed as confirming such days as failed signals.

In Figure 11.16 the very pronounced downside wide-ranging day

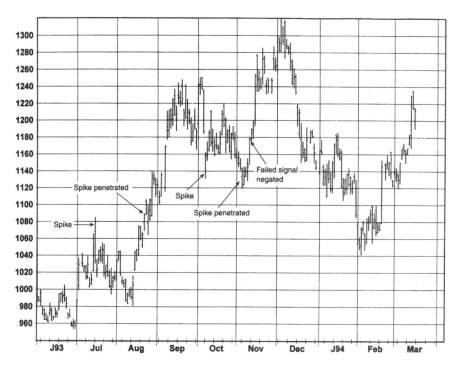

FIGURE 11.15 Spike penetration signal negated: March 1994 cocoa.

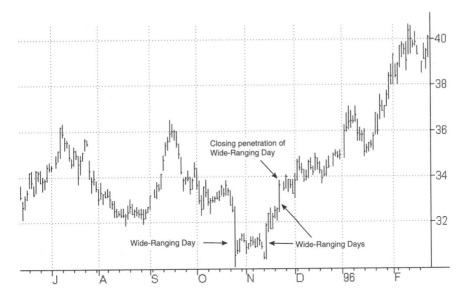

FIGURE 11.16 Penetration of downside wide-ranging day: DuPont. Chart created with TradeStation® by Omega Research, Inc.

formed in late October was followed by a brief consolidation. The market then reversed to the upside with a wide-ranging day, followed roughly a week later by another upside wide-ranging day which closed strongly above the high of the initial October wide-ranging day. This reversal of the original downside wide-ranging day was followed by a protracted price advance in the ensuing months. In Figure 11.17 two downside wide-ranging days formed in close proximity are each penetrated on the upside in the subsequent period. Moreover, note that an upside wide-ranging day materialized between these two penetrations. This confluence of bullish signals proved to be a precursor of a major rally.

Figure 11.18 provides an example of the downside penetration of upside wide-ranging days. The closing downside penetration of the early January wide-ranging day was itself a wide-ranging day and proved to be an early signal of an impending massive price decline.

COUNTER-TO-ANTICIPATED BREAKOUT OF FLAG OR PENNANT

As was explained in Chapter 5, flag or pennant consolidations typically tend to be followed by price swings in the same direction as the price swings that preceded their formation. Therefore, if a flag or pennant

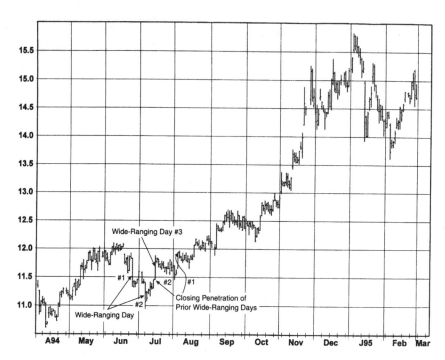

FIGURE 11.17   Penetration of downside wide-ranging days: March 1995 sugar.

FIGURE 11.18   Penetration of upside wide-ranging day: June 1994 Eurodollar.

formation is followed by a breakout in the opposite direction of the preceding price swing, it would qualify the pattern as a failed signal.

In Figure 11.19, just as would have been implied by the chart interpretation guidelines presented in Chapter 5, the flag and pennant formations that evolved during the illustrated downtrend were generally followed by downswings. The one exception, however, was the flag that formed following a downside breakout to a new low for the move in March. In this instance, the flag was followed by an upside breakout. This counter-to-anticipated price action augured a significant rebound. In Figure 11.20 note that both the April and October lows were formed by flags that were penetrated by price swings opposite to the expected direction.

Figure 11.21 depicts a major bottom that was established by a flag that was followed by a counter-to-anticipated breakout. In this instance, however, the breakout was itself followed by a pullback before the sharp price advance ensued. The lesson is that the counter-to-anticipated breakout does not need to be followed by an immediate extension of the price move in order to be a valid confirmation of a failed signal. How much of a

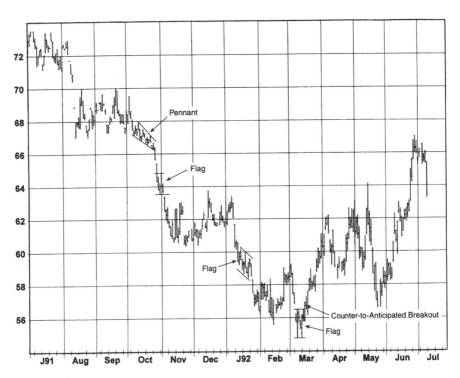

FIGURE 11.19 Counter-to-anticipated breakout of flag pattern: July 1992 cotton.

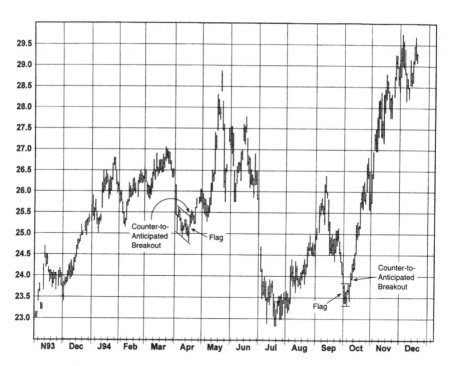

FIGURE 11.20 Counter-to-anticipated breakout of flag patterns: December 1994 soybean oil.

FIGURE 11.21 Counter-to-anticipated breakout of flag pattern followed by pullback: March 1994 cotton.

retracement can be allowed before the interpretation of a failed signal is abandoned? One reasonable approach is to consider the confirmation of a failed signal in force as long as prices do not close beyond the opposite end of the relevant flag or pennant. The retracement in the illustrated example stopped short of such a point.

Figures 11.22 and 11.23 provide examples of downside breakouts of flags or pennants that formed after price advances. In each of these cases, a flag or pennant formed at or near contract highs—normally, a very bullish development. Instead of leading to renewed advances, however, each of these flags or pennants yielded to a sharp downside breakout. In both instances, the failed signals implied by the counter-to-anticipated breakouts provided extraordinarily timely indications of major trend reversals. Although prices witnessed immediate, sustained downtrends in Figure 11.22, note that in Figure 11.23, prices first rebounded back to the pennant before plunging. This pullback, however, did not carry above the pennant; therefore, according to the previously provided rule, the implications of the failed signal would still be considered to be in effect.

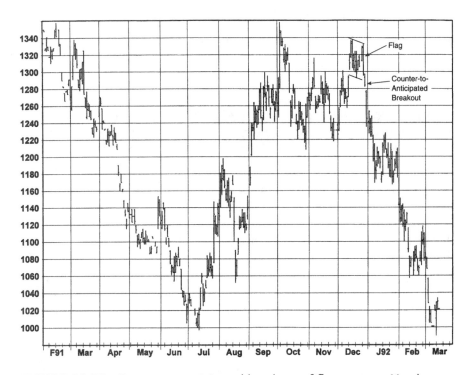

FIGURE 11.22 Counter-to-anticipated breakout of flag pattern: March 1992 cocoa.

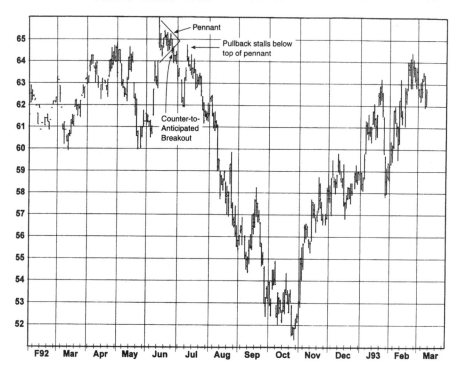

FIGURE 11.23 Counter-to-anticipated breakout of pennant: March 1993 cotton.

OPPOSITE DIRECTION BREAKOUT OF FLAG OR PENNANT FOLLOWING A NORMAL BREAKOUT

In some cases, flags and pennants are followed by breakouts in the anticipated direction, but prices then reverse, closing beyond the opposite extreme of the flag or pennant. This combined price action provides another example of a failed signal, since the anticipated breakout of the flag or pennant is followed by a price reversal instead of a price follow-through. Note that a close beyond the opposite end of the flag or pennant is required to confirm a failed signal, rather than a mere intraday penetration. Although this more restrictive condition will yield slightly less timely confirmations of failed signals in cases when such a conclusion proves valid, it will reduce the number of inaccurate calls of failed signals.

In Figure 11.24 the flag consolidation that formed near the top of a four-month advance was followed by an upside breakout, as might have been anticipated. Instead of witnessing a further advance, how-

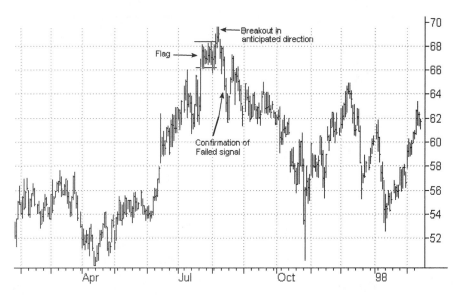

FIGURE 11.24 Opposite direction breakout of flag following normal breakout: DuPont.
Chart created with TradeStation® by Omega Research, Inc.

ever, prices moved higher for only three days (only two of which closed above the upper boundary of the flag) and within four more days had retreated to below the low end of the flag consolidation. This price action qualified the earlier upside breakout above the flag pattern as a failed signal.

Figure 11.25 illustrates a failed downside penetration of a flag that occurred after an extended price slide. This downside breakout led to little further downside movement, and prices soon rebounded back above the top of the pennant, confirming a failed signal and presaging a large advance. Figure 11.26 provides another example in which a rebound above the top of a flag after an initial downside breakout confirmed a relative low and led to a large advance. Note that this chart also contains an example of a failed signal based on a counter-to-anticipated breakout from a flag—an event that occurred at the market top.

PENETRATION OF TOP AND BOTTOM FORMATIONS

The penetration of patterns that are normally associated with major tops and bottoms represents another important type of failed signal in that price has neglected to respect the support or resistance level implied by such

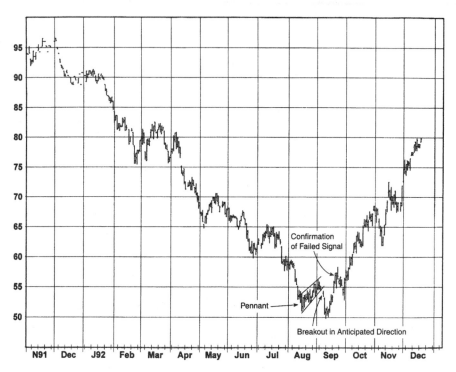

FIGURE 11.25 Opposite direction breakout of pennant following normal breakout: December 1992 coffee.

formations. For example, Figure 11.27 illustrates the double top formed during 1993 in May 1994 coffee and the penetration of this top about seven months later. Figure 11.28, which depicts the July 1994 contract, shows the immense rally that followed this upside breakout. Although in this chart the July–September 1993 double top looks like nothing more than a squiggle in an extended, narrow trading range, Figure 11.27 makes clear that at the time the formation did appear to be a double top. It was only the towering proportions of the subsequent May–July 1994 rally that made the earlier price action look like part of a narrow trading range in comparison.

Penetrations of double-top and double-bottom patterns provide good signals but are relatively rare. Failed signals involving head-and-shoulders patterns are more common and often provide excellent trading indicators. Although the choice of what condition constitutes a confirmation of a failed head-and-shoulders pattern is somewhat arbitrary, I would use the criterion of prices retracing beyond the most recent shoulder. For example, in Figure 11.29 the rebound above the November 1995 shoulder would represent a confirmation of a failed head-and-shoulders top pattern.

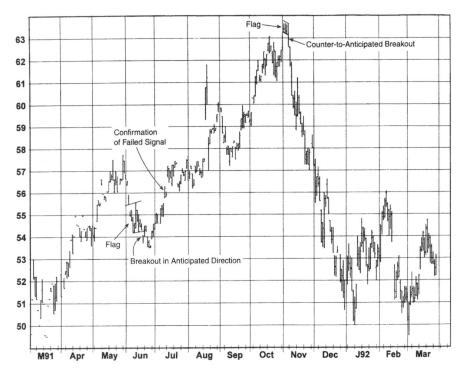

FIGURE 11.26 Opposite direction breakout of flag following normal breakout: April 1992 heating oil.

Figure 11.30 illustrates an example of a failed head-and-shoulders bottom pattern. In analogous fashion to the head-and-shoulders top case, the downside penetration of the more recent shoulder is used as the confirmation condition of a failed signal. Note that prices first rebounded after the confirmation signal before eventually heading sharply lower. As this example suggests, the trader may often benefit by waiting for a retracement before implementing a position based on the confirmation of a failed head-and-shoulders pattern. The trade-off is that such a strategy will result in missing very profitable trades in those cases where there is no retracement or only a very modest retracement.

BREAKING OF CURVATURE

As was discussed in Chapter 5, rounding patterns often provide very reliable trading signals. In this sense, the breaking of a curved price pattern can be viewed as transforming the pattern into a failed signal. For example,

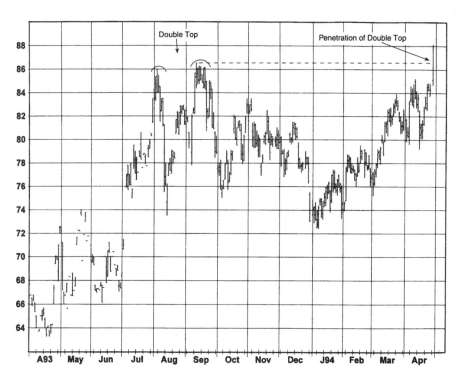

FIGURE 11.27 Penetration of double top: May 1994 coffee.

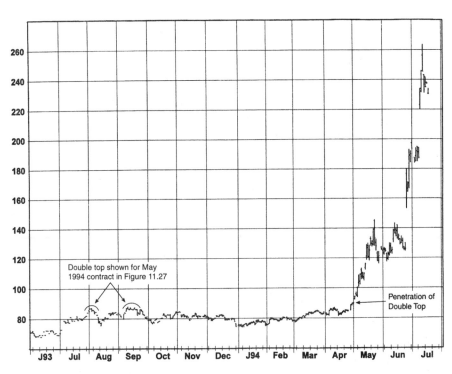

FIGURE 11.28 Penetration of double top: July 1994 coffee.

174

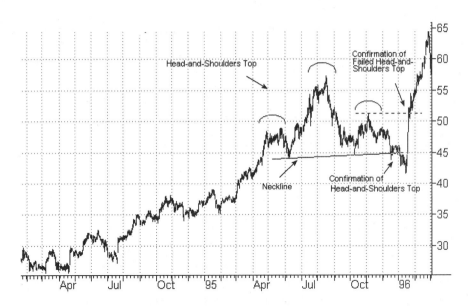

FIGURE 11.29 Failed head-and-shoulders top pattern: IBM. Chart created with TradeStation® by Omega Research, Inc.

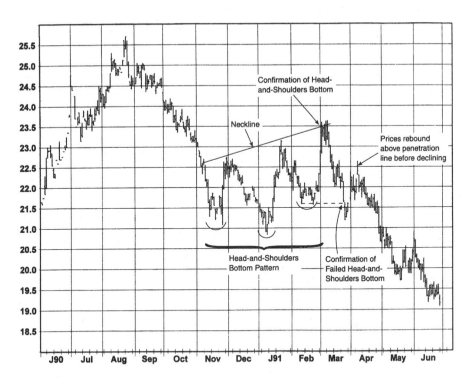

FIGURE 11.30 Failed head-and-shoulders bottom pattern: July 1991 soybean oil.

in Figure 11.31 the breaking of the curvature of what had been an apparent rounding top pattern represented a bullish signal.

THE FUTURE RELIABILITY OF FAILED SIGNALS

There is an inverse relationship between the popularity of an indicator and its efficiency. For example, prior to the 1980s, when technical analysis was used by fewer market practitioners, chart breakouts (price moves above or below prior trading ranges) tended to work relatively well as indicators, providing many excellent signals without an abundance of false signals. In my observation, as technical analysis became increasingly popular and breakouts a commonly used tool, the efficiency of this pattern seemed to deteriorate. In fact, it now seems that price *reversals* following breakouts are more often the rule than the exception.

As stated earlier, I find failed signals considerably more reliable than conventional chart patterns. Although the concept of failed signals is certainly not new—in fact, my own book, *A Complete Guide to the Futures Markets*, written in 1984, contains a section on this topic—I am not aware

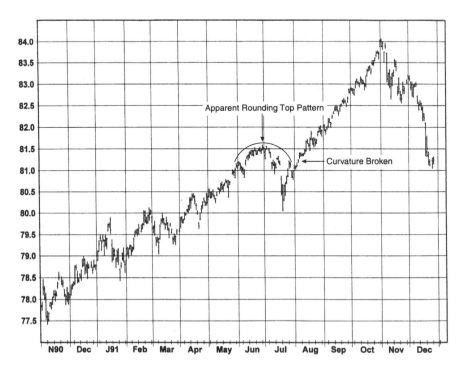

FIGURE 11.31 Breaking of curvature: Canadian dollar continuous futures.

of its usage being strongly emphasized elsewhere. If the use of failed signals were to become significantly more widespread, however, their long-term reliability could be adversely affected.

As a final comment, it should be emphasized that the concept of failed signals in this chapter has been presented in the context of conventional chart analysis as it exists today. In the future—particularly the distant future—what passes for popular chart interpretation may well change. The concept of failed signals, however, can be made dynamic by pegging it to the conventional wisdom. In other words, if a new chart pattern became popular as a technical signal in the future (e.g., in the way breakouts are widely used today), a failure of the pattern could be viewed as more significant than the pattern itself. In this more general sense, the concept of failed signals could prove timeless.

CONCLUSION

The novice trader will ignore a failed signal, riding a position into a large loss while hoping for the best. The more experienced trader, having learned the importance of money management, will exit quickly once it is apparent that he or she has made a bad trade. However, the truly skilled trader will be able to do a 180-degree turn, reversing a position at a loss if market behavior points to such a course of action. In other words, it takes great discipline to capitalize on failed signals, but such flexibility is essential to the effective synthesis of chart analysis and trading.

Chapter 12

Real-World
Chart Analysis

The speculator's chief enemies are always boring from within. It is inseparable from human nature to hope and to fear. In speculation when the market goes against you, you hope that every day will be the last day—and you lose more than you should had you not listened to hope—to the same ally that is so potent a success-bringer to empire builders and pioneers, big and little. And when the market goes your way you become fearful that the next day will take away your profit, and you get out—too soon. Fear keeps you from making as much money as you ought to. The successful trader has to fight these two deep-seated instincts. He has to reverse what you might call his natural impulses. Instead of hoping he must fear; instead of fearing he must hope. He must fear that his loss may develop into a much bigger loss, and hope that his profit may become a big profit.

—Edwin Lefèvre

I t is always easy to analyze a chart with the benefit of hindsight. It is quite another matter to analyze a chart in real time, with actual trading decisions dependent on the outcome. The chart examples in this chapter represent a handful of the trade recommendations I issued in my role as director of futures research at Prudential Securities. For each trade, I noted the reasons for entry and exit, as well as any lessons provided by the trade after the smoke had cleared. To provide a rounded perspective, both winning and losing trades are included. Knowing what can go wrong in a trade is often more important that knowing what can go right.

HOW TO USE THIS CHAPTER

1. Do not read this chapter out of sequence. It is essential that Part One be read before this chapter.

2. For maximum benefit, reading this chapter should be a hands-on experience. It is suggested that the reader first photocopy all the *odd* (right-hand) pages of the charts that follow.

3. Each trade contains the reasons for entering the position. Consider whether you interpret the chart the same way. Even technical analysts using the same patterns may interpret these patterns differently. One analyst's double top is another's trading range consolidation, and so on. In short, second-guessing is strongly encouraged. Remember, many of these trades turned out to be losers.

4. The illustrations in the following charts emphasize the analytical tools and chart patterns that I tend to rely on most heavily. This by no means implies that these methods are the most important or accurate, only that they are the ones I am most comfortable using. Chart analysis is a very subjective endeavor.

   There are many techniques that have been described in this book that are not applied in the following illustrations. Some readers may find these other analytical tools helpful as supplemental input or even as substitute methodologies. The mix of methods I feel most comfortable with is likely to be quite different from the approach that will be most suitable for each individual reader. In essence, each practitioner of chart analysis must choose an individual set of technical tools and define a personal analytical style.

5. Analyze the chart on each odd (right-hand) page using your favorite approach, specifically detailing your own strategy. If you have made photocopies, you can mark these copies up to your heart's content. Then turn to the next (even) page to see how your analysis (and mine) turned out in the real world; this page contains the reasons for trade exit and observations related to the trade.

By following this procedure instead of passively reading the chapter, you will obtain the maximum learning benefit.

REAL-WORLD CHART ANALYSIS

Begin your analysis with the chart on the opposite page. Finish detailing your strategy before turning the page.

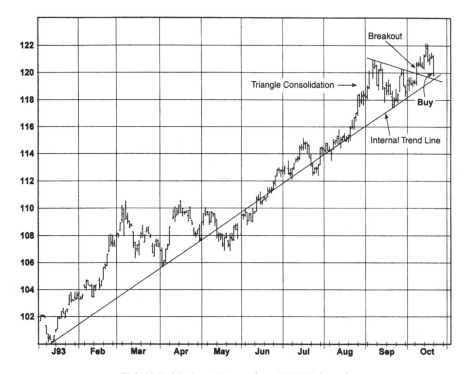

FIGURE 12.1a December 1993 T-bond.

Trade Entry Reasons

1. The breakout above the triangular consolidation implied a continuation of the bull move.

2.. The pullback brought prices close to the major support level indicated by both an extended internal trend line and the top of the triangle.

Do you agree or disagree with the analysis? Evaluate the situation before turning page.

FIGURE 12.1b December 1993 T-bond.

Trade Exit

The significant downside penetration of the lower end of the triangle invalidated the original trade signal.

Comment

A trade should always be liquidated once the primary premise for the trade is violated. In this instance, prices should have held above or near the top of the triangle. Once prices broke meaningfully below the low end of the triangle, the validity of the prior breakout seemed highly questionable. Getting out on the first sign that the market had violated the original trade premise helped keep the loss on the trade relatively small. As can be seen in Figure 12.1b, even a small amount of procrastination would have been very costly.

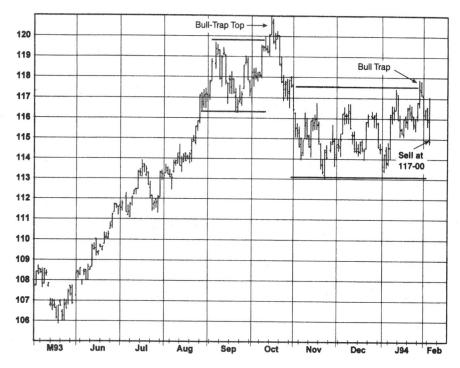

FIGURE 12.2a March 1993 T-bond.

Trade Entry Reasons

1. The October bull-trap top, which formed in record high territory after a very extended price advance, suggested that a major peak had been established. At the time shown, prices had only retraced a small portion of the prior advance, which extended back well before the start of this chart, implying substantial further downside potential.

2. The late January upside breakout above the November–January trading range and the subsequent pullback deep into the range represented another bull trap.

Note that the trade recommendation called for selling on a rebound back to 117-00 as opposed to going short at the market.

**Do you agree or disagree with the analysis?
Evaluate the situation before turning page.**

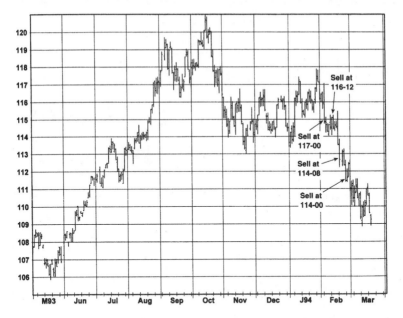

FIGURE 12.2b March 1993 T-bond.

Comment

As can be seen on the chart, the market failed to rebound to the recommended sell point at 117-00. As shown, the sell point was subsequently lowered on three separate occasions. In each instance, the market failed to reach the recommended sell level. As a result, even though the original trade idea was excellent, with the market witnessing a large and rapid price move in the anticipated direction, the trade opportunity was entirely missed.

In every trade there is a trade-off between getting a better entry price and assuring that the position is implemented. This trade highlights the potential pitfall in waiting for a better entry level instead of initiating the position at the market. As in this example, such a more cautious approach can result in missing major winning trades. This observation is not intended to imply that one should always implement intended trades at the market, but it does serve to emphasize the attribute of market orders: They assure that trading opportunities will not be missed. In particular, market orders should be favored in long-term trades that are believed to offer a large profit potential—as was the case in this illustration. Even so, the error made in this trade was not the initial use of a limit order, which could have been justified based on the prevailing trading range pattern, but rather the failure to convert to a market entry approach once the price action (e.g., the flag consolidations formed after the initial recommendation) suggested that a rebound was unlikely.

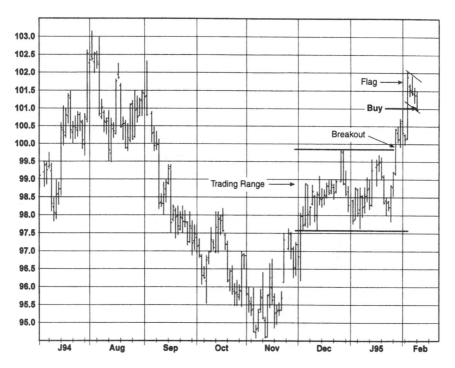

FIGURE 12.3a T-bond continuous futures.

Trade Entry Reasons

1. Sustained upside breakout above prior trading range.
2. Flag consolidation formed above prior trading range.

**Do you agree or disagree with the analysis?
Evaluate the situation before turning page.**

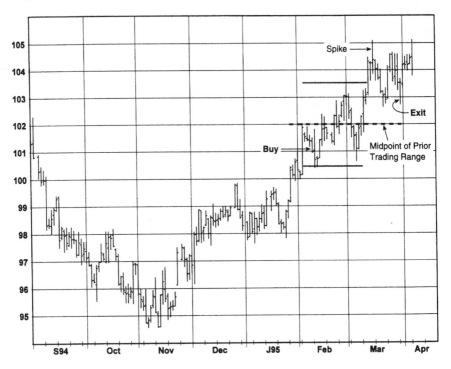

FIGURE 12.3b T-bond continuous futures.

Trade Exit

The trade was liquidated on a raised protective stop. The stop had been brought in relatively close because a spike high that had remained intact for nearly two weeks suggested that a top might be in place.

Comment

The exit on this trade proved highly premature, as the market subsequently moved much higher. Although, as cited, the existence of a spike high provided some justification for a close stop, it is noteworthy that the stop had been raised above the closest meaningful point, which was probably the midpoint of the prior trading range. The lesson is that bringing in stop points closer than meaningful levels will often result in exiting good trades far too early.

FIGURE 12.4a   December 1994 British pound.

Trade Entry Reasons

1. Sustained upside breakout above triangle consolidation.
2. Pennant consolidation following an upswing.

**Do you agree or disagree with the analysis?
Evaluate the situation before turning page.**

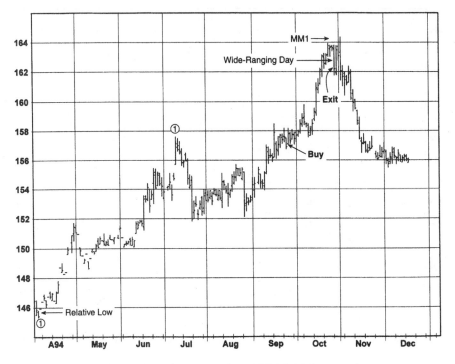

FIGURE 12.4b December 1994 British pound.

Trade Exit

The trade was liquidated on the downside wide-ranging day following the approximate attainment of a major measured move objective (MM1).

Comment

This trade had originally been recommended several weeks before the indicated buy point, using a limit order within the triangle consolidation (see Figure 12.4a), in anticipation of an eventual upside breakout from this formation. This buy point was never reached, and eventually a long position was recommended at the market. This action helped salvage the substantial remaining profit potential in the trade. The general lesson illustrated by this trade is that if a market fails to reach a limit entry price and starts to move in the anticipated direction, it often makes sense to enter the trade somewhat belatedly at a less favorable price, as opposed to abandoning the idea as a missed trade.

This trade also illustrates how using the approach of a measured move objective as an indicator to exit a trade on the first sign of failure can help dramatically limit the surrender of large open profits.

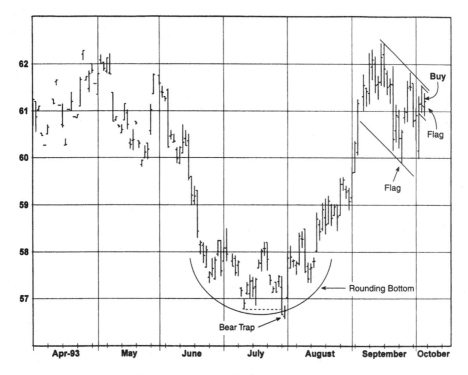

FIGURE 12.5a December 1993 deutsche mark.

Trade Entry Reasons

1. Rounding price base and bear trap low both suggested a major bottom was in place.

2. Both narrow flag and broader flag suggested the likelihood of an upside breakout.

Do you agree or disagree with the analysis?
Evaluate the situation before turning page.

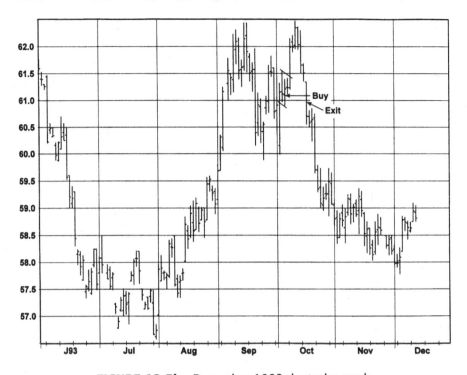

FIGURE 12.5b December 1993 deutsche mark.

Trade Exit

Although the market did break out on the upside initially, there was little follow-through, and the subsequent retracement back below the midpoint of the prior flag pattern suggested a price failure.

Comment

Exit on the first sign of a technical failure kept the loss on the trade very small.

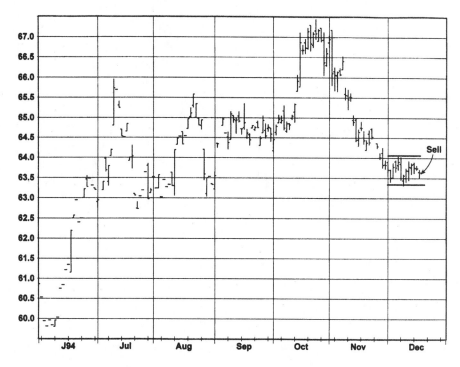

FIGURE 12.6a March 1995 deutsche mark.

Trade Entry Reason

Narrow consolidation formed after steep price slide suggested a probable continuation of downtrend.

**Do you agree or disagree with the analysis?
Evaluate the situation before turning page.**

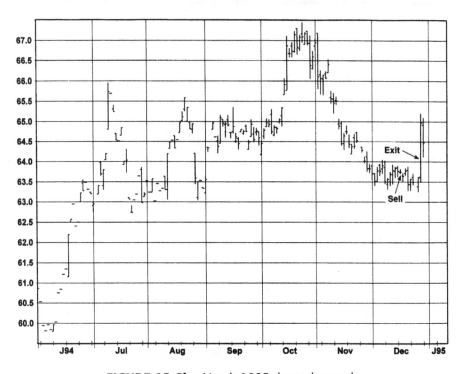

FIGURE 12.6b March 1995 deutsche mark.

Trade Exit

Counter-to-anticipated breakout from consolidation violated a basic premise of trade.

Comment

Exit on the first sign of an invalidation of the trade premise kept the loss small.

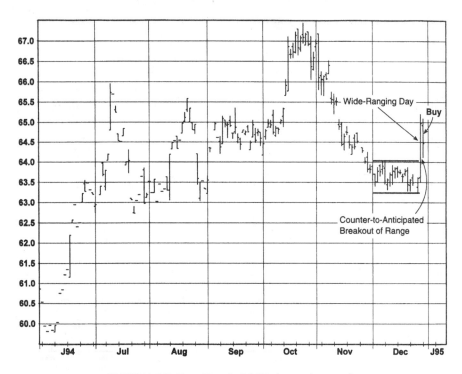

FIGURE 12.7a March 1995 deutsche mark.

Trade Entry Reasons

1. Counter-to-anticipated penetration of a narrow consolidation suggested an upside reversal. (Same reason why prior trade liquidated—see Figure 12.6b.)

2. A wide-ranging day formed near a relative low is often an early sign of a trend reversal.

Do you agree or disagree with the analysis? Evaluate the situation before turning page.

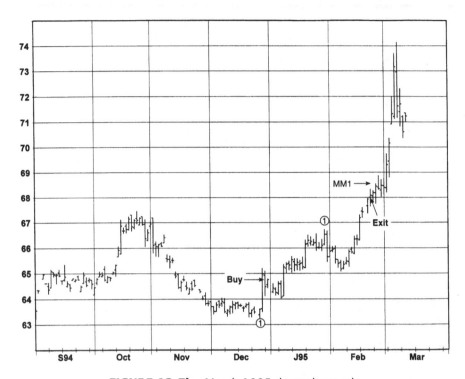

FIGURE 12.7b March 1995 deutsche mark.

Trade Exit

The trade was liquidated on a sharply raised stop because of the proximity of the measured move objective.

Comment

This trade provides a perfect example of the desirability of quickly reversing a trade opinion if market conditions change. Only two days before implementation of a long position in this trade, I had been bearish and short (see Figure 12.6b). However, the same factors that had suggested covering short also supported the idea of going long. Unfortunately, I am usually not this wise without the benefit of hindsight.

  In this instance, getting out of a winning trade because of the proximity of an important objective sacrificed a significant further advance. Sometimes getting out near an objective is the right decision (see, for example, Figure 12.4b); sometimes letting the position ride would be the right decision, as was the case here.

FIGURE 12.8a October 1993 gold.

Trade Entry Reasons

1. Confirmed bull trap top.
2. Sustained downside gap.
3. Wide-ranging down day.
4. Flag consolidation formed after downswing.

**Do you agree or disagree with the analysis?
Evaluate the situation before turning page.**

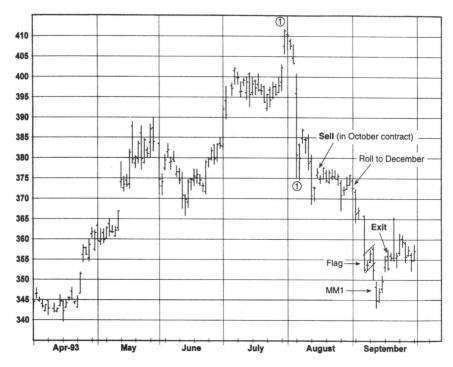

FIGURE 12.8b   October 1993 gold.

Trade Exit

1. Stop brought in very close once the measured move objective (MM1) was achieved.

2. Rebound to upper portion of prior flag provided the first sign of a possible trend reversal.

Comment

Confirmed bull traps are among the most reliable chart signals of a major top. Also note that the achievement of a measured move objective can be used as a signal for bringing in a stop very close—an action that locks in a major portion of profits, while still leaving open the opportunity for additional profits if the price move continues uninterrupted (which, of course, was not the case here).

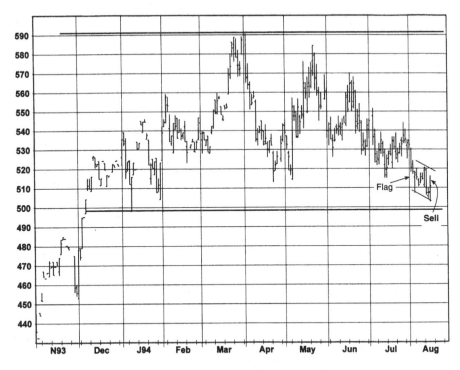

FIGURE 12.9a September 1994 silver.

Trade Entry Reason

Flag pattern formed near the bottom of an extended, broad trading range is often an excellent sell signal.

**Do you agree or disagree with the analysis?
Evaluate the situation before turning page.**

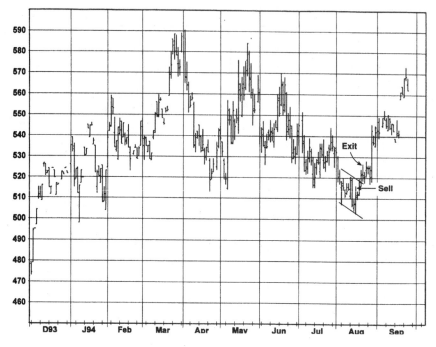

FIGURE 12.9b September 1994 silver.

Trade Exit

Counter-to-anticipated upside breakout of flag pattern violated the trade premise.

Comment

A chart pattern does not need to be right more than 50% of the time—or, for that matter, even close to 50% of the time—to be valuable. For example, when the pattern that motivated this trade—a flag near the low end of a trading range—proves correct, it can allow the trader to capture a major downswing. On the other hand, when it is wrong, evidence of the failure is provided quickly—a modest upside penetration of the flag pattern. In other words, trading this pattern will naturally allow for much larger average gains on winning trades than average losses on losing trades. Consequently, the pattern can be a beneficial tool even if it leads to significantly more losses than gains.

In general, it is a mistake to focus on the percentage of winning trades generated by a system or methodology. The key factor is the *expected gain per trade*. (The expected gain per trade is equal to the percentage of winning trades times the average profit per winning trade minus the percentage of losing trades times the average loss per losing trade.)

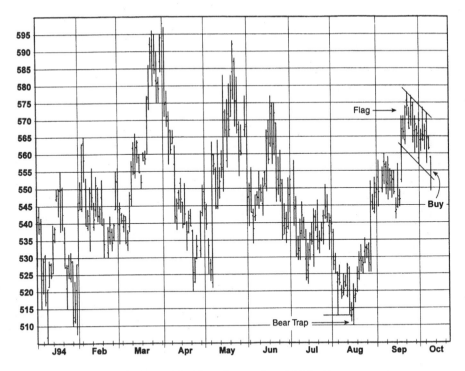

FIGURE 12.10a December 1994 silver.

Trade Entry Reasons

1. Sustained bear trap suggested that a major low had been established.

2. Flag pattern formed following the upswing implied that the next market price swing would on the upside.

3. Buy initiated near support implied at the lower end of the broad flag consolidation.

**Do you agree or disagree with the analysis?
Evaluate the situation before turning page.**

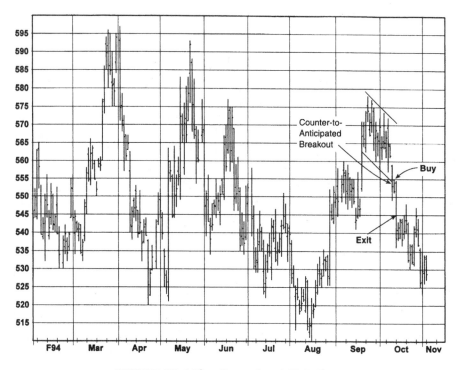

FIGURE 12.10b   December 1994 silver.

Trade Exit

Counter-to-anticipated downside penetration of the flag pattern strongly suggested the trade idea was wrong.

Comment

When the market doesn't behave as expected, get out! Although the loss on this particular trade was relatively small ($500), some readers may wonder if the loss might not have been kept even smaller by getting out closer to the counter-to-anticipated breakout point. Perhaps, but only by a marginal amount. Generally speaking, it is not a good idea to place stops too close to critical points. For example, in the case of flag patterns, the shape of the flag can change as it evolves, or the pattern may of be interrupted by a one-day spike without any follow-through. In both instances, keeping a stop very close to a breakout point can result in liquidating a position even though the flag ultimately remains intact and the original trade idea proves successful.

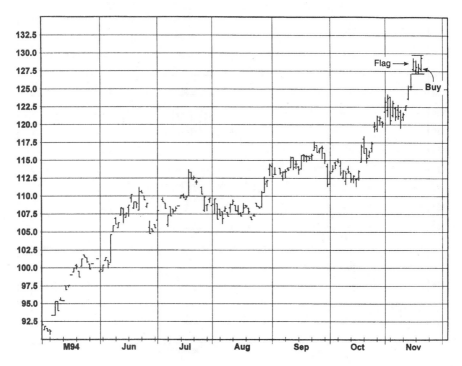

FIGURE 12.11a March 1995 copper.

Trade Entry Reason

A flag consolidation formed in new high ground usually leads to at least a short-term upswing.

**Do you agree or disagree with the analysis?
Evaluate the situation before turning page.**

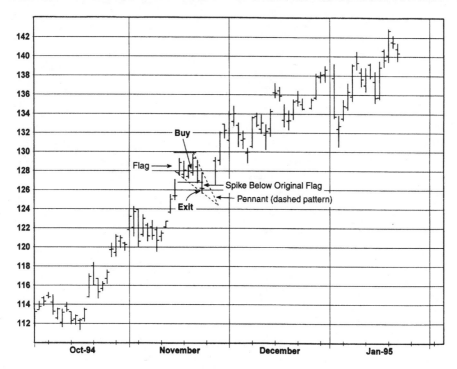

FIGURE 12.11b March 1995 copper.

Trade Exit

Trade liquidated on a downside penetration of the flag pattern.

Comment

Although this trade idea ultimately proved correct and could have been very profitable, in reality, the trade resulted in a loss. The reason for this disappointing outcome is that I was guilty of a trading error: Specifically, the stop was brought in too close. Flag and pennant consolidations frequently change their shape as they evolve. It is also quite common for such consolidations to be interrupted by one-day spikes. Consequently, it is important that stops in such trades allow for a meaningful margin beyond the existing boundary of the pattern. The illustrated trade can be viewed as either one of the aforementioned developments—that is, as either a one-day spike below the original flag pattern or a change in the shape of the consolidation (from a flag to a pennant).

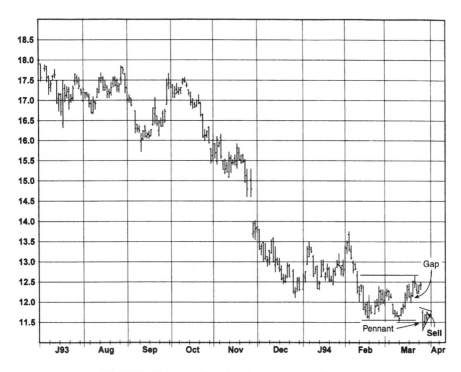

FIGURE 12.12a Crude oil continuous futures.

Trade Entry Reasons

1. Pennant consolidation formed near the low end of the trading range suggested the potential for another downswing.
2. Wide downside gap immediately preceding pennant consolidation.

Do you agree or disagree with the analysis?
Evaluate the situation before turning page.

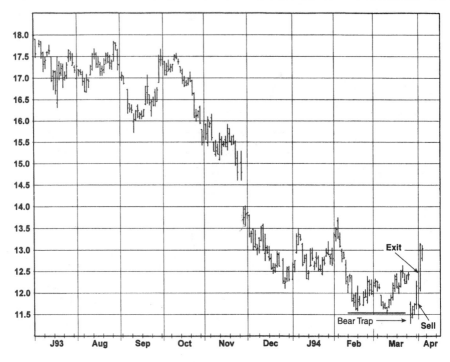

FIGURE 12.12b   Crude oil continuous futures.

Trade Exit

Subsequent rebound back to near the top of the trading range left the low of the pennant consolidation looking like a bear trap reversal.

Comment

See next trade.

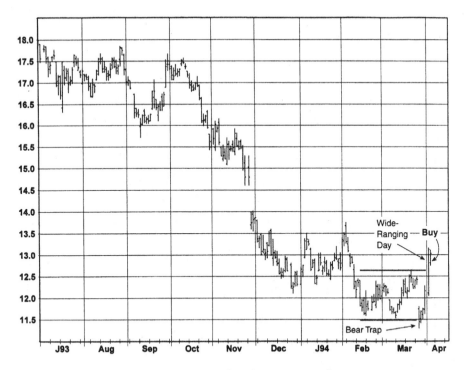

FIGURE 12.13a Crude oil continuous futures.

Trade Entry Reasons

1. Bear trap low.
2. Wide-ranging up day formed near the low of an extended decline.

If this chart looks familiar, it is because the trade was implemented on the day following the activation of the stop in the prior trade.

Do you agree or disagree with the analysis?
Evaluate the situation before turning page.

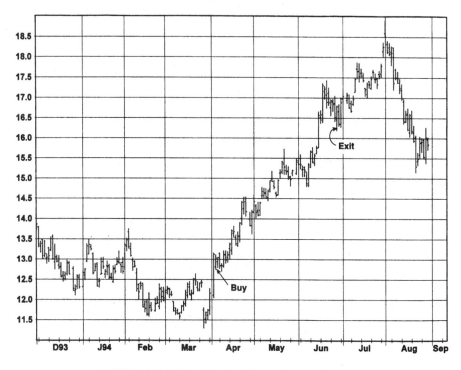

FIGURE 12.13b Crude oil continuous futures.

Trade Exit

Position was liquidated on a trailing stop, which at the time of exit was kept close because of large open profits.

Comment

This trade was motivated by failure signals related to the prior trade. Flexibility in recognizing a trade was wrong and reversing (not merely liquidating) the original position made it possible to capture a large gain in a trade sequence that began by going short at the virtual market bottom! (See Figure 12.12a.) This trade dramatically illustrates the concept that the ability to decisively respond to the market's constantly changing price action is a far more important attribute than skill in making market calls. (Note continuous futures charts were used to illustrate this trade because the position was rolled through several contracts.)

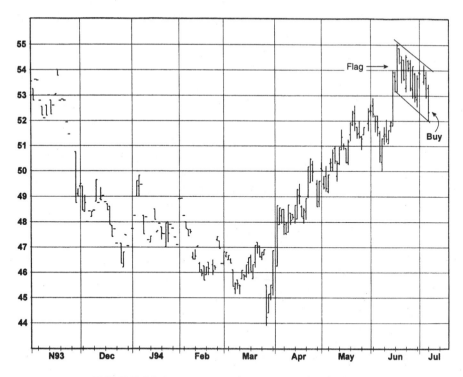

FIGURE 12.14a September 1994 unleaded gas.

Trade Entry Reasons

1. Flag consolidation in an uptrend suggested the likelihood of another upswing.

2. Buy implemented near support implied by lower boundary of flag.

Do you agree or disagree with the analysis?
Evaluate the situation before turning page.

FIGURE 12.14b   September 1994 unleaded gas.

Trade Exit

Trade was liquidated following the counter-to-anticipated penetration of a flag pattern formed after a major measured move objective had been achieved.

Comment

Counter-to-anticipated breakouts from flag patterns can sometimes provide liquidation (or reversal) signals reasonably close to major turning points—particularly when such failure signals occur after a major measured move objective has been attained.

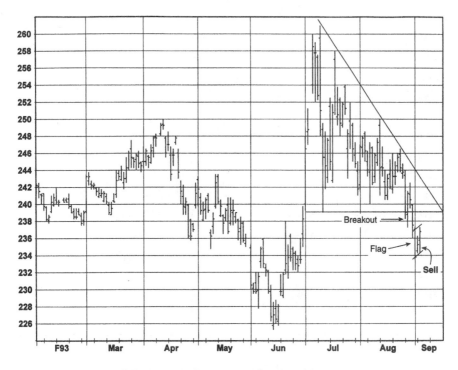

FIGURE 12.15a December 1993 corn.

Trade Entry Reasons

1. Downside breakout of a huge descending triangle.
2. Flag formed below the triangle suggested the likelihood of a continued downtrend.

**Do you agree or disagree with the analysis?
Evaluate the situation before turning page.**

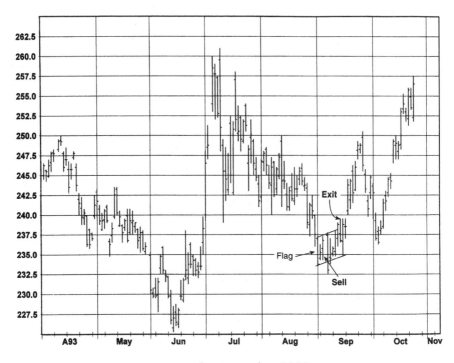

FIGURE 12.15b   December 1993 corn.

Trade Exit

Counter-to-anticipated breakout of flag suggested that an upside reversal had occurred.

Comment

Exiting on the first sign of violation of the trade premise kept loss very small even though the trade idea was dead wrong.

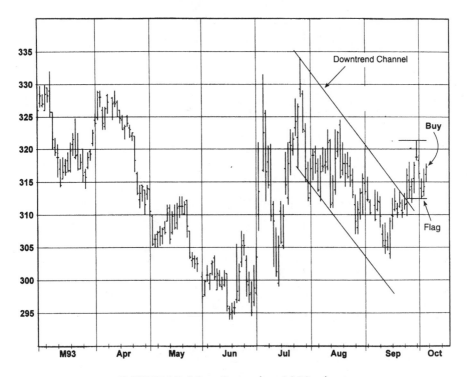

FIGURE 12.16a　December 1993 wheat.

Trade Entry Reason

Flag formed after the breakout above the trend channel suggested the likelihood of a continued price advance.

Do you agree or disagree with the analysis?
Evaluate the situation before turning page.

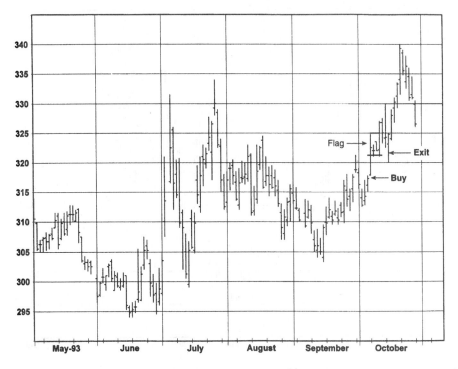

FIGURE 12.16b   December 1993 wheat.

Trade Exit

Pullback to the low end of the most recent flag pattern represented a short-term failure signal.

Comment

Even though this trade was net profitable, placing the protective stop at a point representing the first sign of a market failure resulted in missing the bulk of the price move. There is a trade-off in using stops equivalent to the closest meaningful point: In some cases, this approach will provide very timely exits; In other instances, however, this procedure will result in the highly premature liquidation of good positions (as was the case in this illustration). There is no absolute right or wrong answer regarding the use of such stops; it is largely a matter of personal choice. One possible compromise approach is to avoid bringing the stop in closer than breakeven for the first two weeks of the trade. Such a rule would have prevented the premature exit in this trade.

FIGURE 12.17a July 1994 soybeans.

Trade Entry Reasons

1. Rebound to resistance area implied by the concentration of prior relative highs (denoted by downward-pointing arrows).

2. Apparent peak in place based on the following factors:

   a. Bull trap

   b. Island reversal

   c. Spike

   d. Wide-ranging day

It is noteworthy that all four of the listed bearish patterns occurred on a single day! (Of course, in the case of the island reversal, by definition, the pattern also included the preceding and succeeding days.)

**Do you agree or disagree with the analysis?
Evaluate the situation before turning page.**

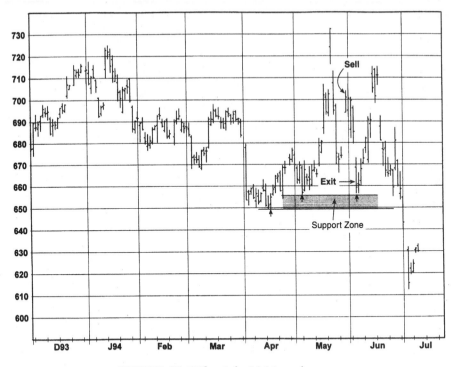

FIGURE 12.17b July 1994 soybeans.

Trade Exit

Trade was liquidated on a retracement to the support zone implied by the concentration of prior relative lows (denoted by upward-pointing arrows).

Comment

Although as a general rule it is desirable to try to ride a trade until there is at least some sign of a reversal, a reasonable exception is provided by trades that meet the following combined conditions:

1. Very quick, pronounced move in anticipated direction.
2. Proximity of major support (or major resistance, in the case of long positions).

The reasoning is that these trades are particularly prone to abrupt pullbacks, and such corrective moves can easily result in trade being liquidated at a much worse price (e.g., activation of protective stop), even if the trend eventually continues.

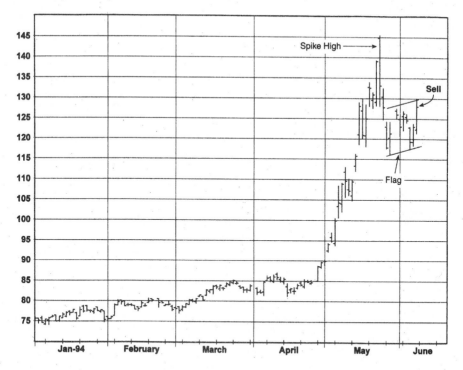

FIGURE 12.18a July 1994 coffee.

Trade Entry Reasons

1. Extreme spike high after an extended advance suggested a possible major top.

2. Flag pattern formed after downswing implied that the next price swing would also be on downside.

**Do you agree or disagree with the analysis?
Evaluate the situation before turning page.**

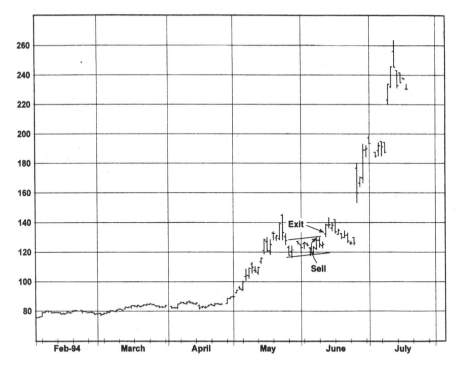

FIGURE 12.18b July 1994 coffee.

Trade Exit

The counter-to-anticipated upside breakout of the flag pattern contradicted one of the basic premises for the trade.

Comment

Sometimes what appears to be a major top proves to be only a minor peak. This trade provides a good example of why traders who do not routinely employ a trade exit plan are unlikely to stay in the game very long.

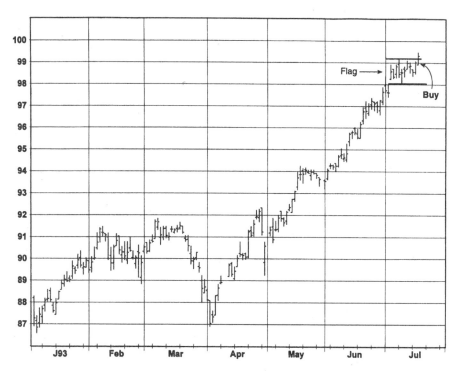

FIGURE 12.19a Italian bond continuous futures (daily).

Trade Entry Reason

Flag consolidation after an uptrend suggested continuation of the uptrend.

**Do you agree or disagree with the analysis?
Evaluate the situation before turning page.**

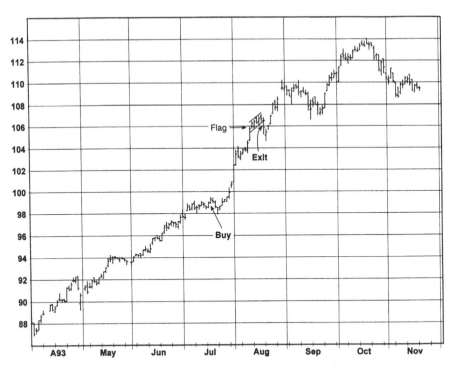

FIGURE 12.19b Italian bond continuous futures (daily).

Trade Exit

Downside penetration of the flag pattern after a large advance suggested danger of at least a temporary reversal. (Continuous futures are used to depict all the Italian bond trades, because virtually all the trading in this market is concentrated in the nearest contract until near expiration, making it impossible to generate individual contract charts of sufficient duration to perform an adequate chart analysis.)

Comment

This trade provides a good illustration of two concepts:

1. Just because the market has already witnessed a large advance does not necessarily mean it's too late to buy.

2. By waiting for an appropriate chart pattern, it is possible to select a relatively close, technically meaningful stop, even if the market has experienced a large advance. (In this trade, the initial stop was placed moderately below the narrow consolidation formed just prior to entry.)

PART THREE

TRADING SYSTEMS

Chapter 13

Charting and Analysis Software

One of the most welcome developments in technical analysis has been the proliferation of powerful computers and software that has liberated traders from the painstaking pencil-and-paper charting techniques of the relatively recent past. There are any number of software programs available which enable traders to load price data, construct various price charts (bar, point-and-figure, close-only, candlestick, daily, weekly, monthly, hourly, etc.), apply a host of analytical tools and indicators, and design and test trading ideas. Such programs are indispensable to the serious trader and technical analyst. This chapter will review the important considerations in selecting such software.

There are dozens of technical analysis software packages, many of which specialize in particular techniques or markets. For example, one piece of software may be specifically for Elliott Wave analysis; another program may be designed solely to analyze mutual fund data. Our concern here, however, is with broader-based programs that allow traders to apply a wide variety of analytical tools (and alternately, trading system testing capabilities) to different data types—stocks, futures, mutual funds, various cash data, and in some cases options.

A WORD ON PRICE DATA

Technical analysis programs, of course, need price data to analyze. The type of analysis and trading a trader wishes to engage in will determine the type of data he or she purchases, which will in turn influence the program used. (Alternately, a trader who has already decided on an analysis program may have a limited selection of data sources.) There are any number of data vendors who specialize in providing price data in a variety of formats. The three most common formats are:

1. *Historical Price Data.* Historical data refers to price data spanning a specific time period: 3 years, 10 years, 20 years, and so on. Data vendors (and often individual stock and futures exchanges) offer various data packages encompassing different markets—U.S. stocks, futures, indexes, mutual funds, etc.—for different time periods, with daily data being the default time scale (historical intraday data is available, but is generally more expensive). The longer the time period, the higher the price. Luckily, the cost of historical daily data has steadily dropped in recent years; many software programs often include a database of historical prices with their product—for example, three years of daily continuous futures prices and 20 years of daily stock prices on disk or CD-ROM.

2. *End-of-Day Price Data.* End-of-day prices are just what they sound like: the high, low, closing, and, usually, opening prices for each day, generally available within a few hours after the markets close. To be able to use such data, your software program must have a price download feature—very common in most mid- to upper-level packages—and you must be able to communicate electronically with your data vendor (usually via modem or Internet, although other mediums are available). The trader can then build a price database of the instruments he or she follows, or add these prices on to an existing historical database. End-of-day data is more expensive than historical data. Some data vendors will give you access to an extended historical price database when you subscribe to their end-of-day service, in effect, killing two birds with one stone.

3. *Real-Time (or "Tick") Price Data.* These are prices transmitted throughout the day, as trades occur, with as little delay (barring technical problems or exceptional market conditions) as a few seconds. This is the most expensive type of data, but is essentially irrelevant to anyone except full-time professional traders who must watch the markets all day, every day. Traders, however, may purchase delayed intraday price quotes—say, 10, 15, or 30 minutes behind the markets—at a fraction of the cost of nondelayed data.

While end-of-day prices are increasingly available for little or no money off the Internet or directly from an exchange, an important service professional data vendors provide is to correct data flaws (prices incorrectly reported or transmitted by exchanges—it happens) and format prices before forwarding them to customers. Traders may opt to gather prices directly themselves, but they must then assume responsibility for "cleaning" the data, and, if necessary, formatting the prices for use in an analysis program—a time-consuming, probably tedious, and potentially impossible task for the computer amateur. Data vendors, however, are not perfect; traders must always be on the lookout for data errors like missing days and inexplicable price spikes.

Using a particular analysis program or data source may limit your choices of the other—that is, certain programs accept only certain "brands" of price data. Most programs, however, will give you a choice of at least a few competitively priced data sources.

Note: Futures traders should make sure they're getting the specific kind of historical data they need: individual futures contract data, nearest futures, or continuous futures. Continuous futures are the most desirable for historical testing of trading systems. (The advantages and disadvantages of each kind of data were discussed in Chapter 2.)

SOFTWARE CONSIDERATIONS

Before purchasing such software, a trader should take an inventory of his or her trading needs and computer skills. Charting and analysis software ranges in price from less than $100 to thousands of dollars; for less experienced traders especially, there is a risk of paying premium prices for high-level features that serve no practical purpose. Furthermore, many vendors that sell both entry-level and more advanced software allow users to upgrade to the more sophisticated product at a reduced price. To help select an appropriate product, it is useful to consider:

✔ *Time Frame/Trading Style.* Except for those interested in very short-term or intraday trading (using hourly, half-hour, 10-minute, etc., charts), trading software that enables you to import and manipulate real-time price data is unnecessary. One of the greatest price differences in software is that between real-time programs and end-of-day programs, which allow you to import and manipulate daily and historical price data only. And as mentioned earlier, the cost of real-time price data is exponentially higher than end-of-day or historical data.

✔ *Analytical Goals.* What do you wish to accomplish with your software? Are you simply looking for a "digital chart"—an easy way to track markets, perform simple chart analysis (draw trend lines and chart patterns, etc.), and apply a few indicators? Or, do you want a program that will help you design and test your own indicators and trading strategies? Not surprisingly, the latter is more expensive than the former. Again, there is no point in paying for features you will not use.

✔ *Computer Skills.* Most lower- to mid-level analytical programs are fairly intuitive and user-friendly, allowing you to perform simple charting and analysis functions without having to be a computer expert. Software programs with system testing capabilities are a different story, however. While most use simplified programming languages (usually complemented by a library of pre-programmed technical studies or systems) designed specifically for non–computer users, the demands on the trader increase with the capabilities of the program and the complexity of the trading ideas being tested. This may make testing sophisticated systems more wishful thinking than a realistic goal unless the trader is committed to mastering basic programming as well as technical analysis skills. A trader who only needs to test fairly straightforward ideas has no need for a demanding (and probably more expensive) program that will only add to the difficulty of performing market analysis. The object of using such tools is to simplify the analytical process, not complicate it.

It is also important to be aware of certain terminology distinctions. Analytical programs—those that allow you to perform your own analysis, based on your own opinions—should not be confused with trading programs, which are packaged mechanical trading systems that generate buy and sell recommendations for whatever price data is fed into them. The issue can become confused because some trading programs include an analysis component in addition to the trading system. In most instances, however, what you're paying for is the system, not the analytical features.

A mid-level technical analysis program might allow you to:

1. Download historical and end-of-day prices (stocks, futures, mutual funds, possibly options).

2. Create several types of charts (bar, close-only, candlestick, point-and-figure) in a variety of time frames (monthly, weekly, daily).

3. Perform chart analysis and apply and modify a variety of technical indicators. For example, you could apply your choice of simple, weighted, or exponential averages, and adjust the number of days in the average as needed.

4. If the program has a testing feature, you might be able to test the

trading performance of various indicator signals, or design and test relatively simple original indicators and trading ideas.

These features would allow you to apply virtually all the techniques described in this book. A lower-level program might only allow you to create bar charts and apply a handful of simple technical indicators and chart analysis drawing tools. A more advanced program might allow you to use real-time data, perform advanced statistical analysis, and construct elaborate trading models, using both technical and fundamental data, on a portfolio of instruments.

RESEARCHING SOFTWARE

Those interested in purchasing analytical software and price data can consult a variety of sources: the Internet (both investment-related web sites and newsgroups), and industry magazines like the *American Association of Individual Investors (AAII) Journal*, *Technical Analysis of Stocks & Commodities*, *Futures*, and *Commodity Traders Consumer Report (CTCR)*. In addition to regular features on software products, some of these publications offer additional supplements exclusively concerned with analytical software. (AAII, for example, publishes an updated investment software guidebook every year.) But the Internet is the prime source of information for traders interested in learning about or sampling the various kinds of available programs. Many software vendors offer downloadable trial or demonstration versions of their products on the Web.

Chapter

Technical Trading Systems: Structure and Design

There are only two types of trend-following systems: fast and slow.

—Jim Orcutt

WHAT THIS BOOK WILL AND WILL NOT TELL YOU ABOUT TRADING SYSTEMS

Be forewarned. If you are expecting to find the blueprint for a heretofore secret trading system that *consistently makes 100% plus per year in real-life trading with minimal risk*, you'll have to look elsewhere. For one thing, I have not yet discovered such a sure-thing money machine. But in a sense, that is beside the point. For obvious reasons, this book will not offer detailed descriptions of the best trading systems I have designed—systems that at this writing are being used to manage about $40 million. Quite frankly, I have always been somewhat puzzled by advertisements for books or computer software promising to reveal the secrets of systems that make 100%, 200%, and more! Why are they selling such valuable information for $99, or even $2,999?

The primary goal of this chapter is to provide the reader with the background knowledge necessary to develop his or her own trading system. The discussion focuses on the following areas:

1. An overview of some basic trend-following systems

2. The key weaknesses of these systems

3. Guidelines for transforming "generic" systems into more powerful systems

4. Countertrend systems

5. *Diversification* as a means of improving performance

Some of this information must be put into the proper trading context. For example, stock traders, few of whom will short the market, should concentrate on those aspects of system design relevant to timing market entry and liquidating long positions, with the goal of bettering the risk/return profile of a buy-and-hold approach.

THE BENEFITS OF A MECHANICAL TRADING SYSTEM

Is paper trading easier than real trading? Most speculators would answer yes, even though both tasks require an equivalent decision process. This difference is explained by a single factor: emotion. Overtrading, premature liquidation of good positions because of rumors, jumping the gun on market entry to get a better price, holding on to a losing position—these are but a few of the negative manifestations of emotion in actual trading. Perhaps the greatest value of a mechanical system is that it eliminates emotion from trading, helping the speculator avoid many of the common errors just described. Furthermore, the removal of the implied need for constant decision making substantially reduces trading-related stress and anxiety.

Another benefit of a mechanical system is that it ensures a consistency of approach—that is, the trader follows all signals indicated by a common set of conditions. This is important, since even profitable trading strategies can lose money if applied selectively. To illustrate this point, consider the example of a market letter writer whose recommendations yield a net profit over the long run (after allowances for commissions and poor executions). Will his readers make money if they only implement trades in line with his recommendations? Not necessarily. Some subscribers will pick and choose trades, invariably missing some of the largest-profit trades. Others will stop following the recommendations after the advisor has a losing streak, and as a result may miss a string of profitable trades. The point is that a good trading strategy is not sufficient; success also depends upon consistency.

A third advantage of mechanical trading systems is that they normally provide the trader with a method for controlling risk. *Money management* is an essential ingredient of trading success. Without a plan for limiting losses, a single bad trade can lead to disaster. Any properly constructed mechanical system will either contain explicit stop-loss rules or specify conditions for reversing a position given a sufficient adverse price move. As a result, following signals generated by a mechanical trading system will normally prevent the possibility of huge losses on individual trades (except in extreme circumstances when one is unable to liquidate a position because a futures market is in the midst of a string of locked limit moves). Thus, the speculator using a mechanical system may end up losing money due to the cumulative effect of a number of negative trades, but at least his or her account will not be decimated by one or two bad trades.

Of course, money management does not necessarily require the use of a trading system. Risk control can also be achieved by initiating a good-till-canceled stop order whenever a new position is taken, or by predetermining the exit point upon entering a trade and sticking to that decision. However, many traders lack sufficient discipline and will be tempted to give the market just a little more time once too often.

THREE BASIC TYPES OF SYSTEMS

The number of categories used to classify trading systems is completely arbitrary. The following three-division classification is intended to emphasize the key conceptual differences in possible trading approaches:

> *Trend-Following.* A trend-following system waits for a specified price move and then initiates a position in the same direction based on the implicit assumption that the trend will continue.

> *Countertrend.* A countertrend system waits for a significant price move and then initiates a position in the opposite direction on the assumption that the market is due for a correction.

> *Pattern Recognition.* In a sense, all systems can be classified as pattern recognition systems. After all, the conditions that signal a trend or a countertrend trade are a type of pattern (e.g., close beyond 20-day high or low). However, the implication here is that the chosen patterns are not based primarily on directional moves as is the case in trend-following and countertrend systems. For example, a pattern-recognition system might generate signals on the basis of spike days. In this case, the key consideration is the pattern itself (e.g., spike) rather than the extent of any preceding price move. Of course, this example is overly simplistic. In practice, the patterns

used for determining trading signals will be more complex, and several patterns may be incorporated into a single system.

It should be emphasized that the division lines between the preceding categories are not always clear-cut. As modifications are incorporated, a system of one type may begin to more closely approximate the behavioral pattern of a different system category.

TREND-FOLLOWING SYSTEMS

By definition, trend-following systems never sell near the high or buy near the low, since a meaningful opposite price move is required to signal a trade. Thus, in using this type of system, the trader will always miss the first part of a price move and may surrender a significant portion of profits before an opposite signal is received (assuming the system is always in the market). There is a basic trade-off involved in the choice of the sensitivity, or speed, of a trend-following system. A sensitive system, which responds quickly to signs of a trend reversal, will tend to maximize profits on valid signals, but it will also generate far more false signals. A nonsensitive, or slow, system will reflect the reverse set of characteristics.

Although in some markets fast systems consistently outperform slow systems, in most markets the reverse is true, as the minimization of losing trades and commission costs in slow systems more than offsets the reduced profits in the good trades. This observation is only intended as a cautionary note against the natural tendency toward seeking out more sensitive systems. However, in all cases, the choice between fast and slow systems must be determined on the basis of empirical observation and the trader's subjective preferences.

There are a wide variety of possible approaches in constructing a trend-following system. In this chapter we focus on two of the most basic methods: moving average systems and breakout systems.

Moving Average Systems

The moving average for a given day is equal to the average of that day's closing price and the closing prices on the preceding $N - 1$ days, where N is equal to the number of days in the moving average. For example, in a 10-day moving average, the appropriate value for a given day would be the average of the 10 closing prices culminating with that day. The term *moving average* refers to the fact that the set of numbers being averaged is continuously moving through time.

Since the moving average is based on past prices, in a rising market the moving average primarily will be below the price series, while in a declining market the moving average primarily will be above the price series. Thus, when a price trend reverses from up to down, prices must cross the moving average from above. Similarly, when the trend reverses from down to up, prices must cross the moving average from below. In the most basic type of moving average system, these crossover points are viewed as trade signals: A buy signal is indicated when prices cross the moving average from below; a sell signal is indicated when prices cross the moving average from above. The crossover should be determined based on closing prices. Table 14.1 illustrates the calculation of a moving average and indicates the trade signal points implied by this simple scheme.

Figure 14.1 illustrates the December 1993 T-bond contract and a 35-day moving average. The nonbordered buy and sell signals indicated on the chart are based on the simple moving average system just described. (For now ignore the diamond-bordered signals; they will be explained later.) Note that although the system catches the major uptrend, it also generates many false signals. Of course, this problem can be mitigated by increasing the length of the moving average, but the tendency toward excessive false signals is a characteristic of the simple moving average system. The reason for this is that temporary, sharp price fluctuations, sufficient to trigger a signal, are commonplace market events.

One school of thought suggests the problem with the simple moving average system is that it weights all days equally, whereas more recent days are more important and hence should be weighted more heavily. Many different weighting schemes have been proposed for constructing moving averages. Two of the most common weighting approaches are the *linearly weighted moving average* (LWMA) and the *exponentially weighted moving average* (EWMA). The formulas for these moving averages are given in the Appendix.

In my view, there is no strong empirical evidence to support the idea that linearly or exponentially weighted moving averages provide a substantive and consistent improvement over simple moving averages. Sometimes weighted moving averages will do better; sometimes simple moving averages will do better. Experimentation with different weighted moving averages probably does not represent a particularly fruitful path for trying to improve the simple moving average system.

A far more meaningful improvement is provided by the *crossover moving average* approach. In this system, trade signals are based upon the interaction of two moving averages, as opposed to the interaction be-

		10-Day	Crossover
Day	Closing Price	Moving Average	Signal
1	80.50		
2	81.00		
3	81.90		
4	81.40		
5	83.10		
6	82.60		
7	82.20		
8	83.10		
9	84.40		
10	85.20	82.54	
11	84.60	82.95	
12	83.90	83.24	
13	84.40	83.49	
14	85.20	83.87	
15	86.10	84.17	
16	85.40	84.45	
17	84.10	84.64	Sell
18	89.50	84.68	
19	83.90	84.60	
20	83.10	84.42	
21	82.50	84.21	
22	81.90	84.01	
23	81.80	83.69	
24	81.60	83.33	
25	82.20	82.94	
26	82.80	82.68	Buy
27	89.40	82.61	
28	83.80	82.64	
29	83.90	82.64	
30	83.50	82.68	

TABLE 14.1 Calculating a Moving Average

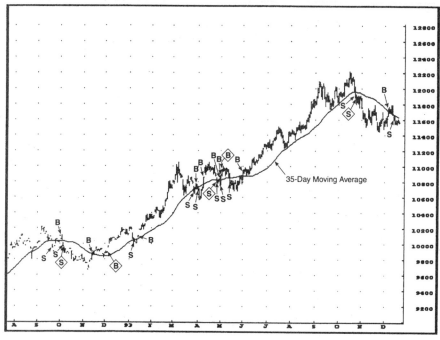

Notes: B = buy signal: prices cross moving average from below and close above
line; S = sell signal: prices cross moving average from above and close below line;
⊕ = buy signal not eliminated by filter; ⊗ = sell signal not eliminated by filter.

FIGURE 14.1 December 1993 T-bond and 35-day moving average.
Source: FutureSource; copyright © 1986–1994; all rights reserved.

tween a single moving average and price. The trading rules are very similar to those of the simple moving average system: A buy signal is generated when the shorter-term (e.g., 10-day) moving average crosses above
the longer-term (e.g., 30-day) moving average; a sell signal is generated
when the shorter-term moving average crosses below the longer-term
moving average. (In a sense, the simple moving average system can be
thought of as a special case of the crossover moving average system, in
which the short-term moving average is equal to 1.) Since trade signals
for the crossover system are based on two smoothed series (as opposed to
one smoothed series and price), the number of false signals is substantially reduced. Figures 14.2, 14.3, and 14.4 compare trading signals indicated by a simple 12-day moving average system, a simple 48-day
moving average system, and the crossover system based on these two averages. Generally speaking, the crossover moving average system is far
superior to the simple moving average. (However, it should be noted that

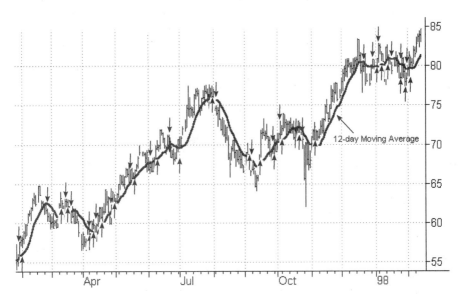

Notes: ↑ = buy signal: prices cross moving average from below and close above line; ↓ = sell signal: prices cross moving average from above and close below line.

FIGURE 14.2 Procter & Gamble and 12-day moving average.
Chart created with TradeStation® by Omega Research, Inc.

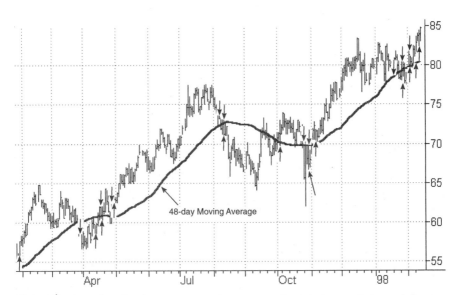

Notes: ↑ = buy signal: prices cross moving average from below and close above line; ↓ = sell signal: prices cross moving average from above and close below line.

FIGURE 14.3 Procter & Gamble and 48-day moving average.
Chart created with TradeStation® by Omega Research, Inc.

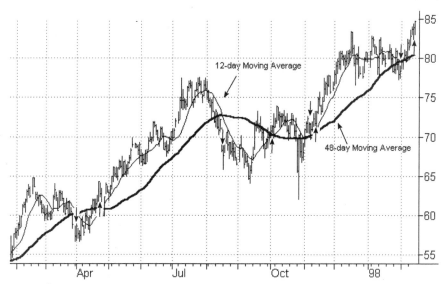

Notes: ↑ = buy signal: short-term moving average (12-day) crosses long-term moving average from below; ↓ = sell signal: short-term moving average crosses long-term moving average from above.

FIGURE 14.4 Procter & Gamble and crossover moving average. Chart created with TradeStation® by Omega Research, Inc.

by including some of the trend-following system modifications discussed shortly, even the simple moving average system can provide the core for a viable trading approach.) The weaknesses of the crossover moving average system and possible improvements are discussed later.

Breakout Systems

The basic concept underlying breakout systems is very simple: The ability of a market to move to a new high or low indicates the potential for a continued trend in the direction of the breakout. The following set of rules provides an example of a simple breakout system:

1. Cover short and go long if today's close exceeds the prior N-day high.

2. Cover long and go short if today's close is below the prior N-day low.

The value chosen for N will define the sensitivity of the system. If a short-duration period is used for comparison to the current price (e.g.,

$N = 7$), the system will indicate trend reversals fairly quickly, but will also generate many false signals. On the other hand, the choice of a longer-duration period (e.g., $N = 40$) will reduce false signals, but at the cost of slower entry. This is analogous to using shorter- or longer-term moving averages in the simple moving average system or the moving average crossover system.

A comparison of the trade signals generated by the preceding simple breakout system using $N = 7$ and $N = 40$ are illustrated in Figures 14.5 and 14.6, respectively. The following observations, which are evidenced in these figures, are also valid as generalizations describing the trade-offs between fast and slow breakout systems:

1. A fast system will provide an earlier signal of a major trend transition. For example, compare the early March 1996 sell signal (the first sell signal in the late February to July 1996 down move) in Figure 14.5 to the April sell signal in Figure 14.6).

2. A fast system will generate far more false signals, e.g., the signals in Figure 14.5 during the July 1997 to February 1998 trading range (as well as the signals immediately following the March 1996 sell signal discussed above).

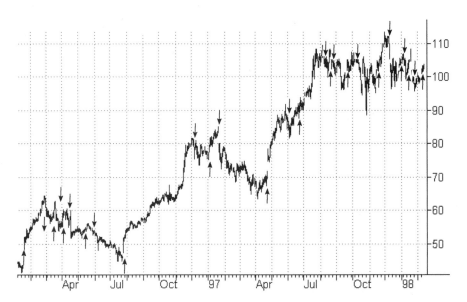

FIGURE 14.5 "Fast" breakout system signals: IBM.
Chart created with TradeStation® by Omega Research, Inc.

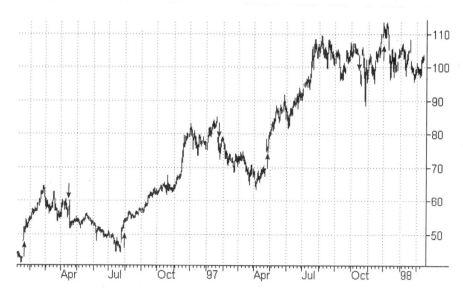

FIGURE 14.6 "Slow" breakout system signals: IBM.
Chart created with TradeStation® by Omega Research, Inc.

3. The loss per trade in the slower system will be greater than the loss for the corresponding trade in the faster system. In some cases, a fast system might even realize a small profit on a minor trend that results in a significant loss in a slower system. For example, from December 1996 to April 1997, the 40-day breakout system in Figure 14.6 generated one sell and one buy signal for a loss of nearly four points. The seven-day system over the same period, by comparison, generated two buy and sell signals, the first pair of which produced a fractional loss while the second produced a seven-point gain.

Although fast and slow systems will each work better under different circumstances, empirical evidence suggests that, in most markets, slower systems tend to work better than fast systems. However, the choice between a fast and slow system must be based on up-to-date empirical testing.

The previous example of a breakout system was based on the current day's close and prior period's high and low. It should be noted that these choices were arbitrary. Other alternative combinations might include current day's high or low versus prior period's high or low; current day's close versus prior period's high close and low close; and current day's high or low versus prior period's high close or low close. Although the choice of the condition that defines a breakout will affect the results, the differences between the variations just given (for the same value of N) will be largely random and not overwhelming.

The pitfalls of breakout-type systems are basically the same as those of moving average systems and are detailed in the following section.

TEN COMMON PROBLEMS WITH STANDARD TREND-FOLLOWING SYSTEMS

1. *Too Many Similar Systems.* Many different trend-following systems will generate similar signals. Thus it is not unusual for a number of trend-following systems to signal a trade during the same one-to-five-day period. In futures markets especially, since many speculators and funds base their decisions on basic trend-following systems, their common action can cause a flood of similar orders that results in poor execution prices.

2. *Whipsaws.* Trend-following systems will signal all major trends; the problem is that they will also generate many false signals. A major frustration experienced by traders using trend-following systems is that markets will frequently move far enough to trigger a signal and then reverse direction. This unpleasant event can even occur several times in succession, hence the term *whipsaw.* For example, Figure 14.7, which indicates the trade signals generated by a breakout system (close beyond prior N-day high or low) for N = 10, provides a vivid illustration of the dark side of trend-following systems.

3. *Failure to Exploit Major Price Moves.* Basic trend-following systems always assume an equal-unit-size position—for example, a fixed-dollar amount or a fixed number of shares, or one futures contract, per buy or sell. As a result, given an extended trend, the best such a system can do is to indicate a one-unit position in the direction of the trend. For example, in Figure 14.8 a breakout system with N = 40 would signal a long position in December 1994 and remain long throughout the entire uptrend. Although this is hardly unfavorable, profitability could be enhanced if the trend-following system were able to take advantage of such extended trends by generating signals indicating increases in the base position size.

4. *Tendency of Nonsensitive (Slow) Systems to Surrender a Large Percentage of Profits.* Although slow variations of trend-following

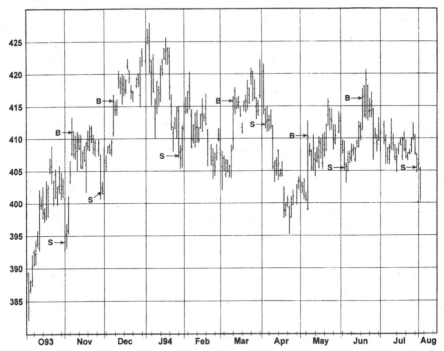

Notes: B = buy signal: close above prior 10-day high; S = sell signal: close below prior 10-day low.

FIGURE 14.7 Breakout signals in trading range market: gold continuous futures.

systems may often work best, one disturbing feature of such systems is that they may sometimes surrender a large portion of open profits. For example, while the breakout signal in Figure 14.8 provided a favorable entry into a massive uptrend, it surrendered almost half the gain before an offsetting signal was received.

5. *Inability to Make Money in Trading Range Markets.* The best any trend-following system can do during a period of sideways price action is to break even—that is, generate no new trade signals. In most cases, however, trading range markets will be characterized by whipsaw losses. This is a particularly significant consideration since sideways price action represents the predominant state of most markets.

6. *Temporary Large Losses.* Even an excellent trend-following system may witness transitory periods of sharp equity retracement.

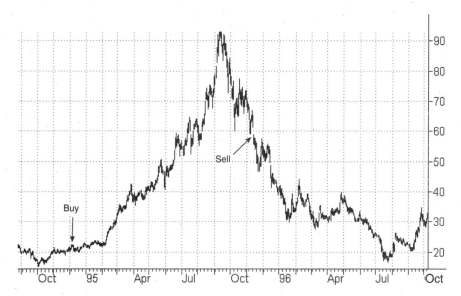

FIGURE 14.8 Failure of system to exploit major price move and surrender of profits: Micron Technology.
Chart created with TradeStation® by Omega Research, Inc.

Such events can be distressing to the trader who enjoys a profit cushion, but they can be disastrous to the trader who has just begun following the system's signals.

7. *Extreme Volatility in Best-Performing Systems.* In some cases, the trader may find that the most profitable trend-following systems are also subject to particularly sharp retracements, thereby implying an unacceptable level of risk.

8. *Systems That Work Well in Testing but Then Bomb.* This is perhaps the most common tale of woe among traders who have used mechanical trading systems.

9. *Parameter Shift.* Frequently, the trader may perform an exhaustive search to find the best *parameter* variation of a system based on past data (e.g., the optimum value of N in a breakout system) only to find that the same variation performs poorly (relative to other variations) in the ensuing period.

10. *Slippage.* Another common experience: The system generates profits on paper, but simultaneously loses money in actual trading. *Slippage* is discussed in Chapter 15.

POSSIBLE MODIFICATIONS FOR BASIC TREND-FOLLOWING SYSTEMS

Based upon the experience of the past two decades, even simple systems, such as moving average or breakout systems, will probably prove profitable if traded consistently over a broad range of markets for a sufficient length of time (e.g., three to five years or longer). However, the simplicity of these systems is a vice as well as a virtue. In essence, the rules of these systems are perhaps too simple to adequately account for the wide variety of possible market situations. Even if net profitable over the long run, simple trend-following systems will typically leave the trader exposed to periodic sharp losses. In fact, the natural proclivity of many, if not most, users of such systems to abandon the approach during a losing period will lead them to experience a net loss even if the system proves profitable over the longer run.

This section discusses some of the primary avenues for modifying basic trend-following systems in an effort to improve their performance. For simplicity, most illustrations are based on the previously described simple breakout system. However, the same types of modifications could also be applied to other basic trend-following systems (e.g., crossover moving average).

Confirmation Conditions

An important modification that can be made to a basic trend-following system is the requirement for additional conditions to be met before a signal is accepted, with the goal of reducing false signals. If these conditions are not realized before an opposite direction signal is received, no trade occurs. The range of possible choices for confirmation conditions is limited only by the imagination of the system designer. Below are three examples:

1. *Penetration.* A trade signal is accepted only if the market moves a specified minimum amount beyond a given reference level (e.g., the trade signal price). Penetration could be measured in either nominal or percentage terms. Figure 14.9 compares the trade signals generated by a standard breakout system with $N = 12$ and the corresponding system with a confirmation rule requiring a close that penetrates the prior N-day high (or low) by at least 2%. Note that in this example, although the confirmation rule results in moderately worse entry levels for valid signals, it eliminates all seven false signals. (The buy signals following the

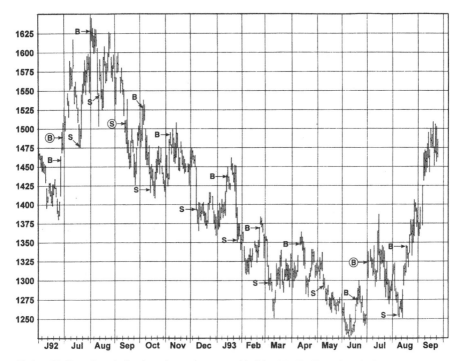

Notes: B, S = signals for breakout system with *N* = 12; Ⓑ,Ⓢ = signals for breakout system with *N* = 12 and 2% closing penetration confirmation.

FIGURE 14.9 Penetration as confirmation condition: cocoa continuous futures.

nonconfirmed sell signals are also eliminated, since the system is already long at that point. Similarly, the sell signals following the nonconfirmed buy signals are also eliminated, since the system is already short at that point.)

2. *Time Delay.* In this approach, a specified time delay is required, at the end of which the signal is reevaluated. For example, a confirmation rule may specify that a trade signal is taken if the market closes beyond the signal price (higher for a buy, lower for a sell) at any time six or more days beyond the original signal date. Figure 14.10 compares the signals generated by a basic breakout system with *N* = 12, and the corresponding system with the six-day time delay confirmation condition. In this case, the confirmation rule eliminates six of the seven false signals.

3. *Pattern.* This is a catchall term for a wide variety of confirmation rules. In this approach, a specified pattern is required to validate

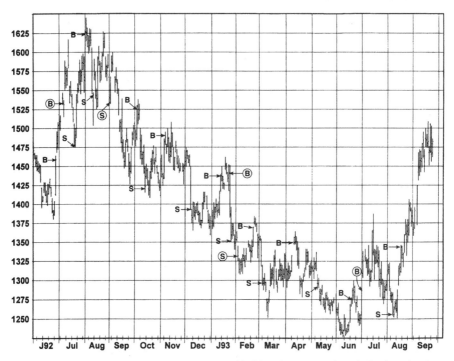

Notes: B, S = signals for breakout system with N = 12; Ⓑ,Ⓢ = signals for breakout system with N = 12 and 6-day time delay confirmation.

FIGURE 14.10   Time delay as a confirmation condition: cocoa continuous futures.

the basic system signal. For example, the confirmation rule might require three subsequent thrust days beyond the signal price. Figure 14.11 compares the signals generated by the basic breakout system with N = 12 and the signals based on the corresponding system using the three-thrust-day validation condition. The thrust day count at confirmed signals is indicated by the numbers on the chart. Here too, the confirmation rule eliminates all seven false signals.

The advantage of confirmation conditions is that they will greatly reduce whipsaw losses. However, it should be noted that confirmation rules also have an undesirable side effect—they will delay entry on valid signals, thereby reducing gains on profitable trades. For example, in Figures 14.9–14.11, note that the confirmation rules result in worse entry prices for the trades corresponding to the June 1992 buy signal, August 1992 sell signal, and the June 1993 buy signals in the basic system. The confirma-

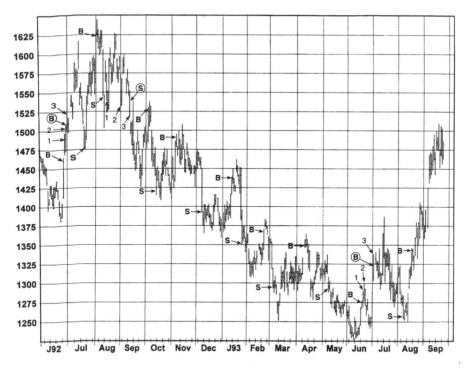

Notes: B, S = signals for breakout system with N = 12; ⓑ,ⓢ = signals for breakout system with N = 12 and 3 thrust day confirmation.

FIGURE 14.11 Example of a pattern confirmation condition: cocoa continuous futures.

tion condition will be beneficial as long as reduced profits due to delayed entry are more than offset by avoided losses. A system that includes confirmation conditions will not always outperform its basic system counterpart, but if properly designed, it will perform significantly better over the long run.

Filter

The purpose of a *filter* is to eliminate those trades that are deemed to have a lower probability of success. For example, the technical system might be combined with a fundamental model that classifies the market as bullish, bearish, or neutral. Technical signals would then be accepted only if they were in agreement with the fundamental model's market designation. In cases of disagreement, a neutral position would be indicated. In most cases, however, the filter condition(s) will also be technical in nature. For example, if one could derive a set of rules that had some accuracy in defining the presence of a trading range market, signals that were received when a trading range market was indicated would not be accepted. In essence, in developing a filter, the system designer is trying to find a common denominator applicable to the majority of losing trades.

We will use the frequently unsatisfactory simple moving average system to provide a specific example of a filter condition. The nonbordered signals in Figure 14.1 illustrate the typical tendency of the simple moving average system to generate many false signals—even in trending markets. These whipsaw trades can be substantially reduced by applying the filter rule that only signals consistent with the trend of the moving average are accepted. For example, prices crossing the moving average from below and closing above the moving average would be accepted as a buy signal only if the moving average was up relative to the previous day's level. This filter condition makes intuitive sense because it adheres to the basic technical concept of trading with the major trend.

Two points should be clarified regarding the application of this rule:

1. A rejected signal could be activated at a later point, if the moving average subsequently turned in the direction of the signal before an opposite direction crossover of the price and moving average.

2. Signals that occur after rejected signals are ignored because the net position is already consistent with the implied trade. This is true because the simple moving average system is always in the market.

The diamond-shaped signals in Figure 14.1 indicate the trades that would have been accepted (either at the time of the crossover or after a delay) if the filter rule just described were applied. As can be seen, on balance the benefits clearly outweigh the disadvantages. Most empirical testing would reveal that, more often than not, the inclusion of the type of filter rule depicted in Figure 14.1 will tend to improve performance.

In fact, a crossover between price and the moving average that is opposite to the direction of the moving average trend can often provide a good signal to add to rather than reverse the original position (per the example of the "Reaction to Long-Term Moving Average" midtrend entry technique described in Chapter 8).

It should be noted that, in a sense, the confirmation conditions detailed in the previous section represent one type of filter, insofar as signals that fulfill a subsequent set of conditions are accepted, while those that do not are eliminated. However, the distinction here is that a filter implies a set of screening rules applied at the time the base system signal is received. Consequently, a system can include both a filter and a confirmation rule. In such a system, only signals that were accepted based on the filter definition and subsequently validated by the confirmation rule(s) would actually result in trades.

Market Characteristic Adjustments

One criticism of simple trend-following systems is that they treat all markets alike. For example, in a breakout system, with $N = 20$, both highly volatile and very quiet markets will require the same conditions for a buy signal—a 20-day high. Market characteristic adjustments seek to compensate for the fact that the best parameter values for a system will depend on market conditions. For example, in the case of a breakout system, instead of using a constant value for N, the relevant value for N might be contingent on the volatility classification of the market. As a specific illustration, the average two-day price range during the past 50-day period might be used to place the market into one of five volatility classifications. The value of N used to generate signals on any given day would then depend on the prevailing volatility classification.

Volatility appears to be the most logical choice for classifying market states, although other criteria could also be tested (e.g., fundamentally based conditions, average volume level, etc.). In essence, this type of modification seeks to transform a basic trend-following system from a static to a dynamic trading method.

Differentiation between Buy and Sell Signals

Basic trend-following systems typically assume analogous conditions for buy and sell signals (e.g., buy on close above 20-day high, sell on close below 20-day low). However, there is no reason to make this assumption automatically. It can be argued that bull and bear markets behave differently. For example, a survey of a broad spectrum of historical price charts would reveal that price breaks from major tops tend to be more rapid than price rallies from major bottoms. This observation suggests a rationale for using more sensitive conditions to generate sell signals than those used to generate buy signals. However, the system designer using such an approach should be particularly sensitive to the danger of *overfitting* the system—a pitfall discussed in detail in Chapter 15.

Pyramiding

One inherent weakness in basic trend-following systems is that they automatically assume a constant unit position size under all conditions. It would seem desirable to allow for the possibility of larger position sizes in the case of major trends, which are almost entirely responsible for the success of any trend-following system. One reasonable approach for adding units to a base position in a major trend is to wait for a specified reaction and then initiate the additional units on evidence of a resumption of the trend. Such an approach seeks to optimize the timing of pyramid units, as well as to provide exit rules that reasonably limit the potential losses that could be incurred by such added positions. An example of this type of approach was detailed in Chapter 8. Another example of a possible pyramid strategy would be provided by the following set of rules:

1. A reaction is defined when the net position is long and the market closes below the prior 10-day low.

2. Once a reaction is defined, an additional long position is initiated on any subsequent 10-day high if the following conditions are met:

   a. The pyramid signal price is above the price at which the most recent long position was initiated.

   b. The net position size is less than three units. (This condition implies that there is a limit of two pyramid units.)

Conditions are reversed for sell signals.

Figure 14.12 illustrates the addition of this pyramid plan to a breakout system with $N = 40$ applied to the September 1992 coffee contract.

Risk control becomes especially important if a pyramiding component is added to a system. Generally speaking, it is usually advisable to use a more sensitive condition for liquidating a pyramid position than the condition required to generate an opposite signal. The following is one example of a set of stop rules that might be employed in a system that uses pyramiding. Liquidate all pyramid positions whenever either condition is fulfilled:

1. An opposite trend-following signal is received.

2. Market closes above (below) the high (low) price since the most recently defined reaction that was followed by a pyramid sell (buy). Figure 14.12 illustrates the stop levels implied by this rule in the case of September 1992 coffee.

Trade Exit

The existence of a trade exit rule in a system would permit the liquidation of a position prior to receiving an opposite trend-following signal. Such a

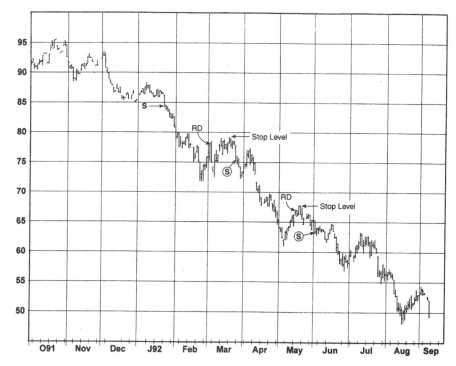

Notes: S = base position sell signal; Ⓢ = pyramid sell signal; RD = reaction defined.

FIGURE 14.12 Pyramid signals: September 1992 coffee.

rule would serve to limit losses on losing trades as well as limit the amount of open profits surrendered on winning trades. Although these are highly desirable goals, the trade-off implied by using a trade exit rule is relatively severe. If a trade exit rule is used, rules must be specified for reentering the position; otherwise, the system will be vulnerable to missing major trends.

The danger in using a trade exit rule is that it may result in the premature liquidation of a good trade. Although the reentry rule will serve as a backstop, the combination of an activated trade exit rule and a subsequent reentry is a whipsaw loss. Thus, it will not be at all uncommon for the addition of a trade exit rule (and implied reentry rule) to have a negative impact on performance. Nevertheless, although it is not easy, for some systems, it will be possible to structure trade exit rules that improve performance on balance. (In terms of return, and usually in terms of *return/risk measures* as well, if a trade exit rule helps performance, the use of the trade exit rule as a reversal signal—as opposed to just a liquidation signal—will help performance even more.) Trade exit rules can also be made dynamic. For example, the trade exit condition can be made increasingly sensitive as a price move becomes more extended in either magnitude or duration.

COUNTERTREND SYSTEMS

General Considerations Regarding Countertrend Systems

Countertrend systems often appeal to many traders because their ultimate goal is to buy low and sell high. Unfortunately, the difficulty of achieving this goal is inversely proportional to its desirability. A critical distinction to keep in mind is that whereas a trend-following system is basically self-correcting, a countertrend system implies unlimited losses. Therefore, it is essential to include some stop-loss conditions in any countertrend system (unless it is traded simultaneously with trend-following systems). Otherwise, the system could end up being long for the duration of a major downtrend or short for the duration of a major uptrend. (Stop-loss conditions are optional for most trend-following systems, since an opposite signal will usually be received before the loss on a position becomes extreme.) One important advantage of using a countertrend system is that it provides the opportunity for excellent diversification with simultaneously employed trend-following systems, thereby reducing overall volatility (see "Diversification" section, below).

Types of Countertrend Systems

The following are some types of approaches that can be used to try to construct a countertrend system.

> *Fading Minimum Move.* This is perhaps the most straightforward countertrend approach. A sell signal is indicated each time the market rallies by a certain minimum amount above the low point since the last countertrend buy signal. Similarly, a buy signal is indicated whenever the market declines by a minimum amount below the high point since the last countertrend sell signal. The magnitude of the price move required to generate a trade signal can be expressed in either nominal or percentage terms. Figure 14.13 illustrates the trade signals that would be generated by this type of countertrend system for a 4% threshold level in the October 1993–July 1994 gold market. Note that this is the same market that was previously used

in this chapter to illustrate whipsaw losses for a sensitive trend-following system (Figure 14.7). This is no accident. Countertrend systems will tend to work best under those types of market conditions in which trend-following systems fare poorly. Additionally, a confirmation condition, such as a thrust day in the direction of the countertrend reversal, can be used to avoid false signals.

Oscillators. A countertrend system could use oscillators (see Chapter 6) as an indicator for generating trade signals. It should be noted, however, that although using oscillators to signal counter-trend trades may work well in a trading-range market, in a trending market such an approach can be disastrous.

Contrary Opinion. A countertrend system might use contrary opinion as an input in timing trades. For example, once the contrary opinion rose above a specified level, a short position would

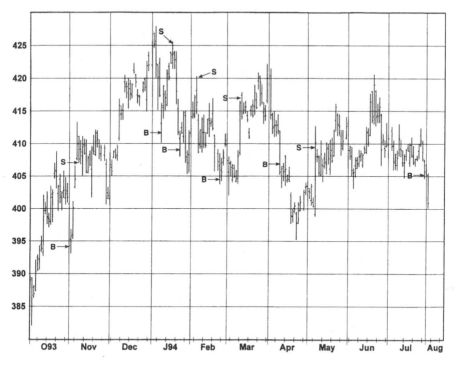

Notes: Percentages are calculated as price changes in continuous futures divided by corresponding *nearest* futures price levels. B = buy signal: 4% decline from prior high; S = sell signal: 4% advance from prior low.

FIGURE 14.13 Countertrend signals: gold continuous futures.

be indicated contingent on confirmation by a very sensitive technical indicator. (Contrary opinion was discussed in Chapter 10.)

DIVERSIFICATION

The standard interpretation attached to the term *diversification* is that trading is spread across a broad range of markets. Although this is the single most important type of diversification (assuming the availability of sufficient funds), there are two additional levels of possible diversification. First, each market can be traded with several systems. Second, several variations of each system can be used. For example, if two lots (100-share units) of a stock are being traded using the breakout system, each lot can be traded using a different value of N (i.e., the number of days whose high or low must be penetrated to trigger a signal).

In the following discussion, we will use the term *single market system variation* (SMSV) to refer to the concept of a specific variation of a given system traded in a single market. Thus, the simple breakout system, with N = 20, traded in the cocoa market would be an example of an SMSV.

There are three important benefits to diversification:

1. *Dampened Equity Retracements.* Different SMSVs will not witness their losses at precisely the same periods. Thus, by trading a wide variety of SMSVs, the trader can achieve a smoother *equity curve.* This means that trading 10 SMSVs with equivalent profit/risk characteristics would require significantly less reserve funds than trading 10 units of a single SMSV, resulting in a higher percent return. Or equivalently, at the same level of fund allocation, the diversified trading portfolio would achieve the same percentage return at a lower risk level. Up to a point, diversification would be beneficial even if the portfolio included SMSVs with poorer expected performance. A key consideration would be a given SMSV's correlation with the other SMSVs in the portfolio.

2. *Ensure Participation in Major Trends.* Since the majority of trades in most trend-following systems will lose money, it is essential that the trader participate in the large-profit trades—that is, major trends. This is a key reason for the importance of diversification across markets.

3. *Bad Luck Insurance.* Systems trading, like baseball, is a game of inches. Given the right combination of circumstances, even a minute difference in the price movement on a single day could

have an extraordinary impact on the profitability of a specific SMSV. If, for example, two versions of an identical breakout system using two slightly different confirmation conditions signal a particular trade one day apart, that difference could be dramatic if the market gaps sharply higher or lower or witnesses a string of locked-limit moves in the case of a futures market.

By trading several variations of a system, the speculator could mitigate the impact of such isolated, abnormally poor results that might result from using only one variation. Of course, in so doing, the trader would also eliminate the possibility of gains far exceeding the average performance of the system. On balance, however, this prospect represents a desirable trade-off, since it is assumed that the basic trading goal is consistent performance rather than windfall profits.

TEN COMMON PROBLEMS WITH STANDARD TREND-FOLLOWING SYSTEMS REVISITED

We are now ready to consider possible solutions to the previously enumerated problems with standard trend-following systems. The problems and the possible solutions are summarized in Table 14.2.

TABLE 14.2 Problems with Standard Trend-Following Systems and Possible Solutions

Problems with Standard Trend-Following Systems	Possible Solutions
1. Too many similar systems	1a. Try to construct original systems in order to avoid the problem of "trading with the crowd."
	1b. If trading more than one contract, spread out entry.
2. Whipsaws	2a. Employ confirmation conditions.
	2b. Develop filter rules.
	2c. Employ diversification.
3. Failure to exploit major price moves	3. Add pyramiding component.

continued

TABLE 14.2 Continued	
Problems with Standard Trend-Following Systems	*Possible Solutions*
4. Tendency of nonsensitive (slow) systems to surrender a large percentage of profits.	4. Employ trade exit rules.
5. Inability to make money intrading range markets	5. Trade trend-following systems in conjunction with countertrend systems.
6. Temporary large losses	6a. If funds permit, trade more than one system in each market.
	6b. When beginning to trade a system, trade more lightly if entering positions at a point after the signal has been received.
7. Extreme volatility in best-performing systems	7. Employ diversification to be able to allocate some funds to a high-profit-potential system that is too risky to trade on its own.
8. Systems that work well in testing but then bomb	8. Reduce the danger of such a development by properly testing systems. This subject is discussed in detail in Chapter 15.
9. Parameter shift	9a. If funds permit, diversify by trading several variations of each system.
	9b. Experiment with systems that incorporate market characteristic adjustments.
10. Slippage	10. Use realistic assumptions (discussed in Chapter 15).

Chapter

Testing and Optimizing Trading Systems

Every decade has its characteristic folly, but the basic cause is the same: people persist in believing that what has happened in the recent past will go on happening into the indefinite future, even while the ground is shifting under their feet.

—George J. Church

Some of the material in this chapter may be somewhat beyond the reach of the novice; it does, however, underscore the unavoidable complexity of the system design and testing process. While some of the concepts may not be immediately applicable, they are crucial to developing sound system testing habits and will become more important to traders as they gain experience in technical system trading. The following section is adapted from an article that first appeared in *Futures* magazine in September 1984.

THE WELL-CHOSEN EXAMPLE

You've plunked down your $895 to attend the 10th annual "Secret of the Millionaires" trading seminar. At that price, you figure the speakers will be revealing some very valuable information.

The current speaker is explaining the Super-Razzle-Dazzle (SRD) trading system. The slide on the huge screen reveals a price chart with "B" and "S" symbols representing buy and sell points. The slide is impressive: All of the buys seem to be lower than the sells.

This point is brought home even more dramatically in the next slide, which reveals the equity stream that would have been realized trading this system—a near-perfect uptrend. Not only that, but the system is also very easy to keep up.

As the speaker says, "All it takes is 10 minutes a day and a knowledge of simple arithmetic."

You never realized making money could be so simple. You could kick yourself for not having attended the first through ninth annual seminars.

Once you get home, you select 10 diversified markets and begin trading the SRD system. Each day you plot your equity. As the months go by, you notice a strange development. Although the equity in your account exhibits a very steady trend, just as the seminar example did, there is one small difference: The trend on your equity chart is down. What went wrong?

The fact is, you can find a favorable illustration for almost any trading system. The mistake is in extrapolating probable future performance on the basis of an isolated and well-chosen example from the past.

A true-life example may help illustrate this point. Back in 1983, when I had been working on trading systems for only a couple of years, I read an article in a trade magazine that presented the following very simple trading system:

1. If the six-day moving average is higher than the previous day's corresponding value, cover short and go long.

2. If the six-day moving average is lower than the previous day's corresponding value, cover long and go short.

The article used the Swiss franc in 1980 as an illustration. Without going into the details, suffice it to say that applying this system to the Swiss franc in 1980 would have resulted in a profit of $17,235 per contract (assuming an average round-turn transaction cost of $80). Even allowing for a conservative fund allocation of $6,000 per contract, this implied an annual gain of 287%! Not bad for a system that can be summarized in two sentences. It is easy to see how traders, presented with such an example, might eagerly abandon their other trading approaches for this apparent money machine.

I couldn't believe such a simple system could do so well. So I decided to test the system over a broader period—1976 to mid-1983—and a wide group of markets.

Beginning with the Swiss franc, I found that the total profit during this period was $20,473. In other words, excluding 1980, the system made only $3,238 during the remaining six and one-half years. Thus, assuming that you allocated $6,000 to trade this approach, the average annual percent return for those years was a meager 8%—quite a comedown from 287% in 1980.

But wait. It gets worse. Much worse.

When I applied the system to a group of 25 markets from 1976 through mid-1983, the system lost money in 19 of the 25 markets. In 13 of the markets—more than half of the total survey—the loss exceeded $22,500, or $3,000 per year, per contract! In five markets, the loss exceeded $45,000, equivalent to $6,000 per year, per contract!

Also, it should be noted that, even in the markets where the system was profitable, its performance was well below gains exhibited for these markets during the same period by most other trend-following systems.

There was no question about it. This was truly a bad system. Yet, if you looked only at the well-chosen example, you might think you had stumbled upon the trading system Jesse Livermore used in his good years. Talk about a gap between perception and reality.

This system witnessed such large, broadly based losses that you may well wonder why fading the signals of such a system might not provide an attractive trading strategy. The reason is that most of the losses are the result of the system being so sensitive that it generates large transaction costs. (Transaction costs include commission costs plus *slippage*. The concept of slippage is discussed later in this chapter.) This sensitivity of the system occasionally is beneficial, as was the case for the Swiss franc in 1980. However, on balance, it is the system's major weakness.

Losses due to transaction costs would not be realized as gains by fading the system. Moreover, doing the opposite of all signals would generate equivalent transaction costs. Thus, once transaction costs are incorporated, the apparent attractiveness of a contrarian approach to using the system evaporates.

The moral is simple: Don't draw any conclusions about a system (or an indicator) on the basis of isolated examples. The only way you can determine if a system has any value is by testing it (without benefit of hindsight) over an extended time period for a broad range of markets.

BASIC CONCEPTS AND DEFINITIONS

A *trading system* is a set of rules that can be used to generate trade signals. A *parameter* is a value that can be freely assigned in a trading system in order to vary the timing of signals. For example, in the basic breakout system, N (the number of prior days whose high or low must be exceeded to indicate a signal) is a parameter. Although the operation of the rules in the system will be identical whether $N = 7$ or $N = 40$, the timing of the signals will be vastly different. (For an example, see Figures 14.5 and 14.6 in Chapter 14.)

Most trading systems will have more than one parameter. For example, in the crossover moving average system there are two parameters: the length of the short-term moving average and the length of the long-term moving average. Any combination of parameter values is called a *parameter set*. For example, in a crossover moving average system, moving averages of 10 and 40 would represent a specific parameter set. Any other combination of moving average values would represent another parameter set. In systems with only one parameter (e.g., breakout), the parameter set would consist of only one element.*

Most "generic" systems are limited to one or two parameters. However, the design of more creative and flexible systems, or the addition of modifications to basic systems, will usually imply the need for three or more parameters. For example, adding a confirmation time delay rule to the crossover moving average system would imply a third parameter: the number of days in the time delay. As a general principle, it is wise to use the simplest form of a system (i.e., least number of parameters) that does not imply any substantial deterioration in performance relative to the more complex versions. However, one should not drop parameters that are deemed important simply to reduce the number of implied parameter sets. In this case, a more reasonable approach would be to limit the number of parameter sets actually tested.

Even in a simple one- or two-parameter-set system, it is not necessary to test all possible combinations. For example, in a simple breakout system in which one wishes to test the performance for values of $N = 1$ to $N = 100$, it is not necessary to test each integer in this range. A far more efficient approach would be to first test the system using spaced values for N (e.g., 10, 20, 30, . . . , 100), and then, if desired, the trader could focus in on any areas that appeared to be of particular interest. For example, if the system exhibited particularly favorable performance for the parameter values $N = 40$ and $N = 50$, the trader might want to test some other values of N in this narrower range as well. Such an additional step, however, is probably unnecessary, since, as is discussed later in this chapter, performance differences in parameter set values—particularly values in such close proximity—are probably a matter of chance and hence lack any significance.

---

*Note that the terms *parameter set* and *system variation* (the latter was used in Chapter 14) refer to identical concepts. The introduction of the term *parameter set* was merely deferred until this chapter because doing so appeared to allow for a more logically ordered presentation of the material.

CHOOSING THE PRICE SERIES

Historical stock prices represent continuous, unbroken data series, suitable for testing purposes (assuming the trade size adjustment discussed in Chapter 2). For futures traders, the first step in testing a system in a given market is choosing the appropriate price series. The issues related to this selection have already been fully detailed in Chapter 2. Generally speaking, a continuous futures series is the preferred choice, although actual contract data could be used for short-term trading systems.

CHOOSING THE TIME PERIOD

Generally speaking, the longer the test period, the more reliable the results. If the time period is too short, the test will not reflect the system's performance for a reasonable range of market situations. For example, a test of a countertrend system on the stock shown in Figure 15.1 that used only two recent years of data (roughly January 1996 to February 1998)—a period dominated by a protracted trading range—would yield highly misleading results in terms of the system's probable long-term performance.

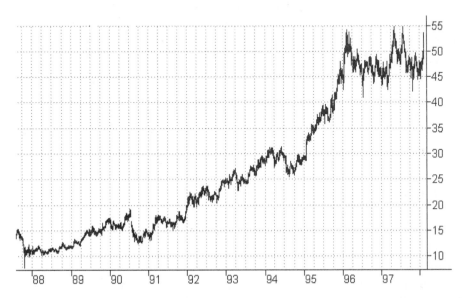

FIGURE 15.1 Trading range as unrepresentative price sample: McDonald's Corp.
Chart created with TradeStation® by Omega Research, Inc.

On the other hand, if too long a period is used for testing a system, the earlier years in the survey period might be extremely unrepresentative of current market conditions. For example, it would probably be better not to extend a test of commodity markets back far enough to include 1973–1976—a time interval that witnessed unprecedented massive price advances and subsequent steep price collapses in a number of commodity markets. An inclusion of this highly unrepresentative period would tend to greatly exaggerate the potential performance of most trend-following systems. In other words, the enormous profits realized by most trend-following systems during this period would be unlikely to be duplicated in the future.

Although it is impossible to provide a decisive answer as to the optimum number of years to be used in testing, 10 to 20 years seems to be a reasonable range. For short-term trading systems (average duration of trades equal to a few weeks or less), a shorter test period (e.g., 5 to 10 years) would probably be sufficient. Trading system test results based on time periods significantly shorter than these guidelines should be suspect. In fact, it is rather incredible that some published studies on trading systems were based on test periods of two years or less.

Ideally, one should test a system using a longer time period (e.g., 15 years) and then evaluate the results for the period as a whole and various shorter time intervals (e.g., individual years). Such an approach is important in determining the degree of *time stability* in the system—the relative consistency of performance from one period to the next. Time stability is important because it enhances confidence regarding a system's potential for maintaining consistent favorable performance in the future. Most people would be quite hesitant about using a system that generated significant net profits over a 15-year period due to three spectacularly performing years, but then witnessed losses or near break-even results in the remaining 12 years—and rightly so. In contrast, a system that registered moderate net gains during the 15-year period and was profitable in 14 of the 15 years would undoubtedly be viewed as more attractive by most traders.

REALISTIC ASSUMPTIONS

Users of trading systems often discover that their actual results are substantially worse than the paper trading results implied by the system. In fact, this situation is so common that it even has its own name: slippage. Assuming that the divergence in the results is not due to errors in the program, slippage is basically a consequence of a failure to use realistic assumptions in testing the system. Basically there are two types of such faulty assumptions:

1. *Transaction Costs.* Most traders don't realize that merely adjusting for actual commission costs in testing a system is not a sufficiently rigid assumption. The reason for this is that commissions account for only a portion of transaction costs. Another less tangible, but no less real, cost is the difference between the theoretical execution price and the actual fill price for stop, market, open, and close orders. A simple way to address this problem is to use a transaction cost per trade assumption much greater than the actual historical commission costs (e.g., $100 per trade).

2. *Limit Days.* Unless it is programmed otherwise, a computerized trading system will indicate executions on the receipt of each signal. However, in the real world, execution may not be possible because a market is locked at the daily permissible limit. If one assumes execution in such a situation, the paper results may dramatically overstate actual performance. Figure 15.2 indicates hypothetical trading signals and the corresponding implied execution

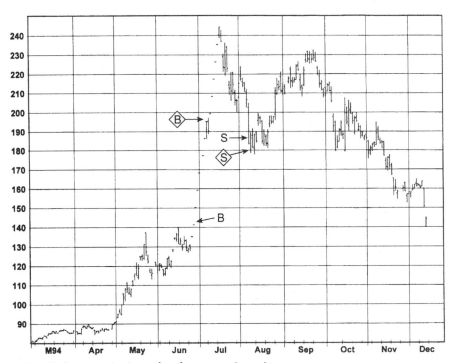

Notes: B, S = signal prices; Ⓑ, Ⓢ = execution prices.

FIGURE 15.2 Wide gap between signal price and actual entry—impact of limit days: December 1994 coffee.

prices. Note that whereas the signal prices suggest a profit of 42.4¢ ($15,900 per contract), the actual trade would have resulted in a loss of 16.2¢ ($6,075 per contract).

The potential systems trader may find that seemingly attractive trading systems disintegrate once realistic assumptions are employed. This is particularly true for very active systems, which generate very large transaction costs. However, it is far better to make this discovery in the analytical testing stage than in actual trading.

OPTIMIZING SYSTEMS

Optimization refers to the process of finding the best-performing parameter set(s) for a given system applied to a specific market. The underlying premise of optimization is that parameter sets that worked best in the past have a greater probability of superior performance in the future. For example, if a trader tested a crossover moving average system on 10 years of price data and found the best-performing combination of short and long moving average lengths was 10 and 40, he or she would trade the system using these values with the expectation that they would produce the best results in future trading. (The question of whether this assumption is valid is addressed later in the section.)

A basic question that must be considered in optimization is what criteria should be used for defining "best performance." Frequently, best performance is simply interpreted as largest equity gain. However, such a definition is incomplete. Ideally, four factors should be considered in performance comparisons:

1. *Percent Return.* Return measured relative to funds needed to trade the system. Two systems that return $10,000 per year may seem equally attractive until you find out one requires a $40,000 trading account and the other a $200,000 account.

2. *Risk Measure.* In addition to percent gain, it is also important to employ some measure of equity fluctuations (e.g., variability in rate of gain, retracements in equity). Consider two systems that each return $10,000 per year and require a $40,000 trading account. However, the maximum drawdown shown in historical testing for one system is $20,000 (50%) while the maximum drawdown for the other is $5,000 (12.5%). Under these circumstances, there is no reason to trade the former system rather than

the latter. Besides the obvious psychological reasons for wishing to avoid parameter sets and systems with high volatility, a risk measure is particularly significant because one might pick an unfavorable starting date for trading the system (i.e., there is no way to know when a drawdown might occur). For example, if a trader using the first system had the misfortune of experiencing the $20,000 drawdown in the first few months of trading it, he or she might be too discouraged to continue trading long enough to profit with the system.

3. *Parameter Stability.* It is not sufficient to find a parameter set that performs well. It is also necessary to ascertain that the parameter set does not reflect a fluke in the system. In fact, the goal of optimization should be to find broad regions of good performance rather than the single best-performing parameter set.

For example, if in testing a simple breakout system one found that the parameter set $N = 7$ exhibited the best percent return/risk characteristics but that performance dropped off very sharply for parameter sets $N < 5$ and $N > 9$, while all sets in the range $N = 25$ to $N = 54$ performed relatively well, it would make much more sense to choose a parameter set from the latter range. Why? Because the exceptional performance of the set $N = 7$ appears to be a peculiarity of the historical price data that is not likely to be repeated. The fact that surrounding parameter sets performed poorly suggests that there is no basis for confidence in trading the parameter set $N = 7$. In contrast, the broad range of performance stability for sets in the region $N = 25$ to $N = 54$ suggests that a set drawn from the center of this range would have a better prospect for success.

4. *Time Stability.* As detailed in a previous section, it is important to ascertain that favorable performance for the period as a whole is truly representative of the total period rather than a reflection of a few isolated intervals of extraordinary performance.

Realistically speaking, many traders will find elaborate performance evaluations impractical. In this regard, the trader can draw solace from the fact that for comparisons involving different parameter sets for the same system, the preceding factors tend to be highly correlated. Generally, the parameter sets with the best gain will also be the sets that exhibit the smallest equity retracements. Consequently, for the optimization of a single system, the use of a basic return/risk measure, or even a simple percent return measure, will usually yield similar results to a complex performance evaluation that incorporates a number of performance measures. However, if one is comparing parameter sets from completely different systems, the explicit consideration of risk, parameter stability, and time stability is more important.

The results of empirical tests I have conducted suggest the following key conclusions regarding optimization:

1. Any system—*any system*—can be made to appear very profitable in historical testing through optimization. If you ever find a system that can't be optimized to show good profits in the past, congratulations—you have just discovered a money machine (by doing the opposite, unless transaction costs are exorbitant). Therefore, a wonderful past performance for a system that has been optimized may be nice to look at, but it doesn't mean very much.

2. Optimization will always—*always*—overstate the potential future performance of a system, usually by a wide margin (say, three trailer trucks' worth). Therefore, optimized results should never—*never*—be used to evaluate a system's merit.

3. For many if not most systems, optimization will improve future performance only marginally, if at all.

4. If optimization has any value, it is usually in defining the broad boundaries for the ranges from which parameter set values in the system should be chosen. Fine-tuning of optimization is at best a waste of time and at worst self-delusion.

5. In view of the preceding items, sophisticated and complex optimization procedures are a waste of time. The simplest optimization procedure will provide as much meaningful information (assuming that there is any meaningful information to be derived).

In summary, contrary to widespread belief, there is some reasonable question as to whether optimization will yield meaningfully better results over the long run than randomly picking the parameter sets to be traded. Lest there be any confusion, let me explicitly state that this statement is not intended to imply that optimization is never of any value. First, as indicated previously, optimization can be useful in defining poorly performing parameter ranges that should be excluded from the selection of parameter set values. Also, it is possible that for some systems, optimization may provide some edge in parameter set selection, even after suboptimal extreme ranges are excluded. However, I do mean to imply that the degree of improvement provided by optimization is far less than generally perceived and that traders would probably save a lot of money by first proving any assumptions they are making about optimization rather than taking such assumptions on blind faith.

TESTING VERSUS FITTING

Perhaps the most critical error made by users of trading systems is the assumption that the performance of the optimized parameter sets during the test period provides an approximation of the potential performance of those sets in the future. Unfortunately, such assumptions will lead to grossly overstated evaluations of a system's true potential. It must be understood that price fluctuations are subject to a great deal of randomness. Thus, the ugly truth is that the question of which parameter sets will perform best during any given period is largely a matter of chance. The laws of probability indicate that if enough parameter sets are tested, even a meaningless trading system will yield some sets with favorable past performance. Evaluating a system based on the optimized parameter sets (i.e., the best-performing sets during the survey period) would be best described as *fitting* the system to past results rather than *testing* the system. If optimization can't be used to gauge performance, how then do you evaluate a system? The following sections describe two meaningful approaches.

Blind Simulation

In the blind simulation approach the system is optimized using data for a time period that deliberately excludes the most recent years. The performance of the system is then tested using the selected parameter sets for subsequent years. Ideally, this process should be repeated several times.

For example, trading system results for a 1985–1992 testing period could be used to determine the best-performing parameter sets for a system, which could then be tested for the years 1993–1994. Next, the system results for the 1987–1994 period could be used to determine the best-performing parameter sets, which could then be tested for the years 1995–1996. Finally, the system results for a 1989–1996 period could be used to determine the best-performing parameter sets, which could then be tested for the years 1997–1998.

Note that the error of fitting results is avoided because the parameter sets used to measure performance in any given period are selected entirely on the basis of prior rather than concurrent data. In a sense, this testing approach mimics real life (i.e., one must decide which parameter sets to trade on the basis of past data). The essential point is that simulation and optimization periods should not be allowed to overlap. Simulations that are run over the same period as the optimization are worthless.

Average Parameter Set Performance

Finding the average parameter set performance requires defining a complete list of all parameter sets that one wishes to test before running any simulations. Simulations are then run for all the parameter sets selected, and the average of all sets tested is used as an indication of the system's potential performance. The important point is that this average should be calculated across all parameter sets, not just those sets that prove profitable.

The blind simulation approach probably comes closest to duplicating real-life trading circumstances. However, the average parameter set performance is probably as conservative and has the advantage of requiring far less calculation. Both approaches represent valid procedures for testing a system.

One important caveat: In the advertised claims for given systems, the term "simulated results" is often used loosely as a euphemism for optimized results (instead of implying that the results are based on a blind simulation process). If this is the case, the weight attached to the results should equal the amount of money invested in the system: zero. The commonplace misuse and distortion of simulated results is examined in detail in the next section.

THE TRUTH ABOUT SIMULATED RESULTS

Although the value of optimization in improving a system's future performance is open to debate, there is absolutely no question that the use of optimized results will greatly distort the implied future performance of a system. The reason for this is that there is very little, if any, correlation between the best-performing parameters in a system for one period and the best-performing parameters in a subsequent period. Hence, assuming that the performance implied by the best-performing parameters could have been achieved in the past is totally unrealistic.

After years of experience, my attitude toward simulated results is summarized by what I call Schwager's corollary of simulations to Gresham's law of money. As readers may recall from Economics 101, Gresham's proposition was that "Bad money drives out good." Gresham's contention was that if two types of money were in circulation (e.g., gold and silver) at some arbitrarily defined ratio (e.g., 16:1), the bad money (i.e., the money overvalued at the fixed rate of exchange) would drive out the good. Thus, if gold were worth more than 16 ounces of silver, a 16:1 ratio would result in silver driving gold out of circulation (as people would tend to hoard it).

My corollary is: "Bad simulations drive out good." The term "bad" means simulations derived based on highly tenuous assumptions, not bad in terms of indicated performance. On the contrary, truly "bad" simulations will show eye-popping results.

I frequently get flyers hawking systems that supposedly make 200%, 400%, or even 600% a year. Let's be conservative—and I use the term loosely—and assume a return of *only* 100% per year. At this level of return, $100,000 would grow to over $1 *billion* in just over 13 years! How can such claims possibly be true, then? The answer is that they can't. The point is that, given enough hindsight, it is possible to construct virtually any type of past-performance results. If anyone tried to sell a system or a trading program based on truly realistic simulations, the results would appear laughably puny relative to the normal promotional fare. It is in this sense that I believe that bad (unrealistic) simulations drive out good (realistic) simulations.

How are simulated results distorted? There are a number of primary means including:

1. *The Well-Chosen Example (revisited).* In constructing a well-chosen example, the system promoter selects the best market, in the best year, using the best parameter set. Assuming a system is tested on 25 markets for 15 years and uses 100 parameter set variations, there would be a total of 37,500 (25 × 15 × 100) one-year results. It would be difficult to construct a system in which not one of these 37,500 possible outcomes showed superlative results. For example, if you tossed a group of 10 coins 37,500 times, don't you think you would get 10 out of 10 heads sometimes? Absolutely. In fact, you would get 10 out of 10 heads on the average of one out of 1,024 times.

2. *Kitchen Sink Approach.* By using hindsight to add parameters and create additional system rules that conveniently take care of past losing periods, it is possible to generate virtually any level of past performance.

3. *Ignoring Risk.* Advertised system results frequently calculate return as a percent of margin or as a percent of an unrealistically

low multiple of margin. This one item alone can multiply the implied returns severalfold. Of course, the risk would increase commensurately, but the ads don't provide those details.

4. *Overlooking Losing Trades.* It is hardly uncommon for charts in system brochures or advertisements to indicate buy and sell signals at the points at which some specified rules were met, but fail to indicate other points on the same chart where the same conditions were met and the resulting trades were losers.

5. *Optimize, Optimize, Optimize.* Optimization (i.e., selecting the best-performing parameter sets for the past) can tremendously magnify the past performance of a system. Virtually any system ever conceived would look great if the results were based on the best parameter set (i.e., the parameter set that had the best past performance) for each market. The more parameter sets tested, the wider the selection of past results, and the greater the potential simulated return.

6. *Unrealistic Transaction Costs.* Frequently, simulated results include only commissions but not slippage (the difference between the assumed entry level and the actual fill that would be realized by using a market or stop order). For fast systems, ignoring slippage can make a system that would wipe out an account in real life look like a money machine.

7. *Fabrication.* Even though it is remarkably easy to construct system rules with great performance for the past, some promoters don't even bother doing this much. For example, one infamous individual keeps on emerging with promotions for various $299 systems that are outright frauds. Bruce Babcock of *Commodity Traders Consumers Report* has labeled this fellow appropriately enough the "$299 man."

The preceding is not intended to indict all system promoters or all those using simulated results. Certainly, there are many individuals who construct simulated results in appropriately rigorous fashion. However, the sad truth is that the extraordinary misuse of simulations over many years has virtually made simulated results worthless. Advertised simulated results are very much like restaurant reviews written by the proprietors—you would hardly expect to ever see a bad review. I can assure you that you will never see any simulated results for a system that shows the system long the S&P as of the close of October 16, 1987. Can simulated results ever be used? Yes, if you are the system developer *and* you know what you're doing (e.g., use the simulation methods detailed in the previous section), or equivalently, if you have absolute faith in the integrity and competence of the system developer.

MULTIMARKET SYSTEM TESTING

The actual application of portfolio system testing is beyond the scope of the beginner. However, an understanding of the subject is nonetheless worthwhile because of the critical importance of diversification, as was detailed in Chapter 14.

Although it is probably unrealistic to expect any single system to work in all markets, generally speaking, a good system should demonstrate profitability in a large majority of actively traded futures markets (e.g., 85% or more). In the case of stocks, assuming that a system is used for timing purchases and liquidating long positions (most traders will not short stocks), a good system should exhibit better return/risk characteristics than a buy-and-hold strategy in a majority of tested stocks. There are, of course, some important exceptions. A system employing fundamental input would, by definition, be applicable to only a single market. In addition, the behavior of some markets is so atypical (e.g., stock indexes) that systems designed for trading such markets might well perform poorly over the broad range of markets.

In testing a system for a multimarket portfolio, it is necessary to predetermine the relative number of shares or futures contracts to be traded in each market. This problem is frequently handled by simply assuming that the system will trade one lot (100 shares) or one futures contract in each market. However, this is a rather naive approach, for two reasons: First, some markets are far more volatile than other markets. For example, a portfolio that included one contract of coffee and one contract of corn would be far more dependent on the trading results in coffee. Second, it may be desirable to trade fewer shares or contracts of highly correlated markets within a portfolio (e.g., two oil stocks like Chevron and Amoco, or deutsche marks and Swiss francs).*

In any case, the percentage allocation of available funds to each market should be determined prior to testing a system. These relative weightings can then be used to establish the number of contracts to be traded in each market. Note that as long as gain is measured in percentage rather

---

*For purposes of real-time trading (as opposed to historical testing), historical performance might be a third relevant factor in determining contract weightings. However, this factor cannot be included as an input in the testing procedure because it would bias the results.

than in nominal terms, the total number of contracts assumed to be traded in each market is irrelevant—only the contract ratios between markets will be important.

NEGATIVE RESULTS

Analyzing the conditions under which a system performs poorly can sometimes reveal important weaknesses in the system that have been overlooked and thus provide clues as to how the system can be improved. The validity of any rule changes in the system would be confirmed only if such revisions generally tended to improve the results for a broad range of parameter sets and markets, not just a select few. The potential value of negative results as a source of ideas for how a system can be improved cannot be overstated. The concept that disorder is a catalyst for thought is a general truth that was perfectly expressed by the late novelist John Gardner: "In a perfect world, there would be no need for thought. We think because something goes wrong."

The idea of learning from poor results is basically applicable to a system that works in most markets and for most parameter sets, but performs badly in isolated cases. However, systems that exhibit disappointing results over a broad range of markets and parameter sets are likely to be lost causes, unless the results are spectacularly poor. In the latter case, a system that exactly reverses the trade signals of the original system might be attractive. For example, if tests of a new trend-following system reveal that the system consistently loses money in most markets, the implication is that one might have accidentally stumbled upon an effective countertrend system. Such discoveries may be difficult on the ego, but they should not be ignored. (The fact that a system exhibits stable poor performance does not necessarily imply that the reverse system would perform favorably, because of the influence of transaction costs.)

STEPS IN CONSTRUCTING AND TESTING A TRADING SYSTEM

1. Obtain all data needed for testing.
2. Define the system concept.
3. Program rules to generate trades in accordance with this concept.
4. Select a small subset of stocks or futures markets and a subset of years for these instruments.

5. Generate system trading signals for these subsets for a given parameter set.

6. Generate charts for these markets and years and make several photocopy sets (futures traders: use continuous futures).

7. Denote trading signals on these charts. (Be sure the same price series was used to generate charts as to test the system.) This is an important step. I find it is much easier to debug a system by visually inspecting signals on charts than by working only with data printouts.

8. Check to see that the system is doing what was intended. Almost invariably, a careful check will reveal some inconsistencies due to either or both of the following reasons:

a. There are errors in the program.

b. Rules in the program do not anticipate some circumstances or create unforeseen repercussions.

Some examples of the latter might include: the system failing to generate a signal, given an event at which a signal is intended; the system generating a signal when no signal is intended; the system rules inadvertently creating a situation in which no new signals can be generated or in which a position is held indefinitely. In essence these types of situations arise because there will always be some missed nuances.

The system rules need to be modified to correct both programming errors and unforeseen inconsistencies. It should be emphasized that corrections of the latter type are concerned only with making the system operate consistently with the intended concept and should be made *without any regard as to whether the changes help or hurt performance in the sample cases used in the developmental process.*

9. After making necessary corrections, repeat steps 7 and 8. Pay particular attention to changes in indicated signals versus previous run for two reasons:

a. To check whether the program changes achieved the desired fix.

b. To make sure the changes did not have unintended effects.

10. Once the system is working as intended and all rules and contingencies have been fully defined, *and only after such a point*, test the system on the entire defined parameter set list across the full price data base. (Be sure the intended trading portfolio has been defined before this test is run.)

11. As detailed earlier in this chapter, evaluate performance based on the average of all parameter sets tested or a blind simulation process. (The former involves far less work.)

12. Compare these results with the results of a generic system (e.g., breakout, crossover moving average) for the corresponding portfolio and test period. The return/risk characteristics of the system should be measurably better than those of the generic system, or equivalent and diversified versus the generic system, if it is to be deemed to have any real value.

The preceding steps represent a rigorous procedure that is designed to avoid generating results that are upwardly biased by hindsight. As such, expect most system ideas to fail the test of merit in step 12. Designing a system with a truly superior performance is more difficult than most people think.

A NOTE ON SYSTEM TESTING SOFTWARE

There are several commercially available software programs that will enable you to execute most of the steps outlined in the previous section: define and program trading rules, organize price data for different tests, create charts showing trade signals, generate system performance statistics for analysis, and so on. The relevant issues regarding software selection were outlined in Chapter 13.

OBSERVATIONS ABOUT TRADING SYSTEMS

1. In trend-following systems, the basic method used to identify trends (e.g., breakout, crossover moving average) may well be the least important component of the system. In a sense, this is merely a restatement of Jim Orcutt's observation that "there are only two types of trend-following systems: fast and slow." Thus, in designing trend-following systems, it may make more sense to concentrate on modifications (e.g., filters and confirmation rules to reduce bad trades, market characteristic adjustments, pyramiding rules, stop rules) than on trying to discover a better method for defining trends.

2. Complexity for its own sake is no virtue. Use the simplest form of a system that does not imply a meaningful sacrifice in performance relative to more complex versions.

3. The well-publicized and very valid reason for trading a broad range of markets is risk control through diversification. However, for futures traders there is another very important reason for trading as many markets as possible: insurance against not missing any sporadic, giant price moves. The importance of catching all such major trends cannot be overstressed—it can make the difference between mediocre performance and great performance. The 1994 coffee market (see Figure 1.2 in Chapter 1) and the 1979–1980 silver market (see Figure 1.1 in Chapter 1) are two spectacular examples of markets that were critical to portfolio performance.

4. If trading funds are sufficient, diversification should be extended to systems as well as markets. Trading several systems rather than a single system could help smooth overall performance. Ideally, the greatest degree of diversification would be achieved if the mix of systems included countertrend and pattern recognition systems as well as trend-following systems. (However, this goal may be difficult to achieve because countertrend and pattern recognition systems are generally significantly harder to design than trend-following systems.)

5. If sufficient funds are available, it is better to trade a number of diversified parameter sets than to trade a single optimized set.

6. Generally speaking, the value of parameter optimization is far overstated.

7. The previous observation strongly suggests that optimized results should never be used for evaluating the relative performance of a system. Two meaningful methods for testing systems were discussed in the text: blind simulation and average parameter set performance.

8. So-called simulated results are frequently optimized results (i.e., derived with the benefit of hindsight) and, as such, virtually meaningless. This caveat is particularly pertinent in regard to advertisement or direct-mail promotions for trading systems, which invariably use very well-chosen examples.

9. An analysis of the results of successful systems will almost always reveal the presence of many markets with one or more years of very large profits, but few instances of very large single-year

losses. The implication is that a key reason for the success of these systems is that their rules adhere to the critical, albeit hackneyed, principle of letting profits run and cutting losses short.

10. A market should not be avoided because its volatility increases sharply. In fact, the most volatile markets are often the most profitable.

11. Isolating negative results for a system that performs well on balance can provide valuable clues as to how the system can be improved.

12. A frequently overlooked fact is that trading results may often reflect more information about the market than the system. For example, in Figure 15.3, a trend-following system that was long in late July or early August 1997 would have seen the profits from the dramatic upward spike evaporate by the time an offsetting sell signal appeared. Such an event would not necessarily reflect inadequate risk control. Any trend-following system would have experienced the same fate.

This example illustrates how the value of a system cannot be judged in a vacuum. In some cases, poor performance may reflect nothing more than the fact that market conditions would have resulted in poor results for the vast majority of systems.

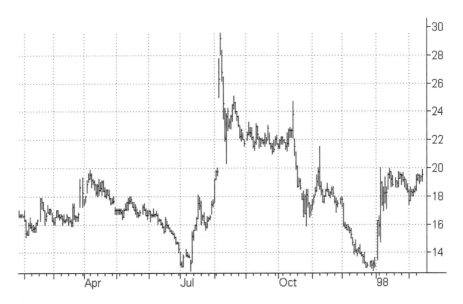

FIGURE 15.3 Trading results reflect market, not system: Apple Computer. Chart created with TradeStation® by Omega Research, Inc.

Similarly, favorable results may also reflect the conditions of the market rather than any degree of superiority in the tested system. These considerations suggest that a meaningful assessment of a new system's performance should include a comparison to a benchmark (e.g., the corresponding performance of standard systems, such as a crossover moving average or a simple breakout, during the same period for the same markets).

13. Use continuous futures prices for testing futures trading systems.

14. Use only a small portion of the database (i.e., some markets for only a segment of the full time period) for developing and debugging a system.

15. Use charts with superimposed signal annotations as an aid to debugging systems.

16. In checking the accuracy and completeness of the signals generated by a system, make changes dictated by deviations from the intended operation of the system (due to oversights related to the full implications of the rules employed or unforeseen situations) with complete disregard to whether such changes increase or decrease profits in the sample tests.

PART FOUR

PRACTICAL TRADING GUIDELINES

Chapter 16

The Planned Trading Approach

If making money is a slow process, losing it is quickly done.
—Ihara Saikaku

I f the amount of money you risk in trading represents a minuscule fraction of your net worth, and your major motivation for speculation is entertainment, the shoot-from-the-hip approach might be fine. However, if your major trading objective is to make money, an organized trading plan is essential. This is not just a platitude. Search out successful speculators, and you will no doubt find that they all use a systematic, disciplined trading approach.

The following seven steps provide general guidelines for constructing an organized trading plan.

STEP ONE: DEFINE A TRADING PHILOSOPHY

How do you plan to make your trading decisions? If your answer is something vague like "when my friend gets a hot tip from his broker," "when I get a trade idea from reading the newspaper," or "on market feel while watching the quote machine," you're not ready to begin trading. A meaningful strategy would be based on either fundamental analysis, chart analysis, technical trading systems, or some combination of these approaches. The same method will not necessarily be used in all markets. For example, in some markets the trader may use a synthesis of fundamental and chart analyses to make trading decisions, while in other markets decisions may be based on chart analysis only.

The more specific the trading strategy, the better. For example, a trader who plans to base trades on chart analysis should be able to specify the types of patterns that would signal trades, as well as other details, such as confirmation rules. Of course, the most specific trading strategy would be one based on a mechanical trading system; however, such a fully automated approach may not appeal to a significant percentage of traders.

STEP TWO: CHOOSE MARKETS TO BE TRADED

After deciding on how he or she plans to pick trades, the speculator must choose the stocks or futures markets that will be followed. For most speculators, constraints related to time and available funds will significantly limit the number of instruments that can be monitored and traded. Three factors might be considered in selecting markets: suitability, diversification, and volatility.

Suitability to Trading Approach

A trader would choose those markets that appear to have the best potential for satisfactory performance, given one's planned approach. Of course, such a determination can only be made on the basis of either past trading experience or historical testing of a specific trading strategy.

Diversification

The multiple benefits of diversification were discussed in Chapter 14. However, the essential point here is that diversification provides one of the most effective means of reducing risk. Diversification can be enhanced by choosing markets that are not closely related. For example, if a speculator wanted to trade gold, then silver and platinum would be poor choices for additional markets, unless available funds were sufficient to permit trading many other markets as well. Similarly, selecting more than one pharmaceutical company, or more than one airline, in a limited stock portfolio would have the same drawback.

Volatility

A trader with limited funds should avoid extremely volatile markets (e.g., coffee), since the inclusion of such markets in one's portfolio will severely limit the total number of markets that can be traded. Unless the speculator's approach is better suited to a given volatile market, he or she will be better off trading a wider variety of less volatile markets (diversification again). (*Volatility* here refers to dollar volatility per contract. Consequently, high volatility could imply relatively large price swings, large-size contracts, or both.)

STEP THREE: SPECIFY RISK CONTROL PLAN

Risk control is typically referred to as "money management," although I believe the former represents the more descriptive label. The rigid control of losses is perhaps the most critical prerequisite for successful trading. A risk control plan should include the following elements:

1. Maximum risk per trade
2. Stop-loss strategy
3. Diversification
4. Reduced leverage for correlated markets
5. Market volatility adjustments
6. Adjusting leverage to equity changes
7. Losing period adjustments

Maximum Risk per Trade

The speculator can substantially increase the probability of long-term success by restricting the percentage of total funds allocated to any given trade. Ideally, the maximum risk on any trade should be limited to 3% or less of total equity. For smaller accounts, adhering to such a guideline will require restricting trading to less volatile stocks and futures (or mini-futures contracts and spreads). Speculators who find that they must risk more than about 7% of their equity on individual trades should seriously reconsider their financial suitability for trading.

The maximum risk per trade also can be used to determine the number of stock shares or futures contracts that can be initiated in any given trade. For example, if the maximum risk per trade is 3% of equity and the speculator's account size is $100,000, a stock trade that required a stop 5 points (dollars) below the market would imply a maximum position size of 600 shares ($5 × 600 = $3,000, or 3% of $100,000). Under the same circumstances, a corn trade that required a stop point 20¢/bu below the market would imply a maximum position size of three 5,000-bushel futures contracts (20¢ × 5,000 = $1,000, or 1% of $100,000). In similar fashion, the maximum risk per trade would also be used in deciding whether pyramid units could be added without upsetting risk control guidelines.

Stop-Loss Strategy

Know where you're going to get out before you get in. The importance of this rule cannot be overemphasized. Without a predetermined exit point, the trader will be vulnerable to procrastinating in the liquidation of a losing position. At the wrong time, one such lapse of trading discipline could literally knock the speculator out of the game.

Ideally, the speculator should place a good-till-canceled (GTC) stop order when entering the trade. However, traders who are fairly certain they can trust themselves can determine a mental stop point at trade entry, and defer the actual placement of the stop order until the stop point is within a given day's permissible range. For a more detailed discussion of strategies regarding the placement of stop orders, see Chapter 9, "Choosing Stop-Loss Points."

It should be noted that the system trader does not necessarily need to employ stop-loss rules to achieve risk control. For example, if a trading system automatically reverses the position given a sufficient trend reversal, the system will inherently perform the major function of a stop-loss rule—the prevention of catastrophic losses on individual trades—without such a rule being explicit. Of course, large cumulative losses can still occur over many trades, but the same vulnerability would still apply if stops were used.

Diversification

Since different markets will witness adverse moves at different times, trading multiple markets will reduce risk. As a very simple example, assume that a trader with a $20,000 account uses a system that witnesses average drawdowns of $3,000 in both gold and soybeans. If two contracts of either market were traded, the average drawdown would be equal to 30% (6,000 ÷ 20,000), whereas if one contract of each were traded, the average drawdown would invariably be less (possibly even less than for *one* contract of a *single* market if the markets were inversely correlated). In fact, the average drawdown could only reach 30% (assuming average drawdowns remain at $3,000 for each market) if drawdowns in the two markets proved to be exactly synchronized, which is exceedingly unlikely. Of course, the risk-reduction benefit of diversification would increase as more unrelated markets were added to the portfolio. Also, as noted in Chapter 14, the concept of diversification applies to trading not only multiple markets but also multiple systems (or approaches) and multiple system variations (i.e., parameter sets) for each market, assuming equity is sufficient to do so.

Although our focus in this section is risk control, it should be noted that diversification can also increase return by allowing the trader to increase average leverage in each market without increasing overall risk. In fact, the addition of markets with a lower average return than other markets in an existing portfolio can actually *increase* the return of the portfolio if the risk reduction gained by diversification is greater than the decline in return and the trader adjusts leverage accordingly. Two other benefits of diversification—ensuring participation in major trends and providing bad luck insurance—were discussed in Chapter 14.

Reduced Leverage for Correlated Markets

Although adding markets to a portfolio allows a trader to increase leverage, it is important to make adjustments for highly correlated markets. For example, both a currency portfolio consisting of the six most active currency futures contracts and a pharmaceutical portfolio consisting of some of the most popular drug stocks would be subject to much greater risk than more broadly diversified six-market portfolios because of the very strong correlations between some of their component instruments. Consequently, the leverage of such homogenous portfolios should be adjusted downward vis-à-vis a more diversified six-market portfolio with equivalent individual market volatilities.

Market Volatility Adjustments

Trading leverage—the number of shares or contracts traded in each market for any given equity size—should be adjusted to account for volatility differences. There are two aspects of this rule. First, fewer shares or contracts would be traded in more volatile markets. Second, even for a single market, the number of shares or contracts would vary in conjunction with fluctuations in volatility. Of course, because futures can't be traded in fractions, speculators with small accounts will be unable to make such volatility adjustments, which is one reason why small accounts will be subject to greater risk. (Other reasons include the unavoidability of the maximum risk per trade exceeding desired levels and an inability to diversify sufficiently.)

Adjusting Leverage to Equity Changes

Leverage should also be changed in accordance with major fluctuations in equity. For example, if a trader begins with a $100,000 account and loses $20,000, all else being equal, the leverage should be reduced by 20%. (Of course, if equity rises instead, the leverage should be increased.)

Losing Period Adjustments (Discretionary Traders Only)

When a trader's confidence is shaken because of an ongoing losing streak, it is often a good idea to temporarily cut back position size or even take a complete trading break until confidence returns. In this way, the trader can keep a losing phase from steamrollering into a disastrous retracement. This advice would not apply to a system trader, however, since for most viable systems a losing period enhances the potential for favorable performance in the ensuing period. Or, to put it another way, confidence and frame of mind are critical to the performance of a discretionary trader but are not relevant to the performance of a system.

STEP FOUR: ESTABLISH A PLANNING TIME ROUTINE

It is important to set aside some time each evening for reviewing markets and updating trading strategies. In most cases, once the trader has established a specific routine, 30 to 60 minutes should be sufficient (less if only a few markets are being traded). The primary tasks performed during this time would be:

1. *Update Trading Systems and Charts.* At least one of these should be employed as an aid in making trading decisions. In those markets in which fundamental analysis is employed, the trader will also have to reevaluate the fundamental picture periodically after the release of important new information (e.g., government crop report).

2. *Plan New Trades.* Determine whether any new trades are indicated for the next day. If there are any, decide on a specific entry plan (e.g., buy on opening). In some cases, a trading decision may be contingent on an evaluation of market behavior on the following day. For example, assume a trader is bullish on a particular stock, and modestly bearish news about the company is received after the close. Such a trader might decide to go long *if* the market is trading higher on the day at any point within one hour of the close.

3. *Update Exit Points for Existing Positions.* The trader should review the stops and objectives on existing positions to see whether any revisions appear desirable in light of the current day's price action. In the case of stops, such changes should only be made to reduce trade risk.

STEP FIVE: MAINTAIN A TRADER'S NOTEBOOK

The planning routine discussed in the previous section implies some systematic form of record keeping. Figure 16.1 provides one sample of a format that might be used for a trader's notebook. The first four columns merely identify the trade.

Column 5 would be used to indicate the intended stop point at time of entry. Revisions of this stop would be entered in column 6. (Some items, such as column 6, will require pencil entries, since they are subject to revision.) The reason for maintaining the initial stop point as a separate item is that this information may be useful to the trader in any subsequent trade analysis—for example, to check whether initial stops tend to be too wide or too close.

Columns 7–10 provide a summary of the implied risk on open positions. By adding these entries for all open positions, the trader can assess current total exposure—information critical in controlling risk and determining whether new positions can be initiated. As a rough rule of thumb, the cumulative implied risk on all open positions should not exceed 25% to 35% of total account equity. (Assuming the maximum risk on any given position is limited to 2% of equity, this constraint would not be relevant unless there were open positions in at least 13 markets.)

The use of objectives (columns 11 and 12) is a matter of individual preference. Although in some cases the use of objectives will permit a better exit price, in other circumstances objectives will result in the premature liquidation of a trade. Consequently, some traders may prefer to forgo the use of objectives, allowing the timing of liquidation to be determined by either a trailing stop or a change of opinion.

Liquidation information is contained in columns 13–15. The reason for recording the exit date is that it can be used to calculate the duration of the trade, information that may be useful to speculators in analyzing their trades. Column 15 would indicate the profit or loss on the trade after deducting commissions.

Columns 16–17 provide room for capsule comments regarding the reasons for entering the trade (made at that time) and a hindsight evaluation of the trade. Such observations can be particularly useful in helping

(1) Trade Entry Date	(2) Long or Short	(3) Units	(4) Market	(5) Entry Price	Stops (6) Initial	Current	Cumulative Implied Risk (7) Initial	(8) Current	As Percentage of Equity (9) Initial	(10) Current	Objective (11) Initial	(12) Current	(13) Exit Date	(14) Exit Price	(15) Net Profit or Loss	(16) Reasons for Entering Trade	(17) Comment

FIGURE 16.1 Sample page from a trader's notebook.

traders detect any patterns in their successes and failures. Of course, the actual trader's notebook must allow more room for these comments than shown in the illustration provided by Figure 16.1. Furthermore, a more extensive description of the trade would be contained in a trader's diary, which is discussed in the next step.

The novice will usually benefit from a period of paper trading before plunging into actual trading. The trader's notebook would be ideally suited for this purpose, since not only would it provide an indication of potential trading success, but it would also get the new trader into the habit of approaching speculation in a systematic and disciplined fashion. Thus, when the transition is made to actual trading, the decision process will have become routine. Of course, the difficulty of trading decisions will increase dramatically once real money is at stake, but at least the new speculator will have a decisive advantage over his or her more typically ill-prepared counterparts.

STEP SIX: MAINTAIN A TRADER'S DIARY

The trader's diary would contain the following basic information for each trade:

1. *Reasons for Trade.* Over time, this information can help the speculator determine whether any trading strategies are particularly prone to success or failure.

2. *How the Trade Turned Out.* This basic background information is necessary for the evaluation of any trade. (Although the gist of this information can be determined from the net profit or loss column in the trader's notebook, it is also helpful to maintain this information along with each trade discussed in the trader's diary.)

3. *Lessons.* The speculator should itemize the mistakes or correct decisions made in the course of the trade. The mere act of keeping such a written record can greatly help a trader to avoid repeating past mistakes—particularly if repeated errors are indicated in capital letters and followed by several exclamation points. The trader's diary should be reviewed periodically to help reinforce these observations. After a while, the lessons will sink in. Speaking from personal experience, this approach can be instrumental in eradicating frequently repeated mistakes.

It may also be useful to augment the written diary with charts illustrating trade entry and exit points (as was done, for example, in Chapter 12).

STEP SEVEN: ANALYZE PERSONAL TRADING

Speculators must not only analyze the markets, but also their own past trades in order to isolate the strengths and weaknesses of their approach. Besides the trader's diary, two useful tools in such an analysis are analysis of segmented trades and the *equity chart*.

Analysis of Segmented Trades

The idea behind segmenting trades into different categories is to help identify any patterns of substantially above- or below-average performance. For example, by breaking down trades into buys and sells, a trader might discover a predilection toward the long side, but a higher average profit for short trades. Such an observation would obviously imply the desirability of correcting a bias toward the long side.

As another example, after breaking down the results by market, a trader may find he or she consistently loses money in certain stocks or futures markets. Such evidence might suggest that overall performance could be improved by not trading these markets. The segmentation of trading results by market can be an extremely important exercise, since many speculators have a poor intuitive sense of their relative degree of success in various markets. The cessation of trading in poorer performing markets need not be permanent. The speculator could attempt to identify the reasons for disappointing results in these markets and then research and test possible trading approach adjustments.

As a final example, a speculator who combines day trading and position trading might find it particularly instructive to compare the net results of each category. My own suspicion is that if such an analysis were performed by all speculators to whom the exercise is relevant, the population of day traders would shrink by 50% overnight.

Of course, there are other criteria that can be used to segment trades. Two other examples of relevant comparisons are fundamentally versus technically oriented trades, and trades that were in agreement with the position of a given trading system versus those that were not. In each case, the trader would be searching for patterns of success or failure. The process of analyzing segmented trades will be greatly simplified by using an electronic spreadsheet to maintain the trader's notebook.

Equity Chart

This is a close-only type of chart in which the indicated value for each day represents the account equity (including the equity on open positions). The primary purpose of such a chart is to alert the trader when there is a precipitous deterioration of performance. For example, if after an extended, steady climb, the account equity experiences a sudden, steep decline, a trader might be well advised to lighten positions and take time to reassess the situation. Such an abrupt shift in performance might reflect a transformation of market conditions, a current vulnerability in the speculator's trading approach, or a recent predilection toward poor trading decisions. A determination of the actual cause is not essential, since any of these factors could be viewed as strong cautionary signals to reduce risk exposure. In short, the equity chart can be an important tool in mitigating equity retracements.

Chapter 17

Eighty-Two Trading Rules and Market Observations

Live long enough and you will eventually be wrong about everything.
—Russell Baker

Few things are easier to ignore than trading advice. Many of the most critical trading rules have been so widely circulated that they have lost their ability to provoke any thought in the new trader. Thus, valid market insights are often dismissed as obvious clichés.

Consider the rule "Cut your losses short"—perhaps the single most important trading maxim. Lives there a speculator who has not heard this advice? Yet there is certainly no shortage of speculators who have ignored this rule. Not surprisingly, there is also no shortage of speculators whose accounts were virtually obliterated by one or two losing trades.

The truth is that most speculators will ignore advice until they have "rediscovered the wheel" through their own trading experience. Moreover, most traders will repeat a mistake many times before the lesson finally sinks in. Thus, I have no illusions that the advice presented in this and the next chapter will spare the reader from committing basic trading errors. However, it is hoped that several readings of these chapters (particularly following periods of negative trading results) will at least help some novice traders reduce the number of times these mistakes are repeated—hardly a trivial achievement.

The observations in this chapter are based on personal experience. Thus, the following 82 rules should be viewed in their proper perspective: empirically based opinions as opposed to proven facts. Overall, there will be substantial overlap with other published expositions of trading guidelines. This is hardly surprising, since a wide range of rules (many of them mundane) are based on such sound principles that they are almost universally accepted as trading truths. For example, I have never met a successful speculator who did not believe that risk control was essential to profitable trading. On the other hand, some of the rules listed below reflect a subjective view that is contradicted by other writers (e.g., using market orders instead of limit orders). In the final analysis, each speculator must discover his or her own trading truths. It is hoped that the following list will help speed the process.

ENTERING TRADES

1. Differentiate between major position trades and short-term trades. The average risk allocated to short-term trades (as implied by the number of shares or contracts in the position and the stop point) should be significantly smaller. Also, the speculator should focus on major position trades, since these are usually far more critical to trading success. A mistake made by many traders is that they become so involved in trying to catch the minor market swings (generating lots of commissions and slippage in the process) that they miss the major price moves.

2. If you believe a major trading opportunity exists, don't be greedy in trying to get a slightly better entry price. The lost profit potential of one missed price move can offset the savings from 50 slightly better execution prices.

3. Entry into any major position should be planned and carefully thought out—never an intraday impulse.

4. *Find a chart pattern that says the timing is right—now.* Don't initiate a trade without such a confirming pattern. (Occasionally, one might consider a trade without such a pattern if there is a convergence of many measured moves and support/resistance points at a given price area and there is a well-defined stop point that does not imply much risk.)

5. Place orders determined by daily analysis. If the market is not close to the desired entry level, record the trade idea and review it each day until either the trade is entered or the trade idea is no longer deemed attractive. Failure to adhere to this rule can result in missing good trades. One common occurrence is that a trade idea is recalled once the market has moved

beyond the intended entry, and it is then difficult to do the same trade at a worse price.

6. *When looking for a major reversal in a trend, it is usually wiser to wait for some pattern that suggests that the timing is right rather than fading the trend at projected objectives and support/resistance points.* This rule is particularly important in the case of a market in which the trend has carried prices to long-term highs or lows (e.g., highs or lows beyond a prior 100-day range). Remember, in most cases of an extended trend, the market will not form V-type reversals. Instead, prices will normally pull back to test highs and lows—often a number of times. Thus, waiting for a top or bottom to form can prevent getting chopped to pieces during the topping or bottoming process—not to mention the losses that can occur if you are highly premature in picking the top or bottom. Even if the market does form a major V top or V bottom, subsequent consolidations (e.g., flags) can allow favorable reward/risk entries.

7. If you have an immediate instinctive impression when looking at a chart (particularly if you are not conscious about which market you are looking at), go with that feeling.

8. *Don't let the fact that you missed the first major portion of a new trend keep you from trading with that trend* (as long as you can define a reasonable stop-loss point).

9. Don't fade recent price failure patterns (e.g., bull or bear traps) when implementing trades, even if there are many other reasons for the trade.

10. *Never fade the first gap of a price move!* For example, if you are waiting to enter a trade on a correction, and the correction is then formed on a price gap, don't enter the trade.

11. In most cases, use market orders rather than limit orders. This is especially important when liquidating a losing position or entering a perceived major trading opportunity—situations in which traders are apt to be greatly concerned about the market getting away from them. Although limit orders will provide slightly better fills for a large majority of trades, this benefit will usually be more than offset by the substantially poorer fills, or missed profit potential, in those cases in which the initial limit order is not filled.

12. Never double up near the original trade entry point after having been ahead. Often, the fact that the market has completely re-

traced is a negative sign for the trade. Even if the trade is still good, doubling up in this manner will jeopardize holding power due to overtrading.

EXITING TRADES AND RISK CONTROL (MONEY MANAGEMENT)

13. Decide on a specific protective stop point *at the time of trade entry*.

14. *Exit any trade if newly developing patterns or market action are contrary to trade*—even if stop point has not been reached. Ask yourself, "If I had to have a position in this market, which way would it be?" If the answer is not the position you hold, get out! In fact, if contradictory indications are strong enough, reverse the position.

15. Always get out *immediately* once the original premise for a trade is violated.

16. If you are dramatically wrong the first day a trade is on, abandon the trade immediately—especially if the market gaps against you.

17. In the event of a major breakout counter to the position held, either liquidate immediately or use a very close stop. *In the event of a gap breakout, always liquidate immediately.*

18. If a given stock or futures market suddenly trades far in excess of its recent volatility in a direction opposite to the position held, liquidate your position immediately. For example, if a market that has been trading in approximate 50-point daily ranges opens 100 to 150 points higher, cover immediately if you are short.

19. *If selling into resistance or buying into support and the market consolidates instead of reversing, get out.*

20. For analysts and market advisers: *If your gut feeling is that a recent recommendation, hot line broadcast, trade, or written report of yours is wrong, reverse your opinion!*

21. If you're unable to watch markets for a period of time (e.g., when traveling), either liquidate all positions or be sure to have GTC stop orders on all open positions. (Also, in such situations, limit orders can be used to ensure getting into the market on planned buys at lower prices or planned sells at higher prices.)

22. Do not get complacent about an open position. Always know where you are getting out even if the point is far removed from the current price. Also, an evolving pattern contrary to the trade may suggest the desirability of an earlier-than-intended exit.

23. *Fight the desire to immediately get back into the market following a stopped-out trade.* Getting back in will usually supplement the original loss with additional losses. The only reason to get back in on a stopped-out trade is if the timing seems appropriate based on evolving price patterns—that is, only if all the conditions and justifications of any new trade are met.

OTHER RISK-CONTROL
(MONEY MANAGEMENT) RULES

24. *When trading is going badly:* (a) *reduce position size (keep in mind that positions in strongly correlated markets are similar to one larger position);* (b) *use tight stop-loss points;* (c) *slow up in taking new trades.*

25. *When trading is going badly, reduce risk exposure by liquidating losing trades, not winning trades.* This observation was memorably related by Edwin Lefèvre in *Reminiscences of a Stock Operator:* "I did precisely the wrong thing. The cotton showed me a loss and I kept it. The wheat showed me a profit and I sold it out. Of all the speculative blunders there are few greater than trying to average a losing game. Always sell what shows you a loss and keep what shows you a profit."

26. Be extremely careful not to change trading patterns after making a profit:

  a. Do not initiate any trades that would have been deemed too risky at the start of the trading program.

  b. Do not suddenly increase the number of shares or contracts in a typical trade. (However, a gradual increase as equity grows is okay.)

27. *Treat small positions with the same common sense as large positions.* Never say, "It's only 50 shares," or "It's only one or two contracts."

28. Avoid holding very large positions into major reports or the release of important government statistics.

29. Futures traders: Apply the same money management principles to spreads as to outright positions. It is easy to be lulled into thinking that spreads move gradually enough so that it is not necessary to worry about stop-loss protection.

30. Don't buy options without planning at what outright price the trade is to be liquidated.

HOLDING AND EXITING WINNING TRADES

31. Do not take small, quick profits in major position trades. In particular, if you are dramatically right on a trade, *never, never* take profits on the first day.

32. Don't be too hasty to get out of a trade with a gap in your direction. Use the gap as initial stop; then bring in stop in trailing fashion.

33. Try to use trailing stops, supplemented by developing market action, instead of objectives as a means of getting out of profitable trades. Using objectives will often work against fully realizing the potential of major trends. *Remember, you need the occasional big winners to offset losers.*

34. The preceding rule notwithstanding, it is still useful to set an initial objective at the time of trade entry to allow the application of the following rule: If a very large portion of an objective is realized very quickly (e.g., 50–60% in one week or 75–80% in two or three weeks), take partial profits, with the idea of reinstating liquidated shares or contracts on a reaction. The idea is that it is okay to take a quick *sizable* profit. Although this rule may often result in missing the remainder of the move on the liquidated portion of the position, holding the entire position, in such a case, can frequently lead to nervous liquidation on the first sharp retracement.

35. If an objective is reached, but you still like the trade, stay with it using a trailing stop. This rule is important in order to be able to ride a major trend. *Remember, patience is important not only in waiting for the right trades, but also in staying with trades that are working. The failure to adequately profit from correct trades is a key profit-limiting factor.*

36. One partial exception to the previous rule is that if you are *heavily* positioned and equity is surging straight up, consider taking

scale-up profits. Corollary rule: *When things look too good to be true—watch out!* If everything is going right, it is probably a good time to begin taking scale-up (or scale-down) profits and using close trailing stops on a portion of your positions.

37. If taking profits on a trade that is believed to still have long-term potential (but is presumably vulnerable to a near-term correction), have a game plan for reentering position. If the market doesn't retrace sufficiently to allow for reentry, be cognizant of patterns that can be used for timing a reentry. Don't let the fact that the reentry point would be worse than the exit point keep you from getting back into a trade in which the perception of both the long-term trend and current timing suggest reentering. *Inability to enter at a worse price can often lead to missing major portions of large trends.*

38. If trading larger positions, *avoid the emotional trap of wanting to be 100% right.* In other words, take only partial profits. Always try to keep at least a partial position for the duration of the move—until the market forms a convincing reversal pattern or reaches a meaningful stop-loss point.

MISCELLANEOUS PRINCIPLES AND RULES

39. *Always pay more attention to market action and evolving patterns than to objectives and support/resistance areas.* The latter can often cause you to reverse a correct market bias very prematurely.

40. When you feel action should be taken either entering or exiting a position—*act, don't procrastinate.*

41. Never go counter to your own opinion of the long-term trend of the market. In other words, don't try to dance between the raindrops.

42. Winning trades tend to be ahead right from the start.

43. Correct timing of entry and exit (e.g., timing entry on a reliable pattern, getting out immediately on the first sign of trade failure) can often keep a loss small even if the trade is dead wrong.

44. Intraday decisions are almost always losers. *Keep screen off intraday.*

45. Be sure to check markets before the close on Friday. Often the situation is clearer at the end of the week. In such cases, a better entry or exit can usually be obtained on Friday near the close

than on the following Monday opening. This rule is particularly important if you are holding a significant position.

46. Act on market dreams (that are recalled unambiguously). Such dreams are often right because they represent your subconscious market knowledge attempting to break through the barriers established by the conscious mind (e.g., "How can I buy here when I could have gone long $2,000 lower last week?")

47. *You are never immune to bad trading habits—the best you can do is to keep them latent. As soon as you get lazy or sloppy, they will return.*

MARKET PATTERNS

48. If the market sets new historical highs and holds, the odds strongly favor a move very far beyond the old highs. Selling a market at new record highs is probably one of the amateur trader's worst mistakes.

49. Narrow market consolidations near the upper end of broader trading ranges are bullish patterns. Similarly, narrow consolidations near the low end of trading ranges are bearish.

50. Play the breakout from an extended, narrow range with a stop against the other side of the range.

51. Breakouts from trading ranges that hold for one to two weeks, or longer, are among the most reliable technical indicators of impending trends.

52. A common and particularly useful form of the above rule is: Flags or pennants forming right above or below prior extended and broad trading ranges tend to be fairly reliable continuation patterns.

53. Trade in the direction of wide gaps.

54. Gaps out of congestion patterns, particularly one-to-two-month trading ranges, are often excellent signals. (This pattern works especially well in bear markets.)

55. If a "breakaway gap" is not filled during the first week, it should be viewed as a particularly reliable signal.

56. A breakout to new highs or lows followed within the next week or two by a gap (particularly a wide gap) back into the range is a particularly reliable form of a bull trap or bear trap.

57. If the market breaks out to a new high or low and then pulls back to form a flag or pennant in the prebreakout trading range, assume that a top or bottom is in place. A position can be taken using a protective stop beyond the flag or pennant consolidation.

58. A breakout from a trading range followed by a pullback deep into the range (e.g., three-quarters of the way back into the range or more) is yet another significant bull or bear trap formation.

59. If an apparent V bottom is followed by a nearby congestion pattern, it may represent a bottom pattern. However, if this consolidation is then broken on the downside and the V bottom is approached, the market action can be read as a sign of an impending move to new lows. In the latter case, short positions could be implemented using protective stops near the top of the consolidation. Analogous comments would apply to V tops followed by nearby consolidations.

60. V tops and V bottoms followed by multimonth consolidations that form in close proximity to the reversal point tend to be major top or bottom formations.

61. Tight flag and pennant consolidations tend to be reliable continuation patterns and allow entry into an existing trend, with a reasonably close, yet meaningful, stop point.

62. If a tight flag or pennant consolidation leads to a breakout in the wrong direction (i.e., a reversal instead of a continuation), expect the move to continue in the direction of the breakout.

63. Curved consolidations tend to suggest an accelerated move in the direction of the curve.

64. The breaking of a short-term curved consolidation (see Chapter 11) in the direction opposite of the curve pathway tends to be a good trend reversal signal.

65. Wide-ranging days (i.e., days with a range far exceeding the recent average range) with a close counter to the main trend usually tend to provide a reliable early signal of a trend change—particularly if they also trigger a reversal signal (e.g., filling of a runaway gap, complete penetration of prior consolidation).

66. Near-vertical, large price moves over a period of two to four days (coming off a relative high or low) tend to be extended in the following weeks.

67. Spikes are good short-term reversal signals. The extreme of the spike can be used as a stop point.

68. In spike situations, look at chart both ways—with and without spike. For example, if when a spike is removed a flag is evident, a penetration of that flag is a meaningful signal.

69. The filling-in of a runaway gap can be viewed as evidence of a possible trend reversal.

70. An island reversal followed shortly thereafter with a pullback into the most recent trading range or consolidation pattern represents a possible major top (or bottom) signal.

71. The ability of a stock or future to hold relatively firm when other related markets are under significant pressure can be viewed as a sign of intrinsic strength. Similarly, a market acting weak when related markets are strong can be viewed as a bearish sign.

72. If a market trades consistently higher for most of the daily trading session, anticipate a close in the same direction.

73. Two successive flags with little separation can be viewed as a probable continuation pattern.

74. View a curved bottom, followed by a shallower, same-direction curved consolidation near the top of this pattern, as a bullish formation ("cup-and-handle"). A similar pattern would apply to market tops.

75. Moderate sentiment in a market that is strongly trending may be a more reliable indicator of a probable continuation of the price move than a high or low sentiment reading is of a reversal. In other words, extreme sentiment readings can often occur in the absence of major tops and bottoms, but major tops and bottoms rarely occur in the absence of extreme sentiment readings (current or recent).

76. A failed signal is more reliable than the original signal. Go the other way, using the high (or low) before the failed signal as a stop. Some examples of such failure patterns are rule numbers 56, 57, 58, 62, 64, and 69.

77. The failure of a market to follow through on significant bullish or bearish news (e.g., an important earnings reporter or a major U.S. Department of Agriculture report) is often a harbinger of an imminent trend reversal. Pay particular attention to such a development if you have an existing position.

ANALYSIS AND REVIEW

78. Review charts every day—especially if you're too busy.

79. Periodically review long-term charts (e.g., every two to four weeks).

80. Religiously maintain a *trader's diary*, including a chart for each trade taken and noting the following: reasons for trade; intended stop and objective (if any); follow-up at a later point indicating how the trade turned out; observations and lessons (mistakes, things done right, or noteworthy patterns); and net profit or loss. It is important that the trade sheet be filled out when the trade is entered so that the reasons for the trade accurately reflect your actual thinking rather than a reconstruction.

81. Maintain a *patterns chart book* whenever you notice a market pattern that is interesting and you want to note how you think it will turn out, or you want to record how that pattern is eventually resolved (in the case where you don't have any bias concerning the correct interpretation). Be sure to follow each chart up at a later date to see the actual outcome. Over time, this process may improve skills in chart interpretation by providing some statistical evidence of the forecasting reliability of various chart patterns (as recognized in real time).

82. Review and update trading rules, trader's diary, and patterns chart book on a regular schedule (e.g., three-month rotation for the three items). Of course, any of these items can be reviewed more frequently, whenever it is felt such a review would be useful.

Market Wiz(ar)dom

There is no such thing as being right or beating the market. If you make money, it is because you understood the same thing the market did. If you lose money, it is simply because you got it wrong. There is no other way of looking at it.

—Musawer Mansoor Ijaz

The previous chapter detailed specific trading rules and market observations. This chapter, which has been adapted from *The New Market Wizards*,* examines the broad principles and psychological factors that are crucial to trading success.

The methods employed by exceptional traders are extraordinarily diverse: Some are pure fundamentalists; others employ only technical analysis, and still others combine the two methodologies. Some traders consider two days to be long-term, while others consider two months to be short-term. Yet despite the wide gamut of styles, I have found that certain principles hold true for a broad spectrum of successful traders. After a score of years analyzing and trading the markets and two books of interviews with great traders, I have come down to the following list of 42 observations regarding success in trading.

1. *First Things First.* First, be sure that you really want to trade. It is common for people who think they want to trade to discover that they really don't.

2. *Examine Your Motives.* Think about why you really want to trade. If you want to trade for the excitement, you might be better off

*The New Market Wizards, Jack Schwager, Harper Business, New York, 1989, pp. 461–478; copyright © 1989 by HarperCollins Publishers; by permission.

riding a roller coaster or taking up hang gliding. In my own case, I found that the underlying motive for trading was serenity or peace of mind—hardly the emotional state typical of trading. Another personal motive for trading was that I loved puzzle solving—and the markets provided the ultimate puzzle. However, while I enjoyed the cerebral aspects of market analysis, I didn't particularly like the visceral characteristics of trading itself. The contrast between my motives and the activity resulted in very obvious conflicts. You need to examine your own motives very carefully for any such conflicts. The market is a stern master. You need to do almost everything right to win. If parts of you are pulling in opposite directions, the game is lost before you start.

How did I resolve my own conflict? I decided to focus completely on mechanical trading approaches in order to eliminate the emotionality in trading. Equally important, focusing on the design of mechanical systems directed my energies to the part of trading I did enjoy—the puzzle-solving aspects. Although I had devoted some energy to mechanical systems for these reasons for a number of years, I eventually came to the realization that I wanted to move in this direction exclusively. (This is not intended as an advocacy for mechanical systems over human-decision-oriented approaches. I am only providing a personal example. The appropriate answer for another trader could well be very different.)

3. *Match the Trading Method to Your Personality.* It is critical to choose a method that is consistent with your own personality and comfort level. If you can't stand to give back significant profits, then a long-term trend-following approach—even a very good one—will be a disaster, because you will never be able to follow it. If you don't want to watch the quote screen all day (or can't), don't try a day trading method. If you can't stand the emotional strain of making trading decisions, then try to develop a mechanical system for trading the markets. The approach you use must be right for you; it must feel comfortable. The importance of this concept cannot be overemphasized. Randy McKay, who met success as both an on-the-floor and off-the-floor trader, asserted: "Virtually every successful trader I know ultimately ended up with a trading style suited to his personality."

Incidentally, the mismatch of trading style and personality is one of the key reasons why purchased trading systems rarely make profits for those who buy them, even if the system is a good one. While the odds of getting a winning system are small—certainly less than 50–50—the odds of getting a system that fits your personality are smaller still. I'll leave it to your imagination to decide on the odds of buying a profitable/moderate risk system and using it effectively.

4. *It Is Absolutely Necessary to Have an Edge.* You can't win without an edge, even with the world's greatest discipline and money management skills. If you could, then it would be possible to win at roulette (over the long run) using perfect discipline and risk control. Of course, that is an impossible task because of the laws of probability. If you don't have an edge, all that money management and discipline will do for you is to guarantee that you will bleed to death gradually. Incidentally, if you don't know what your edge is, you don't have one.

5. *Derive a Method.* To have an edge, you must have a method. The type of method is irrelevant. Some of the supertraders are pure fundamentalists; some are pure technicians; and some are hybrids. Even within each group, there are tremendous variations. For example, within the group of technicians, there are tape readers (or their modern-day equivalent, screen watchers), chartists, mechanical system traders, Elliott Wave analysts, Gann analysts, and so on. The type of method is not important, but having one is critical—and, of course, the method must have an edge.

6. *Developing a Method Is Hard Work.* Shortcuts rarely lead to trading success. Developing your own approach requires research, observation, and thought. Expect the process to take lots of time and hard work. Expect many dead ends and multiple failures before you find a successful trading approach that is right for you. Remember that you are playing against tens of thousands of professionals. Why should you be any better? If it were that easy, there would be a lot more millionaire traders.

7. *Skill versus Hard Work.* Is trading success dependent on innate skills, or is hard work sufficient? There is no question in my mind that many of the supertraders have a special talent for trading. Marathon running provides an appropriate analogy. Virtually any healthy person can run a marathon, given sufficient commitment and hard work. Yet, regardless of the effort and desire, only a small fraction of the population will ever be able to run a 2:12 marathon. Similarly, almost anyone can learn to play a musical instrument. But again, regardless of work and dedication, only a handful of individuals possess the natural talent to become concert soloists. The general rule is that exceptional performance requires both natural talent and hard work to realize its potential. If the innate skill is lacking, hard work may provide proficiency, but not excellence.

In my opinion, the same principles apply to trading. Virtually anyone can become a net profitable trader, but only a few have the inborn talent to become supertraders. For this reason, it may be possible to teach trading success, but only up to a point. Be realistic in your goals.

8. *Good Trading Should Be Effortless.* Wait a minute. Didn't I just list hard work as an ingredient to successful trading? How can good trading require hard work and yet be effortless?

There is no contradiction. Hard work refers to the preparatory process—the research and observation necessary to become a good trader—not to the trading itself. In this respect, hard work is associated with such qualities as vision, creativity, persistence, drive, desire, and commitment. Hard work certainly does not mean that the process of trading itself should be filled with exertion. It certainly does not imply struggling with or fighting against the markets. On the contrary, the more effortless and natural the trading process, the better the chances for success. One trader quoting *Zen and the Art of Archery* made the following analogy: "In trading, just as in archery, whenever there is effort, force, straining, struggling, or trying, it's wrong. You're out of sync; you're out of harmony with the market. The perfect trade is one that requires no effort."

Visualize a world-class distance runner clicking off mile after mile at a five-minute pace. Now picture an out-of-shape, 250-pound couch potato trying to run a mile at a 10-minute pace. The professional runner glides along gracefully—almost effortlessly—despite the long distance and fast pace. The out-of-shape runner, however, is likely to struggle, huffing and puffing like a Yugo going up a 1% grade. Who is putting in more work and effort? Who is more successful? Of course, the world-class runner puts in hard work during training, and this prior effort and commitment are essential to his or her success.

9. *Money Management and Risk Control.* Almost all the great traders I interviewed felt that money management was even more important than the trading method. Many potentially successful systems or trading approaches have led to disaster because the trader applying the strategy lacked a method of controlling risk. You don't have to be a mathematician or understand portfolio theory to manage risk. Risk control can be as easy as the following three-step approach:

1. Never risk more than 1% to 2% of your capital on any trade. (Depending on your approach, a modestly higher number might still be reasonable. However, I would strongly advise against anything over 5%.)

2. Predetermine your exit point before you get into a trade. Many of the traders I interviewed cited exactly this rule.

3. If you lose a certain predetermined amount of your starting capital (e.g., 10% to 20%), take a breather, analyze what went wrong, and

wait until you feel confident and have a high-probability idea before you begin trading again. For traders with large accounts, trading very small is a reasonable alternative to a complete trading hiatus. The strategy of cutting trading size down sharply during losing streaks is one mentioned by many of the traders I interviewed.

10. *The Trading Plan.* Trying to win in the markets without a trading plan is like trying to build a house without blueprints—costly (and avoidable) mistakes are virtually inevitable. A trading plan simply requires combining a personal trading method with specific money management and trade entry rules. Robert Krausz, a hypnotist who has made a specialty of working with traders, considers the absence of a trading plan the root of all the principal difficulties traders encounter in the markets. Richard Driehaus, a very successful mutual fund manager I interviewed, stresses that a trading plan should reflect a personal core philosophy. He explains that without a core philosophy, you are not going to be able to hold on to your positions or stick with your trading plan during really difficult times.

11. *Discipline.* "Discipline" was probably the most frequent word used by the exceptional traders that I interviewed. Often, it was mentioned in an almost apologetic tone: "I know you've heard this a million times before, but believe me, it's really important."

There are two basic reasons why discipline is critical. First, it is a prerequisite for maintaining effective risk control. Second, you need discipline to apply your method without second-guessing and choosing which trades to take, as you will almost always pick the wrong ones. Why? Because you will tend to pick the comfortable trades, and as Bill Eckhardt, a mathematician turned successful commodity trading advisor (CTA), explained, "What feels good is often the wrong thing to do."

As a final word on this subject, remember that you are never immune to bad trading habits; the best you can do is to keep them latent. As soon as you get lazy or sloppy, they will return.

12. *Understanding That You Are Responsible.* Whether you win or lose, you are responsible for your own results. Even if you lost on your broker's tip, an advisory service recommendation, or a bad signal from the system you bought, you are responsible because you made the decision to listen and act. I have never met a successful trader who blamed others for his or her losses.

13. *The Need for Independence.* You need to do your own thinking. Don't get caught up in mass hysteria. Ed Seykota, a futures trader who multiplied the equity in his accounts a thousandfold over an 18-year period, pointed out that by the time a story is making the cover of national periodicals, the trend is probably near an end.

Independence also means making your own trading decisions. Never listen to other opinions. Even if it occasionally helps on a trade or two, listening to others seems to end up invariably costing you money—not to mention confusing your own market view. As Michael Marcus, a very successful futures trader, stated in *Market Wizards*, "You need to follow your own light. If you combine two traders, you will get the worst of each."

A related personal anecdote concerns another trader I interviewed in *Market Wizards*. Although he could trade better than I if he were blindfolded and placed in a trunk at the bottom of a pool, he still was interested in my view of the markets. One day he called and asked, "What do you think of the yen?"

The yen was one of the few markets about which I had a strong opinion at the time. It had formed a particular chart pattern that made me very bearish. "I think the yen is going straight down, and I'm short," I replied.

He proceeded to give me 51 reasons why the yen was oversold and due for a rally. After he hung up, I thought: "I'm leaving on a business trip tomorrow. My trading has not been going very well during the past few weeks. The short yen trade is one of the only positions in my account. Do I really want to fade one of the world's best traders given these considerations?" I decided to close out the trade.

By the time I returned from my trip several days later, the yen had fallen 150 points. As luck would have it, that afternoon the same trader called. When the conversation rolled around to the yen, I couldn't resist asking, "By the way, are you still long the yen?"

"Oh no," he replied, "I'm short."

The point is not that this trader was trying to mislead me. On the contrary, he firmly believed each market opinion at the time he expressed it. However, his timing was good enough so that he probably made money on both sides of the trade. In contrast, I ended up with nothing, even though I had the original move pegged exactly right. The moral is that even advice from a much better trader can lead to detrimental results.

14. *Confidence.* An unwavering confidence in their ability to continue to win in the markets was a nearly universal characteristic among the traders I interviewed. Dr. Van Tharp, a psychologist who has done a great deal of research on traders and was interviewed in *Market Wizards*, claims that one of the basic traits of winning traders is that they believe "they've won the game before the start."

The trader who has confidence will have the courage to make the right decisions and the strength not to panic. There is a passage in Mark Twain's *Life on the Mississippi* that I find remarkably apropos, even though it has nothing to do with trading. In it, the author-protagonist—an apprentice steamboat river pilot—is tricked by his mentor and the crew into panicking in a stretch of river he *knows* to be the easiest in the entire run. The following exchange then ensues with his mentor:

"Didn't you know there was no bottom in that crossing?"
"Yes sir, I did."
"Very well then, you shouldn't have allowed me or anybody else to shake your confidence in that knowledge. Try to remember that. And another thing, when you get into a dangerous place, don't turn coward. That isn't going to help matters any."

15. *Losing Is Part of the Game.* The great traders fully realize that losing is an intrinsic element in the game of trading. This attitude seems linked to confidence. Because exceptional traders are confident that they will win over the long run, individual losing trades no longer seem horrible; they simply appear inevitable—which is what they are. As Linda Raschke, a futures trader with a particularly high ratio of winning to losing trades, explained, "It never bothered me to lose, because I always knew I would make it right back."

There is no more certain recipe for losing than having a fear of losing. If you can't stand taking losses, you will end up either taking large losses or missing great trading opportunities. Either flaw is sufficient to sink any chance for success.

16. *Lack of Confidence and Time-Outs.* Trade only when you feel confident and optimistic. I have often heard traders say: "I just can't seem to do anything right." Or, "I bet I get stopped out right near the low again." If you find yourself thinking in such negative terms, it is a sure sign that it is time to take a break from trading. Get back into trading slowly. Think of trading as a cold ocean. Test the water before plunging in.

17. *The Urge to Seek Advice.* The urge to seek advice betrays a lack of confidence. As Linda Raschke said, "If you ever find yourself tempted to seek out someone else's opinion on a trade, that's usually a sure sign that you should get out of your position."

18. *The Virtue of Patience.* Waiting for the right opportunity increases the probability of success. You don't always have to be in the market. As Edwin Lefèvre put it in his classic *Reminiscences of a Stock Operator*, "There is the plain fool who does the wrong thing at all times anywhere, but there is the Wall Street fool who thinks he must trade all the time."

One of the more colorful descriptions of patience in trading was offered by well-known investor Jim Rogers in *Market Wizards*: "I just wait until there is money lying in the corner, and all I have to do is go over there and pick it up." In other words, until he is so sure of a trade that it seems as easy as picking money off the floor, he does nothing.

Mark Weinstein, a phenomenally consistent futures and stock trader (also interviewed in *Market Wizards*), provided the following apt analogy: "Although the cheetah is the fastest animal in the world and can catch any animal on the plains, it will wait until it is absolutely sure it can catch its prey. It may hide in the bush for a week, waiting for just the right moment. It will wait for a baby antelope, and not just any baby antelope, but preferably one that is also sick or lame. Only then, when there is no chance it can lose its prey, does it attack. That, to me, is the epitome of professional trading."

19. *The Importance of Sitting.* Patience is important not only in waiting for the right trades, but also in staying with trades that are working. The failure to adequately profit from correct trades is a key profit-limiting factor. Quoting again from Lefèvre in *Reminiscences*, "It never was my thinking that made big money for me. It was always my sitting. Got that? My sitting tight!" Bill Eckhardt offered a particularly memorable comment on this subject: "One common adage . . . that is completely wrongheaded is: You can't go broke taking profits. That's precisely how many traders *do* go broke. While amateurs go broke by taking large losses, professionals go broke by taking small profits."

20. *Developing a Low-Risk Idea.* One of the exercises Dr. Van Tharp uses in his seminars is having the participants take the time to write down their ideas on low-risk trades. The merit of a low-risk idea is that it combines two essential elements: patience (because only a small portion of ideas will qualify) and risk control (inherent in the definition). Taking the time to think through low-risk strategies is a useful exercise for all traders. The specific ideas will vary greatly from trader to trader, depending on the markets traded and methodologies used. At the seminar I attended, the participants came up with a long list of descriptions of low-risk ideas. As one example: a trade in which the market movement required to provide convincing proof that you are wrong is small. Although it had nothing to do with trading, my personal favorite of the low-risk ideas mentioned was: "Open a doughnut shop next door to a police station."

21. *The Importance of Varying Bet Size.* All traders who win consistently over the long run have an edge. However, that edge may vary significantly from trade to trade. It can be mathematically demonstrated that in any wager game with varying probabilities, winnings are maximized by adjusting the bet size in accordance with the perceived chance for a successful outcome. Optimal blackjack betting strategy provides a perfect illustration of this concept.

If the trader has some idea as to which trades have a greater edge—say, for example, based on a higher confidence level (assuming that it is a reliable indicator)—then it makes sense to be more aggressive in these situations. As Stanley Druckenmiller, a highly profitable hedge fund manager, expresses it, "The way to build [superior] long-term returns is through preservation of capital and home runs. . . . When you have tremendous conviction on a trade, you have to go for the jugular. It takes courage to be a pig." For a number of Market Wizards, keen judgment as to when to really step on the accelerator and the courage to do so have been instrumental to their achieving exceptional (as opposed to merely good) returns.

Some of the traders I interviewed mentioned that they varied their trading size in accordance with how they were doing. For example, McKay indicated that it was not uncommon for him to vary his position size by as much as a factor of 100 to one. He finds this approach helps him reduce risk during losing periods while enhancing profits during the winning periods.

22. *Scaling In and Out of Trades.* You don't have to get in or out of a position all at once. Scaling in and out of positions provides the flexibility of fine-tuning trades and broadens the set of alternative choices. Most traders sacrifice this flexibility without a second thought because of the innate human desire to be completely right. (By definition, a scaling approach means that some portions of a trade will be entered or exited at worse prices than other portions.) Some traders also noted that scaling enabled them to stay with at least a portion of long-term winning trades much longer than would otherwise have been the case.

23. *Being Right Is More Important than Being a Genius.* I think one reason why so many people try to pick tops and bottoms is that they want to prove to the world how smart they are. Think about winning rather than being a hero. Forget trying to judge trading success by how close you can come to picking major tops and bottoms, but rather by how well you can pick individual trades with favorable return/risk characteristics. Go for consistency on a trade-to-trade basis, not perfect trades.

24. *Don't Worry about Looking Stupid.* Last week you told everyone at the office, "My analysis has just given me a great buy signal in the S&P. The market is going to a new high." Now as you examine the market action since then, something appears to be wrong. Instead of rallying, the market is breaking down. Your gut tells you that the market is vulnerable. Whether you realize it or not, your announced prognostications are going to color your objectivity. Why? Because you don't want to look stupid after telling the world that the market was going to a new high. Consequently, you are likely to view the market's action in the most favorable light possible. "The market isn't breaking down; it's just a pullback to knock out the weak longs." As a result of this type of rationalization, you end up holding a losing position far too long. There is an easy solution to this problem: Don't talk about your position.

What if your job requires talking about your market opinions (as mine does)? Here the rule is: Whenever you start worrying about contradicting your previous opinion, view that concern as reinforcement to reverse your market stance. As a personal example, in early 1991 I came to the conclusion that the dollar had formed a major bottom. I specifically remember one talk in which an audience member asked me about my outlook for currencies. I responded by boldly predicting that the dollar would head higher for years. Several months later, when the dollar surrendered the entire gain it had realized following the news of the August 1991 Soviet coup before the coup's failure was confirmed, I sensed that something was wrong. I recalled my many predictions over the preceding months in which I had stated that the dollar would go up for years. The discomfort and embarrassment I felt about these previous forecasts told me it was time to change my opinion.

In my earlier years in the business, I invariably tried to rationalize my original market opinion in such situations. I was burned enough times that I eventually learned a lesson. In the preceding example, the abandonment of my original projection was fortunate, because the dollar collapsed in the ensuing months.

25. *Sometimes Action Is More Important than Prudence.* Waiting for a price correction to enter the market may sound prudent, but it is often the wrong thing to do. When your analysis, methodology, or gut tells you to get into a trade at the market instead of waiting for a correction, do so. Caution against the influence of knowing that you could have gotten in at a better price in recent sessions, particularly in those situations when the market witnesses a sudden, large move (often due to an important surprise news item). If you don't feel the market is going to correct, that consideration is irrelevant. These types of trades often work because they are so hard to do.

26. *Catching Part of the Move Is Just Fine.* Just because you missed the first major portion of a new trend, don't let that keep you from trading with that trend (as long as you can define a reasonable stop-loss point). McKay commented that the easiest part of a trend is the middle portion, which implies always missing part of the trend prior to entry.

27. *Maximize Gains, Not the Number of Wins.* Eckhardt explains that human nature does not operate to maximize gain but rather the chance of a gain. The problem with this is that it implies a lack of focus on the magnitudes of gains (and losses)—a flaw that leads to nonoptimal performance results. Eckhardt bluntly concludes: "The success rate of trades is the least important performance statistic and may even be inversely related to performance." Jeff Yass, a very successful options trader, echoes a similar theme: "The basic concept that applies to both poker and option trading is that the primary object is not winning the most hands, but rather maximizing your gains."

28. *Learn to Be Disloyal.* Loyalty may be a virtue in family, friends, and pets, but it is a fatal flaw for a trader. Never have loyalty to a position. Novice traders will have lots of loyalty to their original positions, ignoring signs of being on the wrong side of the market, and riding a trade into a large loss while hoping for the best. More experienced traders, having learned the importance of money management, will exit quickly once it is apparent they have made a bad trade. However, truly skilled traders will be able to do a 180-degree turn, *reversing* a position at a loss if market behavior points to such a course of action. Druckenmiller made the awful error of reversing his stock position from short to long on the very day before the October 19, 1987, crash. His ability to quickly recognize his error and, more important, to unhesitatingly act on that realization by reversing back to short at a large loss helped transform a potentially disastrous month into a net profitable one.

29. *Pull Out Partial Profits.* Pull a portion of winnings out of the market to prevent trading discipline from deteriorating into complacency. It is far too easy to rationalize overtrading and procrastination in liquidating losing trades by saying, "It's only profits." Profits withdrawn from an account are much more likely to be viewed as real money.

30. *Hope Is a Four-Letter Word.* Hope is a dirty word for a trader, not only in regard to procrastinating in a losing position, hoping the market will come back, but also in terms of hoping for a reaction that will allow for a better entry in a missed trade. If such trades are good, the hoped-for reaction will not materialize until it is too late. Often the only way to enter such trades is to do so as soon as a reasonable stop-loss point can be identified.

31. *Don't Do the Comfortable Thing.* Eckhardt offers the rather provocative proposition that the human tendency to select comfortable choices will lead most people to experience worse than random results. In effect, he is saying that natural human traits lead to such poor trading decisions that most people would be better off flipping coins or throwing darts. Some of the examples Eckhardt cites of the comfortable choices people tend to make that run counter to sound trading principles include gambling with losses, locking in sure winners, selling on strength and buying on weakness, and designing (or buying) trading systems that have been overfitted to past price behavior. The implied message to the trader is: Do what is right, not what feels comfortable.

32. *You Can't Win If You Have to Win.* There is an old Wall Street adage: "Scared money never wins." The reason is quite simple: If you are risking money you can't afford to lose, all the emotional pitfalls of trading will be magnified. Early in his career, when the bankruptcy of a key financial backer threatened the survival of his fledgling investment firm, Druckenmiller "bet the ranch" on one trade in a last-ditch effort to save his firm. Even though he came within one week of picking the absolute bottom in the T-bill market, he still lost all his money. The need to win fosters trading errors (e.g., excessive leverage and a lack of planning in the example just cited). The market seldom tolerates the carelessness associated with trades born of desperation.

33. *Think Twice When the Market Lets You Off the Hook Easily.* Don't be too eager to get out of a position you have been worried about if the market allows you to exit at a much better price than anticipated. If you had been worried about an adverse overnight (or over-the-weekend) price move because of a news event or a technical price failure on the previous close, it is likely that many other traders shared this concern. The fact that the market does not follow through much on these fears strongly suggests that there must be some very powerful underlying forces in favor of the direction of the original position. This concept, which was first proposed in *Market Wizards* by Marty Schwartz, who compiled an astounding track record trading stock index futures, was illustrated by the manner in which Bill Lipschutz, a large-scale currency trader, exited the one trade he admitted had scared him. In that instance, on Friday afternoon, a time when the currency markets are particularly thin (after Europe's close), Lipschutz found himself with an enormous short dollar position in the midst of a strongly rallying market. He had to wait over the weekend for the Tokyo opening on Sunday evening to find sufficient liquidity to exit his position. When the dollar opened weaker than expected in Tokyo, he didn't just dump his position in relief; rather, his trader's instincts told him to delay liquidation—a decision that resulted in a far better exit price.

34. *A Mind Is a Terrible Thing to Close.* Open-mindedness seems to be a common trait among those who excel at trading. For example, Gil Blake, a mutual fund timer who has made incredibly consistent profits, actually fell into a trading career by attempting to demonstrate to a friend that prices were random. When he realized he was wrong, he became a trader. In the words of Driehaus, "The mind is like a parachute—it's only good when it's open."

35. *The Markets Are an Expensive Place to Look for Excitement.* Excitement has a lot to do with the image of trading, but nothing to do with success in trading (except in an inverse sense). In *Market Wizards*, Larry Hite, the founder of Mint Management, one of the largest CTA firms, described his conversation with a friend who couldn't understand his absolute adherence to a computerized trading system. His friend asked, "Larry, how can you trade the way you do? Isn't it boring?" Larry replied, "I don't trade for excitement; I trade to win."

36. *The Calm State of a Trader.* If there is an emotional state associated with successful trading, it is the antithesis of excitement. Based on his observations, Charles Faulkner, a Neuro-Linguistic Programming (NLP) practitioner who works with traders, stated that exceptional traders are able to remain calm and detached regardless of what the markets are doing. He describes Peter Steidlmayer's (a successful futures trader who is best known as the inventor of the Market Profile trading technique) response to a position that is going against him as being typified by the thought, "Hmmm, look at that."

37. *Identify and Eliminate Stress.* Stress in trading is a sign that something is wrong. If you feel stress, think about the cause, and then act to eliminate the problem. For example, let's say you determine that the greatest source of stress is indecision in getting out of a losing position. One way to solve this problem is simply to enter a protective stop order every time you put on a position.

I will give you a personal example. An element of one of my former jobs was to provide trading recommendations to brokers in my company. This task is very similar to trading, and, having done both, I believe it's actually more difficult than trading. At one point, after years of net profitable recommendations, I hit a bad streak. I just couldn't do anything right. When I was right about the direction of the market, my buy recommendation was just a bit too low (or my sell price too high). When I got in and the direction was right, I got stopped out—frequently within a few ticks of the extreme of the reaction.

I responded by developing a range of computerized trading programs and technical indicators, thereby widely diversifying the trading advice I provided to the firm. I still made my day-to-day subjective calls on the market, but everything was no longer riding on the accuracy of these recommendations. By widely diversifying the trading-related advice and information, and transferring much of this load to mechanical approaches, I was able to greatly diminish a source of personal stress—and improve the quality of the research product in the process.

38. *Pay Attention to Intuition.* As I see it, intuition is simply experience that resides in the subconscious mind. The objectivity of the market analysis done by the conscious mind can be compromised by all sorts of extraneous considerations (e.g., one's current market position, a resistance to change a previous forecast). The subconscious, however, is not inhibited by such constraints. Unfortunately, we can't readily tap into our subconscious thoughts. However, when they come through as intuition, the trader needs to pay attention. As the Zen-quoting trader mentioned earlier expressed it, "The trick is to differentiate between what you *want* to happen and what you *know* will happen."

39. *Life's Mission and Love of the Endeavor.* In talking to the traders interviewed in *Market Wizards*, I had the definite sense that many of them felt that trading was what they were meant to do—in essence, their mission in life. In this context, Charles Faulkner quoted NLP cofounder John Grinder's description of mission: "What do you love so much that you would pay to do it?" Throughout my interviews, I was struck by the exuberance and love the Market Wizards had for trading. Many used game-like analogies to describe trading. This type of love for the endeavor may indeed be an essential element for success.

40. *The Elements of Achievement.* Faulkner has a list of six key steps to achievement based on Gary Faris's study of successfully rehabilitated athletes, which appears to apply equally well to the goal of achieving trading success. These strategies are:

1. Using both "Toward" and "Away From" motivation.
2. Having a goal of full capability plus, with anything less being unacceptable.

3. Breaking down potentially overwhelming goals into chunks, with satisfaction garnered from the completion of each individual step.

4. Keeping full concentration on the present moment—that is, the single task at hand rather than the long-term goal.

5. Being personally involved in achieving goals (as opposed to depending on others).

6. Making self-to-self comparisons to measure progress.

41. *Prices Are Nonrandom = The Markets Can Be Beat.* In reference to academicians who believe market prices are random, Monroe Trout, a CTA with one of the best risk/return records in the industry, says, "That's probably why they're professors and why I'm making money doing what I'm doing." The debate over whether prices are random is not yet over. However, my experience in interviewing scores of great traders left me with little doubt that the random walk theory is wrong. It is not the magnitude of the winnings registered by the Market Wizards, but the consistency of these winnings in some cases, that underpins my belief. As a particularly compelling example, consider Blake's 25:1 ratio of winning to losing months and his average annual return of 45% compared with a worst drawdown of only 5%. It is hard to imagine that results this lopsided could occur purely by chance—perhaps in a universe filled with traders, but not in their more finite numbers. Certainly, winning at the market is not easy—and, in fact, it is getting more difficult as professionals account for a constantly growing proportion of the activity—but it can be done!

42. *Keep Trading in Perspective.* There is more to life than trading.

Additional Concepts and Formulas

T his chapter contains miscellaneous definitions and formulas too involved to discuss at great length in the body of the book. Most of these are more sophisticated versions of concepts presented elsewhere in the text. They offer opportunities for additional study for traders seeking to move beyond the basics.

REACTION COUNT

This is a trend reentry technique similar to the one outlined in Chapter 8 in the "Reversal of a Minor Reaction" section. A "reaction" is identified whenever the reaction count reaches 4. The reaction count is initially set to 0. In a rising market, the count would be raised to 1 any day in which the high and low were equal to or lower than the corresponding points on the day on which the high of the move was set. The count would be increased by 1 each day the high and low are equal to or lower than the high and low of the most recent day on which the count was increased. The count would be reset to 0 anytime the market moved to new highs. Analogous conditions would apply to a declining market.

The resumption of the major trend would be indicated whenever the *thrust count* reached 3. The thrust count would initially be set to 0 and would begin being monitored after a reaction was defined. In the case of a reaction in a rising market, the thrust count would increase by 1 on each upthrust day and would be reset to 0 anytime the reaction low was penetrated. Once a signal was received, the reaction low could be used as a stop-loss reference point. For example, the position might be liquidated anytime the market closed below the reaction low. Once again, an analogous set of conditions could be used for defining a resumption of the trend in a declining market.

Figure A.1 illustrates the reversal of minor reaction approach using the specific definitions just detailed. The points at which reactions are defined are denoted by the symbol RD, with the numbers prior to these points indicating the reaction count values. Buy signals are indicated at the points at which the thrust count equals 3, with the letters prior to these points indicating the thrust count values. For any given entry point, stop-loss liquidation would be signaled by a close below the most recent stop level, which in the example provided occurs in January 1995. Note that the last RD point is never followed by a buy signal because the market closes below the most recent stop level before the thrust count can build.

RELATIVE STRENGTH INDEX (RSI)

The RSI belongs to that group of technical indicators known as momentum oscillators (see Chapter 6). Welles Wilder Jr. introduced the RSI in

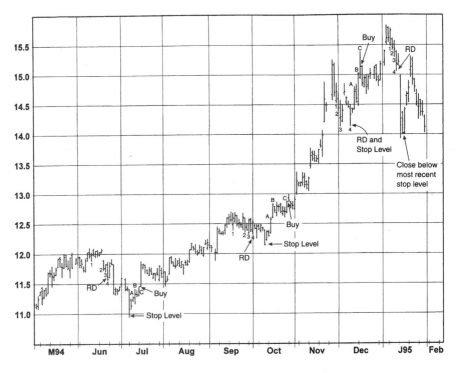

FIGURE A.1   Reversal of minor reaction: March 1995 Sugar.

his 1978 book *New Concepts in Technical Trading Systems* (Trend Research). The formula is:

$$RSI = 100 - [100/(1 + RS)]$$

where

RS = Relative strength = the average of the up closes over the calculation period divided by the average of the down closes over the calculation period

Relative strength (RS) is the key calculation in the formula. The rest of the math simply normalizes the scale of the RSI to a constant range of zero to 100.

The RS for a 14-day period is calculated by dividing the 14-day up close average by the 14-day down close average. "Up closes" and "down closes" refer to the absolute change in price from close to close (a one-day momentum calculation). For example, if today's close is higher than yesterday's close, today is an "up" day, and the difference between the two closes becomes the up close amount for the day. If today's close is lower than yesterday's close, today is a "down" day and the absolute value of the difference of the closes becomes today's down day figure. If a 14-day period contains eight up closes and six down closes, the gains for the eight up days are summed and divided by 14, as are the losses for the six down days (again, the absolute values of the down day figures are used, not negative numbers). In effect, the up close value for a day that closed lower than the previous day is zero, and vice versa. RS is the average up close figure divided by the average down close figure; it is plugged into the formula above to generate the RSI. (Wilder also used an additional smoothing method to simplify continued RSI calculations after the initial period.)

Examples of the RSI appear in Chapters 6 and 10.

RUN DAYS

A *run day* is a strongly trending day. Essentially, a run day is a more powerful version of a thrust day (see Chapter 5), although it is possible for a run day to fail to meet the thrust day condition. Run days are defined as follows.

Up Run Day

An *up run day* meets the following two conditions:

1. The true high of the run day is greater than the maximum true high of the past N days (e.g., $N = 5$).
2. The true low on the run day is less than the minimum true low on the subsequent N days.

Down Run Day

A *down run day* that meets the following two conditions:

1. The true low of the run day is less than the minimum true low of the past N days.
2. The true high on the run day is greater than the maximum true high on the subsequent N days.

(*Note:* See "True Range and Average True Range" section later in the Appendix for definitions of the true high and true low.)

As can be seen by these definitions, run days cannot be defined until N days after their occurrence. Also, note that although most run days are also thrust days, it is possible for the run day conditions to be met on a day that is not a thrust day. For example, it is entirely possible for a day's low to be lower than the past five-day low, its high to be higher than the subsequent five-day high, and its close to be *higher* than the previous day's low.

Figures A.2 and A.3 provide examples of run days (based on a definition of $N = 5$). As can be seen, run days tend to occur when the market is in a trend run—hence the name. The materialization of up run days, particularly in clusters, can be viewed as evidence that the market is in a bullish phase (see Figure A.2). Similarly, a predominance of down run days provides evidence that the market is in a bearish state (see Figure A.3).

SPIKE DAY FORMULA

Spike days, as discussed in Chapter 5, are easy to understand and identify on price charts. It also is possible, though, to construct a mathematically precise definition for them. An example of such a definition for a spike

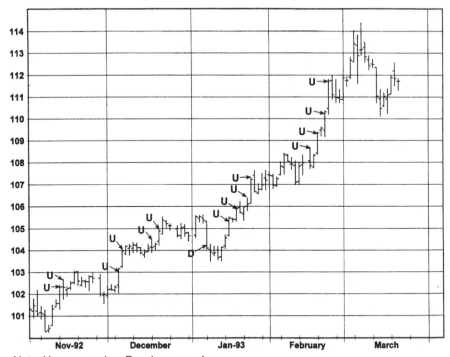

Note: U = up run day; D = down run day.

FIGURE A.2 Run days in bull market: March 1993 T-Bond.

high might be a day that fulfilled all of the following conditions (the definition for a spike low day would be analogous):

1. $H_t - \text{Max}(H_{t-1}, H_{t+1}) > k \cdot \text{ADTR}$

where

H_t = high on given day

H_{t-1} = high on preceding day

H_{t+1} = high on succeeding day

k = multiplicative factor that must be defined (e.g., $k = 0.75$)

ADTR = average daily true range during past 10 days (see "True Range and Average True Range" section, below, for ADTR definition)

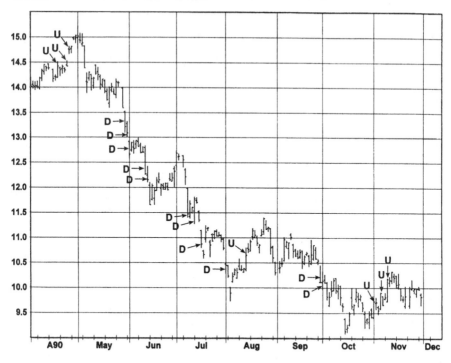

Note: U = up run day; D = down run day.

FIGURE A.3   Run days in bear market: March 1991 sugar.

2. $H_t - C_t > 3 \cdot (C_t - L_t)$

where

    C_t = close on given day

    L_t = low on given day

3. H_t > maximum high during past N days

where

    N = constant that must be defined (e.g., $N = 50$)

The first of the preceding conditions guarantees that the spike high will exceed the surrounding highs by an amount at least equal to three-quarters of the past 10-day average true range (assuming the value of k is defined as 0.75). The second condition assures us that the day's low will be in the lower quartile. The third condition, which requires that the day's high exceed the highest high during the past 50 days (assuming $N = 50$), guarantees that the day was preceded by an upswing. (Generally speaking, higher values of N will require larger prior advances.)

The three-part definition just provided for a spike high day is only intended to offer an example of how a mathematically precise definition can be constructed. Many other definitions are possible. Examples of spike days are provided in Chapter 5.

STOCHASTICS

Another oscillator, stochastics measures momentum by comparing the recent close to the absolute price range (high of the range minus low of the range) over an N-day period. For example, for a 10-day stochastic, the difference between today's close and the lowest low of the past 10 days would be divided by the difference between the highest high and lowest low of the past 10 days; the result would then be multiplied by 100. The formula for the first line, called %K, is:

$$\%K = 100 * (C_t - L_n)/(H_n - L_n)$$

where

   C_t is today's closing price

   H_n is the highest price of the last n days

   L_n is the lowest price of the last n days

The second line of the stochastic indicator, %D, is simply a moving average of the %K line (default value of three days).

$$\%D = \text{a three-period moving average of } \%K = \text{average}(\%K,3)$$

Because of the noisiness of the raw %K and %D lines (commonly calculated over a five-day period, and referred to as "fast stochastics"), an additionally smoothed version of stochastics called "slow stochastics" is usually used by most software programs, and is most frequently referred to simply as "stochastics." The original %D line becomes the new "slow" %K line; in turn, this line is smoothed with a three-day moving average to create the new "slow" %D line.

An example of stochastics is provided in Chapter 6.

TRUE RANGE AND AVERAGE TRUE RANGE

The *true range* formula was developed by Welles Wilder Jr. and explained in his 1978 book *New Concepts in Technical Trading Systems.*

The range (R) of a given day is simply the high (H) minus the low (L): H – L = R. The true range (TR), however, is defined as the *true high* (TH) minus the *true low* (TL): TH – TL = TR. The true high and true low are defined as follows:

> *True high:* The high or previous close, whichever is higher.
>
> *True low:* The low or previous close, whichever is lower.

The true range formula more accurately reflects market activity, because it accounts for gaps between days. The *average daily true range* (ADTR) is simply a moving average of daily true range values (it could just as easily be calculated for weekly, monthly, or intraday time periods). It is a commonly used as a market volatility measurement.

Figure A.4 compares range and true range. Notice that price gaps higher from day 1 to day 2. The standard range calculation for day 2 would be the high minus the low for that day. The true range calculation, however, would be the high of day two (the true high) minus the close of day one (the true low). Plainly, the true range calculation better reflects the essence of price activity by incorporating the gap between days 1 and 2.

WEIGHTED MOVING AVERAGES*

The simple moving average, which was defined in Chapter 3 and used as a component of technical trading systems in Chapter 14, weights every day in the calculation period equally (e.g., a 10-day moving average is the sum of the closing prices of the last 10 days divided by 10). The linearly weighted moving average (LWMA), by contrast, assigns the oldest price in the moving average a weight of 1, the second oldest price a weight of 2, and so on. The weight of the most recent price would be equal to the number of days in the moving average. The LWMA is equal to the sum of the weighted prices divided by the sum of the weights. Or, stated as an equation:

---

*The following two sources were used as references for this section: (1) Perry Kaufman, *The New Commodity Trading Systems and Methods*, John Wiley & Sons, New York, 1987; (2) *Technical Analysis of Stocks & Commodities*, bonus issue 1995, sidebar, page 66.

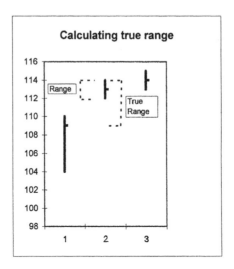

FIGURE A.4 Comparison of range and true range.

$$\text{LWMA} = \frac{\sum\limits_{t=1}^{n} P_t \cdot t}{\sum\limits_{t=1}^{n} t}$$

where

t = time indicator (oldest day = 1, second oldest = 2, etc.)

P_t = price at time t

n = number of days in moving average

For example, for a 10-day LWMA, the price of 10 days ago would be multiplied by 1, the price of 9 days ago by 2, and so on through the most recent price, which would be multiplied by 10. The sum of these weighted prices would then be divided by 55 (the sum of 1 through 10) to obtain the LWMA.

The exponentially weighted moving average (EWMA) is calculated as the sum of the current price multiplied by a smoothing constant between 0 and 1, denoted by the symbol a, and the previous day's EWMA multiplied by $1 - a$. Or, stated as an equation,

$$\text{EWMA}_t = aP_t + (1 - a)\text{EWMA}_{t-1}$$

This linked calculation wherein each day's value of the EWMA is based on the previous day's value means that *all* prior prices will have some weight, but the weight of each day drops exponentially the further back in time it is. The weight of any individual day would be:

$$a(1 - a)^k$$

where

k = number of days prior to current day (for current day, $k = 0$ and term reduce to a)

Since a is *a* value between 0 and 1, the weight of each given day drops sharply moving back in time. For example, if $a = 0.1$, yesterday's price would have a weight of 0.09, the price two days ago would have a weight of 0.081, the price 10 days ago would have a weight of 0.035, and the price 30 days ago would have a weight of 0.004.

An exponentially weighted moving average with a smoothing constant, a, corresponds roughly to a simple moving average of length n, where a and n are related by the following formula:

$$a = \frac{2}{(n+1)}$$

or

$$n = \frac{(2-a)}{a}$$

Thus, for example, an exponentially weighted moving average with a smoothing constant equal to 0.1 would correspond roughly to a 19-day simple moving average. As another example, a 40-day simple moving average would correspond roughly to an exponentially weighted moving average with a smoothing constant equal to 0.04878.

WIDE-RANGING DAY

Wide-ranging days, which were discussed in Chapter 5, can be mathematically defined as days for which the volatility ratio (VR) is greater than k (e.g., $k = 2.0$). The VR is equal to today's true range divided by the true range of the past N-day period (e.g., $N = 15$).

Glossary

Average daily true range   *see* **True range.**

Bar chart   a chart that represents each trading day as a vertical line ranging from the daily low to the daily high. The day's closing value is indicated by a horizontal protrusion to the right of the bar. Additionally, the day's opening value is often (but not always) indicated by a horizontal protrusion to the left of the bar.

Bear trap   major downside breakouts quickly followed by upward price reversals.

Bottom pattern   a pattern that implies a significant market low point. See Chapter 5.

Breakout   a price move that forces through the upper or lower boundaries of a trading range (or another type of price congestion pattern, such as a triangle—see Chapter 5).

Bull trap   major upside breakouts quickly followed by downward price reversals.

Candlestick chart   adds dimension and color to the simple bar chart by depicting the segment of the bar between the open and close as a two-dimensional "real body" (which is usually shaded white for an up day and black for a down day), while the extensions beyond this range to the high and low are shown as lines (called shadows).

Classic divergence   in an upmove, a new price high accompanied by a lower momentum oscillator high; in a downmove, a new price low accompanied by a higher momentum low (see Figure 6.8).

Close-only chart   a chart that is based on closing values and ignores high and low price information. Also called a line chart. Some price series (like cash prices and spreads) can be depicted only in close-only chart format because intraday data are not readily available.

Confirmation   a secondary market event that strengthens the validity of a primary technical trade signal. For example, an upside breakout of a long-standing resistance level may be confirmed by price closing above the level five consecutive days after the initial breakout.

Continuation pattern   one of various chart formations that imply a perpetuation of the trend in place before the formation occurred.

Contrary opinion   a theory that suggests whenever a large majority of speculators are bullish/bearish, those who want to be long/short are already long/short. Consequently, there will be a paucity of potential new buyers/sellers, and the market will be vulnerable to a reversal.

Countertrend   an indicator or system that waits for a significant price move and then initiates a position in the opposite direction on the assumption the market is due for a correction.

Crossover moving average system   a system that generates buy signals when a shorter-term moving average (say, 10 days) crosses above a longer-term moving average (say, 30 days) and generates sell signals when the shorter-term average crosses below the longer-term average.

Divergence   the phenomenon of price and momentum moving in opposite directions.

Diversification   trading multiple markets, multiple systems, or variations of a system in the same or different markets.

Double top/double bottom   a formation in the form of twin price peaks or troughs. The two tops (or bottoms) that make up the pattern need not be exactly the same, only in the same general price vicinity. Double tops and bottoms that materialize after large price moves should be viewed as strong indicators of a major trend reversal.

Down run day   *see* **Run day**.

Downthrust day   *see* **Thrust day**.

Drawdown   a trading loss measured from an equity curve peak to a trough. If a trading account reaches an equity peak of $75,000 and then experiences a $25,000 drop due to a series of losing trades, a 33.3% drawdown has occurred.

Equity curve   a close-only type chart that tracks the rise and fall of trading funds in an account.

Failed signal   when a market fails to follow through in the direction of a chart signal. Such events strongly suggest the possibility of a significant move in the opposite direction.

Filter   a rule or condition designed to eliminate lower-probability trades. A filter differs from a confirmation rule in that it is applied at the time of the trade signal, not after.

Fitting   (or, overfitting) creating highly optimized trading rules that perform well on a specific set of historical data. Evaluating a system based on the optimized parameter sets (i.e., the best performing sets during the survey period) rather than *testing* the system would be best described as *fitting* the system to past results.

Flag   a shorter-term (generally one to three weeks) continuation pattern in which the upper and lower boundary lines are parallel.

Gap a break in prices that occurs when the current day's low is higher than the previous day's high, or the current day's high is lower than the previous day's low.

Good-till-canceled (GTC) a trade order that remains active for an extended period rather than being canceled automatically at the end of a trading day (like a standard order).

Head and shoulders a three-part top formation in which the middle high (the "head") is above high points on either side (the "shoulders"). Similarly, the head-and-shoulders bottom is a three-part formation in which the middle low is below low points on either side.

Internal trend line a trend line drawn to best approximate the majority of relative highs or relative lows without any special consideration being given to extreme highs or lows.

Island bottom a chart pattern formed when prices gap lower after an extended decline, trade one or more days leaving the gap open, and then gap higher.

Island top a chart pattern formed when prices gap higher after an extended advance, trade one or more days leaving the gap open, and then gap lower.

Momentum the rate or speed of price change.

Money management rules that limit risk on a trade (and, as an extension, determine how many shares or contracts to trade in a given situation).

Money stop a protective stop-loss point determined by a dollar-risk level rather than a significant technical level or pattern.

Moving average a calculation that smoothes a price series and makes any trends more discernible. The most basic type, a simple moving average, is defined as the average close of the past N days, ending in the current day. Linearly and exponentially weighted moving averages use special weighting calculations that emphasize current prices over more distant prices.

Neckline a line that connects the relative lows between the shoulders of a head-and-shoulders top or the relative highs between the shoulders of a head-and-shoulders bottom (see Figures 5.38 and 5.39).

Optimization the process of finding the best-performing parameters (say, the length of the moving average in a simple moving average system) for a trading system.

Oscillators a group of countertrend, momentum-based indicators that typically move above and below a horizontal axis representing neutral market momentum. They are mostly used to locate overbought or oversold price levels. Examples include the relative strength index and stochastics.

Overbought   when prices have risen too far too fast and are ripe for a downward correction.

Oversold   when prices have fallen too far too fast and are ripe for an upward correction.

Parameter   a value that can be freely assigned in a trading system to vary the timing of signals. For example, in a simple moving average system, the number of days used to calculate the moving average is a parameter.

Pattern recognition system   price patterns based not primarily on directional moves, as with trend-following and countertrend systems. The key consideration is the pattern itself (e.g., spike or wide-ranging day) rather than the extent of any preceding price move.

Pennant   a shorter-term (generally one to three weeks) continuation pattern in which the upper and lower boundary lines converge.

Point-and-figure chart   a chart that depicts all trading as a single continuous stream (and hence ignores time) using a series of columns of X's and O's (some types of charting software use rectangles or other symbols instead of O's). Each X represents a price move of a given magnitude called the box size. As long as prices continue to rise, X's are added to a column for each increment equal to the box size. However, if prices decline by an amount equal to or greater than the reversal size (usually quoted as a multiple of the box size), a new column of O's is initiated and plotted in descending fashion.

Price envelope band   method of identifying support and resistance levels. The upper boundary of a price envelope band is defined as a moving average plus a given percent of the moving average. Similarly, the lower boundary of the price envelope band is defined as the moving average minus a given percent of the moving average. The resulting indicator encompasses most price action.

Pyramiding   adding additional long or short positions to an existing position.

Quarterly cycle   a common rotation of contract months used in the futures industry: March, June September, December.

Range   the price difference from high to low in a given time period. For example, the daily range would be the day's high minus the day's low, the weekly range would be the week's high price minus the week's low price, and so on.

Relative high   a daily high that is higher than the N preceding and succeeding days. For example, if N = 5, the relative high is defined as a high that is higher than any high in the prior five days and the succeeding five days.

Relative low   a low that is lower than any low in the prior N days and succeeding N days.

Resistance   a price level to which prices repeatedly rally, than pull back, as if they were hitting a ceiling.

Retracement a price move of a certain magnitude in the opposite direction of the preceding price move. For example, a stock that gains 30 points and then loses 15 points has experienced a 50% retracement.

Return/risk measure a measure that places the profitability of a trade or system in the context of the risk required to achieve it. A simple example would be to divide the average winning trade of a system by the average losing trade. The higher the return/risk ratio, the more desirable the system.

Reversal high day a new high in an upmove that closes below the previous day's close. (A stronger version would require a close below the previous day's low.)

Reversal low day a new low in a decline that closes above the previous day's close. (A stronger version would require a close above the previous day's high.)

Rollover when one futures contract month approaches expiration and the next futures contract month in the cycle becomes the new current, or "front" month. For example, a rollover would occur when the March S&P 500 contract is reaching its end and positions are "rolled over" into the June contract.

Rounded top/rounded bottom a formation characterized by a relatively smooth curvature of prices, rather than distinct peaks or troughs. The main criterion is whether the outer perimeter of the formation conforms to a rounding shape.

Run day a strongly trending day. An up run day is a day whose high is greater than the high of the past N days and whose low is less than the low of the next N days, where N is a number that has to be specified. A down run day would be a day whose low is less than the low of the past N days and whose high is greater than the high of the next N days.

Signal line a moving average of an indicator (as found in the MACD and stochastics) that generates buy and sell signals when the indicator crosses above and below it.

Slippage the difference between hypothetical execution costs and real costs resulting from poor fills and limit days (in futures markets).

Spike high a day whose high is sharply above the high of the preceding and succeeding days. Frequently, the closing price on a spike high day will be near the lower end of the day's trading range.

Spike low a day whose low is sharply below the low of the preceding and succeeding days. Frequently, the closing price on a spike low day will be near the upper end of the day's trading range.

Spread a chart that depicts the price difference between two instruments (e.g., corn and wheat) or different months of the same futures contract (e.g., July corn and December corn). Spread can also refer to the price difference between a futures contract and its underlying cash instrument.

Stop-loss   a predetermined price level at which a trade will be liquidated to prevent further losses.

Support   a price level to which prices repeatedly fall, and bounce off, as if hitting a floor.

Thrust day   a day that closes above the high of the previous day (upthrust day) or below the low of the previous day (downthrust day). A series of upthrust or downthrust days suggests pronounced price strength or weakness, respectively. See Chapter 5.

Time stability   comparability of a trading system's performance from one test period to another.

Top pattern   a price formation that suggests the development of a significant market high point.

Trading range   a period of price congestion during which prices move sideways between relatively restricted upper and lower price levels.

Trailing stop   a protective stop that is intermittently raised (in a rising market) or lowered (in a falling market) to lock in profits on a trade.

Trend   a discernible pattern of advancing or declining prices over time. An uptrend is a succession of higher highs and higher lows; a downtrend, a succession of lower highs and lower lows. The higher highs or lower lows are not necessarily consecutive.

Trend channel   set of parallel lines that enclose a trend.

Trend-following system   an indicator or system that waits for a specified price move and then initiates a position in the same direction based on the implicit assumption that the trend will continue.

Trend line   a line that connects a series of chart low points to define an uptrend or a series of chart high points to define a downtrend. See Figures 3.4–3.7.

Triangle   a congestion pattern in which prices gradually converge to a point. Among the most common continuation patterns, triangles can be top and bottom formations as well.

Triple top/triple bottom   similar to the double top and double bottom formations, except the price forms three peaks or troughs instead of two.

True high   the high or previous close, whichever is higher (see true range).

True low   the low or previous close, whichever is lower (see true range).

True range   the true high minus the true low (see definitions above). It is a common measure of market volatility. True range more accurately reflects market activity than the standard range calculation, because it accounts for gaps between days. The average daily true range (ADTR) is simply a moving average of daily true range values (it can also be calculated for weekly, monthly, or intraday time periods).

Up run day   *see* **Run day**.

Upthrust day   *see* **Thrust day**.

Volatility   the amount of price instability a market exhibits. A "choppy" market, one that swings up and down from one price extreme to another, is exhibiting high volatility.

V top/V bottom   turn-on-a-dime type of formation where the market quickly rallies or falls to a top or bottom and just a quickly reverses, giving little or no other technical evidence of a reversal.

Wedge   a pattern in which prices edge steadily higher (in a rising wedge) or lower (in a declining wedge) in a converging pattern. Wedges can sometimes take years to complete.

Whipsaw   to witness repeated, abrupt, sharp trend reversals in prices, causing most trend-following systems to generate many false signals and a string of losses (see Figure 3.21).

Wide-ranging day   a price bar that is significantly bigger than the days preceding it (i.e., a day whose volatility significantly exceeds the average volatility of recent trading days).

Index